A TOUR OF THE
BULGE
BATTLEFIELDS

A TOUR OF THE BULGE BATTLEFIELDS

WILLIAM C C CAVANAGH
& KARL CAVANAGH

Pen & Sword
MILITARY

First published in Great Britain in 2001
and reprinted in 2004, 2007, 2010, 2013 and again in this format in 2015 by
PEN & SWORD MILITARY
An imprint of
Pen & Sword Books Ltd
47 Church Street
Barnsley, South Yorkshire
S70 2AS

ISBN 978 1 47382 814 8

Printed and bound in England
By CPI Group (UK) Ltd, Croydon, CR0 4YY

Pen & Sword Books Ltd incorporates the Imprints of Aviation, Atlas,
Family History, Fiction, Maritime, Military, Discovery, Politics, History,
Archaeology, Select, Wharncliffe Local History, Wharncliffe True Crime,
Military Classics, Wharncliffe Transport, Leo Cooper, The Praetorian Press,
Remember When, Seaforth Publishing and Frontline Publishing.

For a complete list of Pen & Sword titles please contact
PEN & SWORD BOOKS LIMITED
47 Church Street, Barnsley, South Yorkshire, S70 2AS, England
E-mail: enquiries@pen-and-sword.co.uk
Website: www.pen-and-sword.co.uk

AMANDA FOODY is a *New York Times, USA Today*, and indie bestselling author of YA and children's fantasy novels, including the Wilderlore series, the All of Us Villains duology, the Shadow Game series, and more. She lives in Massachusetts with her partner and their feline Beastly companion, Jelly Bean. Visit her at AmandaFoody.com or on Instagram @AmandaFoody.

> "A charming and earnest sequel."
> —*Kirkus Reviews*

ADVENTURE IS CALLING, AND BARCLAY THORNE IS READY TO ANSWER.

Something is wrong at the Sea. The weeping tide, a carnivorous algae bloom, is eating up all the fish. Beasts are terrorizing the nearby Elsewheres. And Lochmordra, the Legendary Beast, is rising at random and swallowing ships whole.

Barclay's teacher, the famous Guardian Keeper Runa Rasgar, has been summoned to investigate, and as her apprentice, Barclay gets to join too. But Runa's nemesis has also been called to the Sea, and he's brought apprentices of his own. When the not-so-friendly competition between them grows fierce, it's Barclay—the only one from the Elsewheres—who can't seem to keep up.

As the flood of the weeping tide encroaches, time is running out to stop Lochmordra. If the rival groups can't cast aside old grudges and learn to work together, soon the Sea will be destroyed completely. And all the while Barclay must ask himself: Is there truly a place for him in the Wilderlands?

DISCOVER THE WORLDS OF THE WILDERLANDS, STARTING WITH *THE NEW YORK TIMES* BESTSELLER, *THE ACCIDENTAL APPRENTICE*!

Cover illustration © 2022 by Petur Antonsson
Cover design by Karyn Lee © 2022 by Simon & Schuster, Inc.

MARGARET K. McELDERRY BOOKS
Simon & Schuster • New York
Ages 8–12 | 0123
EBOOK EDITION ALSO AVAILABLE
AmandaFoody.com

Visit us at simonandschuster.com/kids

CONTENTS

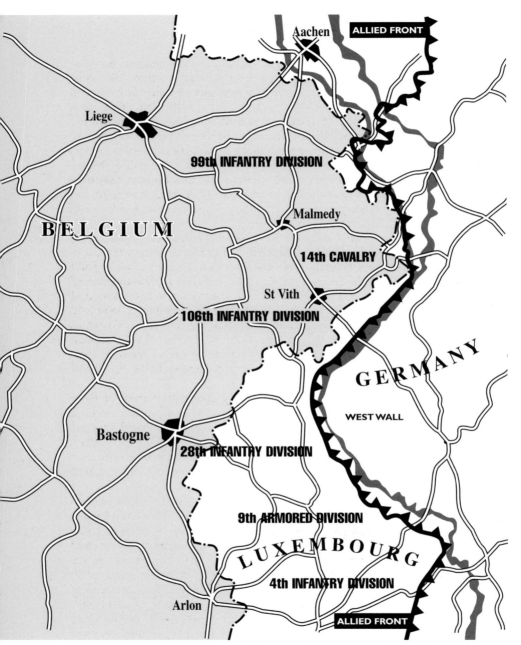

December 1944, five divisions and one cavalry group were in position in a quiet part of the line, facing the frontier defences of the German homeland.

PREFACE

To the south side of the road leading from the east downhill into Stavelot, Belgium the keen-eyed traveller can spot a moss-covered low stone foundation, all that remains of a whitewashed brick structure built over 60 years ago and used as a guard post by Belgian soldiers in 1940. Four years on, in December 1944, another group of soldiers, this time American engineers warily stood guard in the late afternoon dark as the might of Hitler's elite inched toward them down the narrow winding road in what today we call The Battle of the Bulge.

Miles southwest of Stavelot at Dinant, on the east bank of the mighty Meuse River, beneath its imposing ancient citadel, a spectacular rock outcrop named Le Rocher Bayard marks the westernmost point reached by German forces in this last gasp offensive. Noted military historian, Dr. Martin Blumenson once referred to the offensive as 'The Climactic Battle in the West'.

Today, the traveller passing through this pastoral landscape, can almost be forgiven for not realising they are treading hallowed ground where thousands of young Americans, Germans, Belgians and a few British died in a great battle. Since those cold, far off days of the Second World War, a profusion of monuments and plaques recall the suffering of a past generation and bear witness to the valour of the young American soldiers who selflessly liberated the people of mainland Europe. Nowhere is this more evident than in the drab market town of Bastogne, where thousands flock to visit the Historical Centre and nearby Mardasson monument honouring those who served. This somewhat dreary town, in large part, owes its present day prosperity to its wartime prominence as the 'Bastion of the Battered Bastards' of the 101st Airborne Division.

The more keen-eyed visitor, however, can easily spot telltale signs of those momentous times all over the battlefield. At the Baracken road junction north of Rocherath, the farmhouse in which Captain Charles B. MacDonald met his battalion commander, Lieutenant Colonel Paul V. Tuttle, still stands a silent witness to a small episode in a great story. At the eastern edge of Ettlebruck a magnificent bronze statue of Lieutenant General George S. Patton Jr. stands guard over the road to Diekirch.

On the Ourthe river bridge at Hotton, a plaque recalls the valour of the soldiers of Lieutenant Colonel 'Scrappy' Fraser's 51st Engineer Combat Battalion, whilst in the woods near Foy, fast-disappearing foxholes dug by men of the 101st Airborne still dot the forest floor at the time of writing. Houses on the hill leading down into Stavelot from the east still sport traces of machine-gun bullets fired by the soldiers of Kampfgruppe Peiper as they entered the town early on the morning of 18 December 1944. Along the German border, 'Dragon Teeth' anti-tank obstacles of Hitler's 'Westwall' provide yet another reminder of the region's turbulent past. Last, but most of all not least, military and civilian cemeteries in Belgium and Luxembourg bear lasting testimony to the suffering endured by so many over half a century ago.

INTRODUCTION

A multitude of books, films, museums, collector's clubs, re-enactment groups and travel agencies cater to the whims of historians, veterans, collectors, serving soldiers and others interested in World War Two. Despite subsequent conflict of one kind or another, if someone uses the term 'during the war', we still tend to presume that they are referring to the Second World War. No other war has captivated the interest and imagination of so many people world-wide. In post-war Britain, the baby-boom generation grew up with the immediate effects of THE war ever present. Our elders made frequent references to such phenomena as 'powdered eggs, Deanna Durbin or the Blitz'. The government introduced some of the severest rationing after the cessation of hostilities and it didn't end until 1954! At school, we swapped Nazi flags and medals and an uncle proudly showed me the Samurai sword he 'liberated' from one of Hirohito's 'supermen'. The draft had sent some off to war in France, Singapore and other far-off places while some risked life and limb down coal mines doing their bit for the war effort. My late father made armoured cars and served as an air raid warden while his future wife, a Belgian lived under the heel of enemy occupation in her hometown of Verviers.

On 9 September 1944, the U.S. 3rd Armored Division liberated Verviers and my mother, a fluent English speaker, went to work for U.S. First Army C2G1 Civil Affairs under Major Alan Brown as an interpreter in their headquarters at the 'Crédit Anversois', a local bank. Three months later the joy of liberation turned sour as Hitler launched a desperate counter offensive through eastern Belgium and Luxembourg. As his spearheads raced toward the Meuse River, the staff at C2G1 frantically loaded documents and type-writers onto waiting trucks for evacuation to the rear. Briefly, it looked as if the Nazi War machine might just snatch a last minute victory from impending defeat; such was Hitler's plan. The idea originated with him

Marthe Close, interpreter at C2G1 Civil Affairs Detachment Verviers. (Author's collection)

and he took the leading role in planning the attack. One crucial factor he overlooked was the capacity of the American soldier to absorb, stop and ultimately reverse the tide of the German attack. Frequent childhood visits to my late mother's family in Belgium, kindled my interest in what Winston Churchill later called, an ever-famous American Victory. An entire generation of Belgians never forgot the debt of gratitude they owed their liberators from overseas.

In the early sixties, I wrote a letter to the Center of Military History in Washington DC. In turn, I received a reply from one of their leading historians, the late Colonel Charles MacDonald, himself a veteran of the battle and author of several works including 'Company Commander', a classic account of his own experiences as a front line Rifle Company commander. He knew my grandmother's home village of Waimes quite well and had first returned there on a post war bicycle tour in June of 1949.

In 1969, Mac asked that I assist him in guiding a returning group of veterans most of whom were returning to Europe for the first time since World War Two. I well remember taking Ray Fary, a veteran of the 82nd Airborne Division back to the village of Bra where he and a fellow veteran met Joseph Fourgon, who as a boy, remembered their anti-tank gun being positioned close to his home. Over the next twenty years we took thousands of returning veterans back to the fields and forests in which they fought, froze and bled. I assisted 'Mac' in the research for his book *A Time for Trumpets* as well as the production of several video documentaries including *D-Day to the Rhine*.

This guidebook is a small tribute to the thousands of young GIs like Mac in the fervent hope that future generations will not forget what he and his generation did in the name of freedom.

Over thirty years of contact with veterans, serving soldiers, historians, collectors, history buffs and tour guides I've met the full range of 'experts' on the battle. As in any field, some are capable, for example the true perfectionists in Luxembourg who can show visitors the precise location where *Generalleutnant* Kurt Moehring, commanding general of the 276th Volksgrenadier Division, died in a hail of machine gun fire on his way from Beaufort to the Mullerthal. These same avid students of the battle are responsible for the meticulous attention shown to detail in the splendid war museum of Diekirch in Luxembourg.

While some excel in their grasp of events and detail, others leave much to be desired. At the very least,

Charles B. MacDonald, veteran of the battle, returned to Europe on a bicycle tour in 1949.
(Author's collection-courtesy Moire MacDonald).

The author and Charles MacDonald during filming of the television documentary D-Day To the Rhine. *(Author's collection).*

anyone regarding himself as a guide to the battlefield should be familiar with the terrain and possess a sound knowledge of the events that took place, the people involved and the meaning of wartime terms and abbreviations such as 'Pozit', 'OKW' and so on. This guidebook attempts to fill such criteria and if read in conjunction with parts of the relevant books, can help visitors reap the very best from their time in the area, be it long or short. An extensive bibliography is included for readers with plenty of time on their hands. Since most people do not fall into this category, the author recommends that the visitor limits himself to reading MacDonald's *A Time For Trumpets*, published by William Morrow in New York 1985. This book is a detailed account of the intelligence, planning and operational aspects of the battle, as well as a veritable 'gold mine' of human interest.

The U.S. Army official history of the battle, *The Ardennes, Battle of the Bulge*, by Dr. Hugh M. Cole, published by the U.S. Government printing Office in Washington DC in 1965, is a first rate reference source for the serious student of the battle.

ACKNOWLEDGEMENTS

The following people all helped in one way or another, some have passed away since the start of the project:

United States: William D. Amorello, Francis H. Aspinwall, Carlo Biggio, Lyle J. Bouck, George Bodnar, Neil Brown, Richard H. Byers, Tony Calvanese, Frances W. Doherty, Colonel Robert H. Douglas, Sam Doss, Jerry W. Eades, Paul B. Ellis, Ray Fary, Roger V. Foehringer, Brigadier General Harvey Fraser, Jim Gableman, Al Goldstein, Bob Hammons, Colonel William F. Hancock, Major General John. M. Hightower, Colonel William. E. Holland, Sarah Holland, Herbert Hunt, CSM Joseph E. Keirn, Robert. I. Kennedy, Harry and Pat Krig, William.P. Kirkbride, Bob Linkous, Samuel Lombardo, Joe Ludwig, Colonel Charles B. MacDonald, Owen McDermott, Harold R. Mayer, Colonel James F. McKinley, General Frank T. Mildren, George W. Neil, Kendall M. Ogilvie, Colonel James O'Hara, Danny S. Parker, Roger D. Phillips, Thornton 'Moe' Piersall, Moire Queen, Thor Ronningen, Donald Rubendall, Luther Symons, Colonel Paul V. Tuttle, Bill Warnock, Rex Whitehead, Byron Whitmarsh, Byron Wilkins, Grant Yager, and Robert B. Yates.

Germany: Generalmajor Friederich Kittel, Colonel Richard Schulze Kossens, General Meinrad von Lauchert, and General Hasso E. von Manteuffel.

England: James Barrows, Keith Bell, Ralph G. Bennett, Fiona C., Karl, Teri-Anne and Denise Cavanagh, Keith Holyman, Michael F. Mason, Paul Morgan, James G. Rutter, Malcolm Stothard, Henry Wilson and Roni Wilkinson.

Belgium: Guy Blockmans, Madeleine Gourdange, Gerard Grégoire, Marcel and Julia Ozer, Henri Rogister, Nicholas and Sany Schugens and Adolph Schur.

South Africa: Donald Campbell.

Luxembourg: Roland Gaul.

TRAVEL TIPS

Depending upon personal preference, the best way to visit the 'Bulge' is to fly into Brussels, Luxembourg or Frankfurt, all of which lie within about a two hour drive from some spot on the battlefield. The North flank of the battle lies about an hour and a half's drive from Brussels International airport (Zaventem). Upon leaving the airport by car, follow signs leading to highway **E-40** turning southeast in the direction of **Liege** (Luik). Follow E-40 past exit 31 then follow signs for **Aachen**. **Exit** E-40 at **Eupen** and follow **N-67** over the German border and onto Monschau, close to the northern sector of the battlefield.

For the South flank, you can do likewise as far as Liege to pick up **E-25** in the direction of Bastogne, Arlon and Luxembourg City. In **Luxembourg City**, you then follow signs for **Echternach** at which point you are about two miles north of Osweiler and the southern tip of the German attack.

For the North flank, head north on the **N-7** in the direction of Ettelbruck at the southern edge of which you **turn right** at the traffic lights following N-7 around town to the Northeast. Continue north on N-7 to **Wemperhardt** then **turn right** in the direction of St.Vith. Here you follow **N-676** to Amel and **N-658** to Büllingen. Then follow the **N-658** via **Wahlerscheid** where you **turn left** (northwest) on Bundestrasse 258 through Höfen and onto Monschau and the North flank of the battlefield.

* * * *

For those arriving at Frankfurt, airport, Germany: for the North shoulder follow the German autobahn network north to **Aachen** from where **Bundestrasse 258** takes you to Monschau, close to the North shoulder.

For the South shoulder, follow the autobahn network to **Trier** then **Autobahn 48** to **Luxembourg City**. Here take the main road northwest to **Echternach** at which point you are about two miles north of Osweiler on the South shoulder.

Throughout the battlefield, most of the major roads have more than their fair share of twists and turns so always allow yourself sufficient time to get from place to place. Since Belgium is a tri-lingual country, (Flemish, French and German) road signs can appear in one or more languages. Signs are the same throughout the country but place names vary depending upon where you are. When approaching from the west, driving along highway A-3 (E-40), and looking for Liege, you may see signs for 'Luik' and when approaching from the east signs read 'Luttich'. Let your map be the guide since they tend to name big cities in both Flemish and French. Throughout the country most business people speak two of the three languages and sometimes, a smattering of English.

Most of the big car rental companies operate out of Brussels, Luxembourg and

Frankfurt. Travellers from the United States are best advised to arrange car rental stateside with a reputable company that can offer quotes on insurance etc. Be prepared for the fact that fuel is considerably more expensive than in the U.S. At the time of writing it is cheaper in Luxembourg than either Belgium or Germany. The transportation of fuel in jerry cans between Luxembourg and Belgium is forbidden and heavy fines apply to offenders if caught. Drivers and passengers must wear seat belts at all times.

Many travellers choose to combine their battlefield tour with visits to other European destinations and as the cockpit of Europe, Belgium makes an ideal starting point for such trips. By car, the entire country can be crossed in four hours and an extensive highway system gives access to major highways in neighboring countries. For the visitor not wishing to drive, a Eurail pass can serve to get you to most large towns by rail. Frequently, train stations often serve as bus termini but beware most small villages are only served by bus at wide intervals, sometimes as rarely as twice per day. Public transport is definitely not the ideal manner in which to tour the battlefield. For cheap bus travel you can purchase tickets at post offices or on the bus.

For the fit and adventurous there is the option of cycling; recent years have seen a marked rise in the popularity of mountain bike hire in many places, especially so in smaller towns.

ACCOMMODATION

A wide range of accommodation is available, mostly in small, family-run hotels and inns whose owners play an active part in the day-to-day running of the business. In the case of a large group travelling together, the smaller hotels do not have the capacity; therefore the solution in such cases would be to select a chain hotel in one of the larger cities like Liege or Aachen.

Food in both Belgium and Luxembourg is varied rich and a true delight, especially in the hunting season when venison and wild boar grace many a host's table. The privately-run hotels offer gastronomic weekends, in which their chefs excel themselves in the culinary arts. Freshly caught trout is served in a multitude of ways, often accompanied by a fine bottle of Moselle wine. Personal experience leads the author to recommend staying in one of the smaller family-run establishments. Don't be afraid to ask to see the room prior to checking in. Local specialities include pastries, chocolate, smoked hams, waffles, mussels, cheeses and a host of quality Trappist beers brewed by monks in ancient monasteries following an age-old recipe.

A warning to the unwary traveller perhaps tempted to order A la Carte: Filet American consists of raw minced steak topped with a raw egg and parsley. Make sure you ask for clarification of such terms prior to ordering. When eating out in Belgium and Luxembourg be prepared to take your time, since from ordering your food to drinking your coffee can take up to two hours. Long drawn out lunches take up time, which can be better spent visiting the battlefield.

Visitors from the United States frequently make the expensive mistake of using the local or hotel phones to call relatives back home: compared to the U.S., phone charges are very high in Europe and many hotels add to the cost of a call by charging a supplement. To avoid this, consult any of the large U.S. phone companies, all of whom provide a list of numbers which allow the caller direct access to the American operator and stateside call rates. Public telephones in Belgium and Luxembourg are coin or card operated. Cards may be purchased from post offices, railway stations, newspaper stores and telephone sales offices (Téléboutiques) in Belgium.

Post Offices in Belgium open 09:00 through till 17:00 on weekdays, in smaller villages they may close at 16:00. In some of the larger towns, (Malmédy for example) the post office also opens from 10:00 till 12:00 on Saturdays. Banks open weekdays from 09:00 till 16:00 and a few on Saturday mornings. In towns of about 5,000 inhabitants, one can usually locate an ATM that will accept major credit cards and instructions in English. Most banks and businesses accept major credit cards but one can experience difficulty in changing high denomination banknotes.

Public holidays in Belgium include New Year's Day, Easter Monday, May 1, Ascension Day, Whit Monday, July 21, August 15, November 1 and 11 and Christmas Day. In Luxembourg, holidays are much the same with the exception that June 23 replaces July 21 and November 11 is a working day.

Shops' opening hours vary but a good guide would be from 09:00 till 12:30 then from 14:00 till 18:00 Monday till Saturday. Most close on Sundays and some on Monday mornings.

For a 'Battle of the Bulge Tour':
www.tours-international.com
Or write to:
Tours International
1 Sheffield Road
Royal Tunbridge Wells
Kent TN4 0PD
England
Telephone: International + 44 1892 515825.
Fax: International + 44 1892 515815

USING THIS GUIDE

Given the complexity of events which took place during the battle and the extensive area over which they occurred, this guidebook focuses upon numerous places of interest as highlighted in Macdonald's *A Time For Trumpets*. A chronological account of the battle is included so as to inform the reader of what happened throughout the battlefield on a daily basis. It covers the deployment of all major units involved in the battle and can be used in conjunction with the recommended maps so as to plan visits to places and events not specifically mentioned in MacDonald's book. The suggested circuits cover such diverse locations as the Verdenne Pocket, Assenois, the Lausdell Crossroads, '88 Corner' Dasburg, Noville, Wallendorf and Manhay to name but a few. They are designed to enable the reader to follow as few or as many as he or she wishes in whatever order. Using the recommended maps, chronology of the battle and relevant books, the discerning traveller can visit places not covered by the circuits, but nonetheless of interest to them.

A starting point for each circuit is given and can be found in relation to St. Vith, Malmédy, Bastogne or Luxembourg City. The distances from these cities to the suggested starting points are approximate and based 'As the crow flies', eg: Marche is +/- (plus or minus) 54 kilometres southwest of St. Vith.

For the reader wishing to visit places not covered in the itineraries, the chronology gives a day-by-day account of the movements of all units involved in the battle. By extracting relevant details relating to a particular unit, readers can produce their own itineraries.

For a most informative web site devoted to the battle, take a look at the following:

www.criba.be

MAPS OF THE BATTLEFIELD

In a letter to the author on the subject of clear and concise maps, *Generalmajor* Friederich Kittel, wartime commander of the 62nd Volksgrenadier Division stated that he and other German commanders frequently relied upon the commercially available Michelin tourist maps. Numbers 213 and 214 in that series cover the entire battlefield and can be purchased at many Belgian filling stations, supermarkets and bookstores.

For the visitor requiring the very best detail possible it is recommended that maps are acquired from the Belgian National Geographic Institute and the Luxembourg Topographic Administration. They produce quality 1:10,000, 1:25,000and 1:50,000 Ordnance Survey maps. These can be purchased from numerous outlets or directly from the organizations:

Belgian National Geographic Institute,
www.ngi.be/FR/FR0.shtm

Luxembourg Topographic Administration,
www.geoportal.lu/Portail/index.jsp?lang=en

Generalmajor *Friederich Kittel,
commanding general 62nd
Volksgrenadier Division during
the battles for St. Vith.
December 1944.*

(Author's collection courtesy of General Kittel).

15

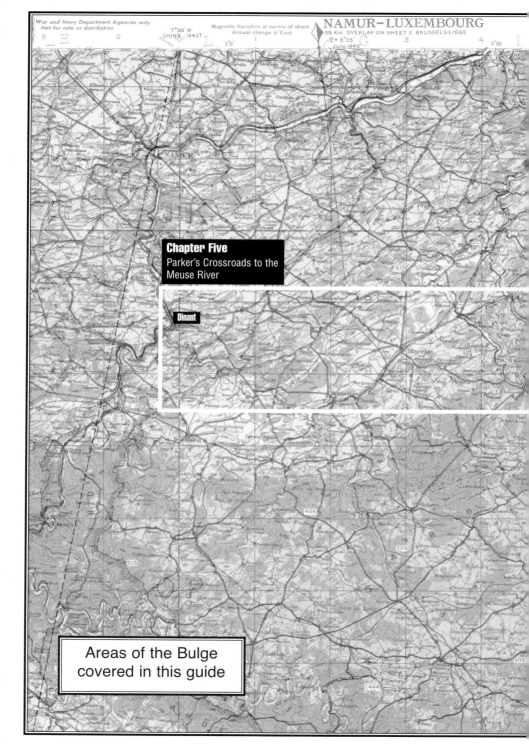

Chapter Five
Parker's Crossroads to the
Meuse River

Dinant

Areas of the Bulge
covered in this guide

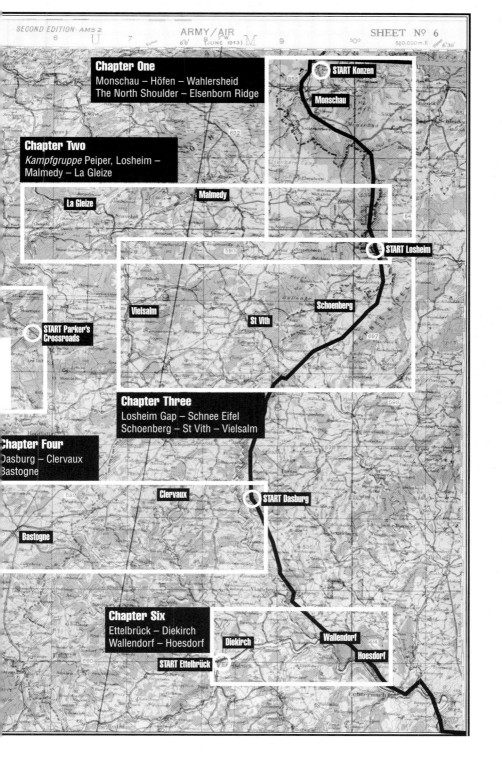

Chapter One
Monschau – Höfen – Wahlersheid
The North Shoulder – Elsenborn Ridge

START Konzen

Monschau

Chapter Two
Kampfgruppe Peiper, Losheim –
Malmedy – La Gleize

La Gleize

Malmedy

START Losheim

Vielsalm

St Vith

Schoenberg

START Parker's
Crossroads

Chapter Three
Losheim Gap – Schnee Eifel
Schoenberg – St Vith – Vielsalm

Chapter Four
Dasburg – Clervaux
Bastogne

Clervaux

START Dasburg

Bastogne

Chapter Six
Ettelbrück – Diekirch
Wallendorf – Hoesdorf

Diekirch

Wallendorf

Hoesdorf

START Ettelbrück

PRELUDE

BACKGROUND TO THE GERMAN ATTACK

By mid September 1944, the Allied advance through Belgium, Luxembourg and Holland had lost much of its momentum at, or just across the western border of Nazi Germany.

Having established the initial American foothold in Normandy, the US Third Army broke out of its beachhead. With the capture of St. Lo and the destruction of German forces near Montmorel (Falaise), American troops raced through France, Belgium and Luxembourg to the German border, a distance of about 750 miles. This put them about 75 miles away from the industrial heart of the Ruhr on the east bank of the Rhine. The capture of Aachen on October 21st and subsequent heavy fighting in the Hürtgen forest, southeast of the city, served to slow down, then stop the American advance into Germany. Another factor contributing to the slowdown was the over-extension of supply lines, meaning that the 'Red Ball Express' was still bringing supplies to the front from depots in Normandy and around Paris. This was costly in terms of manpower and vehicles. In First Army, its theoretical strength of 1,010 medium tanks was down to 85%. In the case of the 3rd Armored Division, of an authorised medium tank strength of 232, only 70 were in condition for frontline duty. The manpower shortage further aggravated the situation, thus contributing to the stabilisation of positions along the German border.

Having withdrawn to positions within the Westwall (Siegfried Line) and facing mounting pressure on the eastern front, Hitler was in desperate need of breathing space. After the daily conference of Saturday, 16 September 1944, convened in the *Wolfsschanze*, (Hitler's field headquarters in East Prussia), the Führer called a meeting of his household military staff. *Generaloberst* Alfred Jodl and *Generalfeldmarschall* Wilhelm Keitel were present, as was *Generaloberst* Heinz Guderian, the acting Chief of Staff of the *Oberkommando der Wehrmacht* (OKW). Guderian was holding direct responsibility for the conduct of military operations on the eastern front. Also in attendance was *Reichmarschall* Herman Goering's Luftwaffe (Air Force) representative, General *der Flieger*, Werner Kreipe. In conflict with direct orders to the contrary, Kreipe kept a diary in which he recorded notes of each daily conference. The meeting began with a briefing by Jodl in which he tried to downplay the effect of his gloomy report of the status quo on the western front. By that stage in the war, those in attendance were well aware of Hitler's tendency to fling violent tantrums when faced with news that he found distasteful. As Jodl gave an overview of the situation in the west, Hitler suddenly cut him short and, after a few moments of strained silence stated, 'I have just made a

Adolf Hitler explains his war strategies to Reichsmarschall *Göring and* Generalfeldmarschall *Keitel.*

momentous decision. I shall go over to the counterattack, that is to say, out of the Ardennes, with the objective of Antwerp'!

He then went on to outline his plan for what was to become the last major offensive in the West.

HITLER'S PLAN

In Hitler's opinion, the situation wasn't quite as desperate as some of his staff might suggest. The slow down and stabilisation of the Allied advance in the West, coupled with an expected seasonal loss of momentum of the Russian attacks in the East, might just give him the respite he so urgently sought. Despite intense Allied air raids, Hitler's armaments chief, Albert Speer and his staff had done a first rate job of maintaining, and in some cases, improving industrial output. Production of fighter aircraft rose from a monthly rate of 1,016 in February 1944, to 3,301 in September of the same year. The Führer's present optimism, spurred on by his inner circle of advisors, led him to believe mistakenly that a German offensive through the Ardennes could succeed. A new mobilisation plan launched by *Reichminister* Josef Goebbels on 24 August 1944, would, in Hitler's eyes, give him the manpower needed to undertake the planned attack.

By late 1944, major decision-making at the level of the OKW, was the responsibility of one man, Adolf Hitler, who despite every indication to the contrary, believed in his own ability as a military genius. He likened his predicament to that of his idol, Frederick the Great, who, when facing certain defeat, at the commencement of the Seven Years' War, defeated armies twice the strength of his own. He thus succeeded in buying time during which the Allied coalition fighting him collapsed. To Hitler, this constituted a precedent for his own dilemma in 1944. He believed that in capturing Antwerp, he'd deal the Allies such a blow that the shaky alliance facing him would disintegrate. He hoped that his offensive would isolate the British 21st Army Group, enabling him to surround British and Canadian armies before the Americans could react. Had not the hilly-forested area east of the Ardennes lent itself to the huge troop build-up required for the successful *Blitzkrieg* attack in May 1940. Hitler believed that he could repeat, to a certain extent, what he'd tried before. This time however, his attacking troops could not count on effective air support, so an attack late in the year would have to gamble on the hope that bad weather would keep Allied fighters grounded.

Initially, Hitler planned to attack between the 20 and 30 November on an eighty-mile front running from Monschau in the north to Echternach in the south. Seizure of bridges over the Meuse River would be followed by a race to capture Antwerp itself, after which, British and Canadian forces north of the line Bastogne-Liège-Antwerp would be annihilated. The plan called for the use of 35 divisions, of which 10 would be armoured. Massive artillery and rocket support would be given to two attacking panzer armies in the lead with their flanks covered by two armies largely composed of infantry divisions. Whatever limited air support there

Adolf Hitler greets Mussolini at Berchtesgaden in 1942. The SS officer behind Hitler is Obersturmbannführer *Richard Schulze Kossens who in December 1944, would lead the attack against Charles MacDonald's company.*

was, s would be made available and all planning would aim at securing tactical surprise and speed. Absolute secrecy was crucial to the build-up with only Hitler's closest advisors let in on the plan. Jodl and his staff presented Hitler with five different attack scenarios, of which they recommended two in particular, Operation HOLLAND and Operation LIÈGE-AACHEN. The first would consist of a single thrust attack aimed at destroying enemy forces between Liège and Aachen. Hitler opted for a combination of the two, a double envelopment known to the planners as the Grand Slam or the Big Solution.

Up to this point, the two major field commands concerned, *Generalfeldmarschall* Gerd von Rundstedt's *Oberbefehlshaber West* (Ob West) – headquarters of the C-in-C Western Front – and *Generalfeldmarschall* Walther Model's Army Group B, had not yet been let in on the plan to regain the initiative in the west. On 22 October, their respective Chiefs of Staff, General *der Kavallerie* Siegfried

Westphal and General *der Infanterie* Hans Krebs went to Hitler's headquarters requesting further reinforcements to defend Germany's industrial heartland of the Ruhr.

After the daily conference, Hitler told them of his plan and their respective roles therein. Both signed a pledge of secrecy upon pain of death concerning the new operation, by then code-named WACHT AM RHEIN (Watch on the Rhine). Hitler then went on to stipulate required troop strengths, asserting that he would personally assure their availability. Keitel then promised both generals that he'd make 4,250,000 gallons of fuel available as well as fifty trainloads of ammunition. As Westphal and Krebs prepared to leave, Hitler ordered that Ob West should prepare a draft plan for the first phase of the operation.

General der Kavallerie Siegfried Westphal, Chief of Staff to Feldmarschall Gerd von Rundstedt.

(Author's collection. Courtesy of General Westphal).

Despite the fact that Belgians often refer to the battle as the 'Von Rundstedt Offensive', the attack was the *Feldmarschall's* in name only. Hitler detested the Old Prussian intensely and saw him as representative of the haughty officer corps. Many of them thought of Hitler as a usurper in his role as commander of the OKW. He'd dismissed Rundstedt twice and brought him out of retirement as a figurehead behind whom the troops would rally in the forthcoming attack.

On 27 October, Rundstedt and his staff went to Model's Army Group B headquarters at Fichtenhain near Krefeld, to discuss the plan with Model. By then, the operations plan drawn up by Ob West for presentation at Army Group B headquarters, was code-named Operation MARTIN. Rundstedt and Model thoroughly disapproved of the 'Big Solution' deeming it over-ambitious. Their alternative, the 'Small Solution', proposed an operation aimed at destroying Allied forces in the Aachen-Maastricht-Liège salient.

The army commanders designated to lead the attack were present at this meeting. General *der Panzertruppen* Hasso E. von Manteuffel would command Fifth Panzer Army, *Obergruppenführer der Waffen-SS,* Josef 'Sepp' Dietrich, Sixth Panzer Army and General *der Panzertruppen* Erich Brandenberger Seventh Panzer Army. The participating generals agreed that the 'Big Solution' was over-ambitious and suggested that they should attack no further than the Meuse River. The result of this meeting was that Model agreed to produce a new plan, largely following the lines of Operation MARTIN. This plan arrived at Ob West on 28 October pending receipt of additional written instructions from Jodl. These instructions arrived at Rundstedt's headquarters on the night of 2 November. In this message, Jodl referred to the objective of Antwerp as 'unalterable', adding 'Although from a strictly technical standpoint, it appears to be disproportionate to our available forces, in our present situation, however, we must not shrink from staking everything on one card'.

German emblem for the counteroffensive. The sketch is one made from memory by O/Gefr Wilhelm Scodzic, 1129 Volksgrenadier Regiment.

Over the page: *Adolf Hitler congratulates General Hasso von Manteuffel on the occasion of the General's birthday. This highly competent officer was given command of 5. Panzer-Armee in September 1944 and commanded it during Hitler's offensive in the west.*
(Author's collection courtesy of General von Manteuffel)

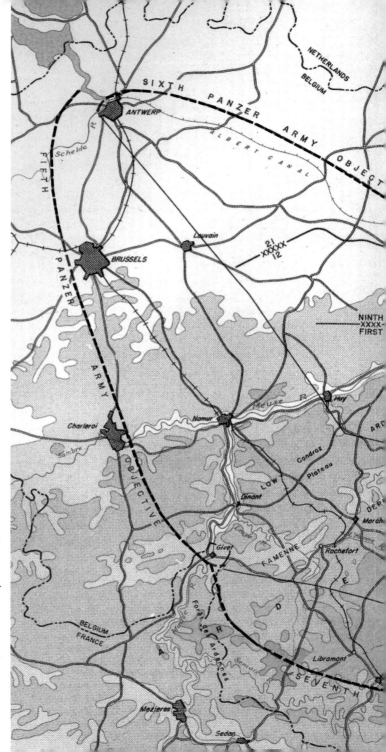

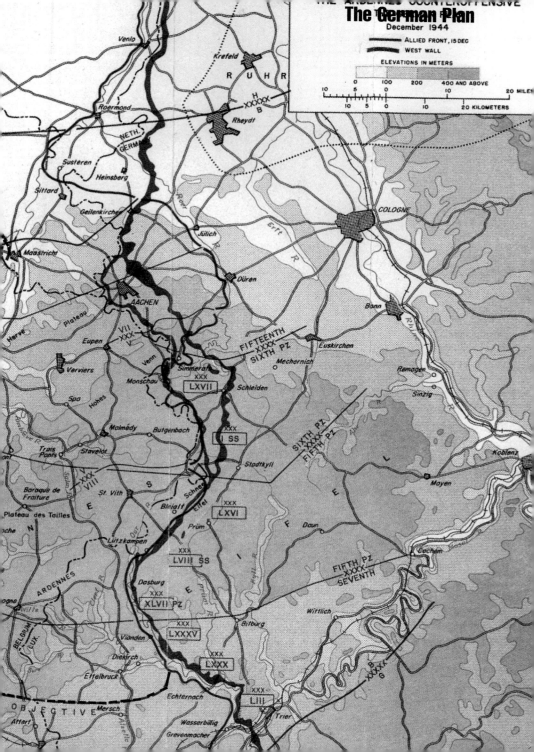

THE ARDENNES COUNTEROFFENSIVE
The German Plan
December 1944

ALLIED FRONT, 15 DEC
WEST WALL

ELEVATIONS IN METERS
0   100   200   400 AND ABOVE

CHAPTER 1

MONSCHAU-HÖFEN-WAHLERSCHEID-THE NORTH SHOULDER-ELSENBORN RIDGE

STARTING POINT: THE VILLAGE OF KONZEN, GERMANY ON BUNDESTRASSE 258 NORTH OF MONSCHAU AND IMGENBROICH, GIVE OR TAKE 20 KILOMETRES NORTHEAST OF MALMÉDY, BELGIUM.

*D*rive north out of Konzen on 258 past the junction to Gemund-Simmerath. Continue until you see the former railway line (now a cycle path) to your left as well as a parking lot. Park here. This parking lot used to be the location of Konzen Station. With your back to the former railway, the Germans attacked from across 258 and the defending Americans held positions along the railroad bed.

As the northernmost American unit involved in the battle, Lieutenant Colonel Robert E. O'Brien's 38th Cavalry Reconnaissance Squadron out-posted Monschau to the North along this railroad track between Monschau and Konzen station.

Konzen Railway Station. Soldiers of Lieutenant Colonel Robert E. O'Brien's 38th Cavalry Reconnaissance Squadron held this area to the west of the railway tracks against attacks by Generalmajor *Erwin Kaschner's 326th Volksgrenadier Division.*

Bundestrasse 258

Monschau

38TH CAVALRY →

Railroad track

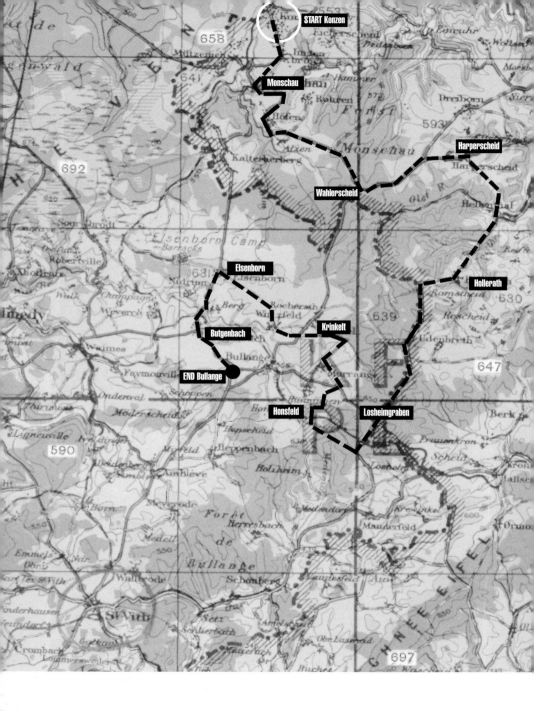

The 38th Cavalry Squadron held a continuous line using fifty dismounted machine-guns dug-in behind mines, barbed wire and trip flares covering approaches from the east. The right flank of the squadron, out posting Monschau, was at some disadvantage as a result of the deep, rocky draws leading into and past the town. Here, to the north, the terrain was less cut up and offered good fields of fire for the machine-gunners positioned on the slopes west of the railroad.

Return to Konzen taking the road to your right sign posted Mutzenich. Cross the former railroad and follow the twisting road about halfway to the village stopping on the high ground overlooking the track.

With its assault gun troop in Mutzenich, the 38th Cavalry was also reinforced by a platoon of self-propelled guns from the 823rd Tank Destroyer Battalion covering the road into the village. Lieutenant Colonel Donald V. Bennett's 62nd Armored Field Artillery Battalion provided much needed artillery support. All things considered, the defense in the Monschau-Höfen sector was well set as the assault battalions of the 326th Volksgrenadier Division moved to their attack positions on the night of 15 December 1944.

The German artillery and *Nebelwerfer* rocket-launcher barrage opened fire at 05.25, rolling over the forward lines, then off to the west along the road to Eupen hitting American artillery positions and cutting telephone wire on its way. Sergeant Jerry W. Eades of Battery B, 62nd Field Artillery Battalion, well remembers that barrage which started upon his return from a forty-eight hour pass to Paris:

'Just about the time I was very sleepily waking up and trying to find my boots, I was really jarred awake in a hurry when we received a tremendous barrage of 88s. In fact, it was one of the most intense barrages I'd ever experienced since the North African campaign and they really used to plaster us with 88's down there. In addition to 88s, larger calibre weapons were firing into our unit. During my absence

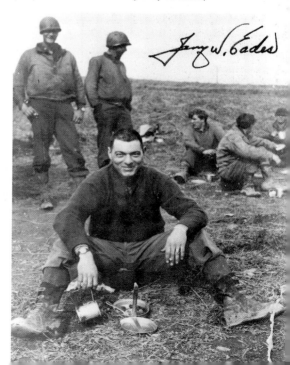

Sergeant Jerry W. Eades of Battery B, 62nd Field Artillery Battalion takes a well-earned break after the hectic events of the 'Bulge'.
(Author's collection - courtesy Jerry W. Eades)

from the battalion, a battery of 'Long Tom' 155mm guns had moved directly in the back of our position and those things began to fire counter-battery. It was just one terrific explosion what with the concussion from their guns directly behind us, and the incoming shells exploding. We were in quite a state of confusion there for a few minutes.'

Neither the infantry in Höfen, nor the cavalry (gone well to ground) suffered much from this fire; heavy though it was, but many buildings in Höfen caught fire, some of which were totally destroyed. Under the specific direction of *Feldmarschall* Model, Monschau escaped this artillery barrage. When it stopped, shock companies of the 326th Volksgrenadier Division spearheaded the attack but the cavalrymen stopped them dead in their tracks using heavy artillery canister, radio adjusted artillery and mortar fire, machine-guns and rifles.

The next day at about 04.00, the cavalry outposts north of Monschau heard enemy troops moving along a draw, or valley, from the east. Quick and accurate response by American gunners ended this move. Three hours later, the German batteries opened up, shelling the thin line of troopers deployed along the railroad cut north of Monschau. When this fire ceased a wave of German infantry headed for the railroad but American machine-gun fire stopped this advance. More Germans appeared, extending the assault from the north edge of Monschau to a hill beyond Mutzenich. American firepower – artillery, tank destroyers, tank guns and the numerous machine-guns stopped this first assault. By 09.00, the enemy had succeeded in gathering a battalion on the north flank poised against the Troop B front Northeast of Mutzenich. In short rushes, the Germans filtered into the Troop B area. Even the Luftwaffe took a hand; at least two squadrons making strafing runs over the cavalry positions. Although some German troops broke through the thin cavalry screen, a sharp shelling administered by Sergeant Eades and his buddies stopped the main assault troops short of the railroad. More Germans could be seen assembling in Imgenbroich, but friendly aircraft were on their way to help out the cavalrymen. Gunners of the 62nd Armored Field Artillery Battalion marked the village with red smoke and the fighter-bombers went in strafing and bombing. This ended the daylight phase of the fray. Elements of the 47th Infantry, 9th Infantry Division moved in to support the cavalry and together, they ended the immediate German threat. The 38th Cavalry reported a count of 200 German dead in front of its lines. Generalmajor Erwin Kaschner's 326th Volksgrenadier Division was finding its position at the pivot of the Sixth Panzer Army offensive a costly one!

Return to Konzen and turn right (south) on 258 in the direction of Monschau. Pass through Imgenbroich and at the southern end of the village to the right of 258 and opposite a VW car dealership note a stretch of the Siegfried Line (Westwall) 'dragon teeth' antitank obstacles. Continue on 258 and pass the right turn to

The scenic beauty spot of Monschau was spared major damage during the battle which raged around it.

> *Eupen with Monschau in the valley to your front left. Park at the second layby on the right. Walk across the road to the overlook above Monschau.*
>
> *As a town that escaped major damage during the battle, Monschau makes an ideal stopping off point, while visiting the north shoulder. A rumour told Model's staff that he wished to save its historic latticed houses from possible destruction. Parking is a problem in the narrow streets, so the best solution is to park at a specified parking lot on the south edge of town. To get there, continue on 258 past the town swimming pool (on your right) then turn left alongside the river to the parking lot outside the local glass factory. For those intent on sticking to this itinerary, from this overlook, on the high ground to your front right is the village of Höfen, held by Lieutenant Colonel McClernand Butler's 3rd Battalion, 395th Infantry of the 99th Infantry Division.*
>
> *Continue on 258 in the direction of Trier. Opposite the right turn toward Malmédy, is a left turn down a dead end marked 'Perlenau'. Turn left here and park.*

The men of the 3rd Battalion, 395th Infantry constituted the northernmost element of the 99th Infantry Division. The bulk of the division held positions east of the twin villages of Krinkelt-Rocherath, and participated in an attack toward the Roer Dams a few days prior to the German counter offensive. The Division Reconnaissance Troop patrolled the almost impenetrable forest between them and Butler's men at Höfen. In 1944, the lake across 258 didn't exist, nor did the post-war Highway Bridge. Private George W. Neil of Company L, 395th and his buddies of the 2nd Platoon, had a 'ringside seat' here at Perlenau for the opening German artillery barrage. In a letter to the author he wrote:

'Artillery shells began landing directly on our positions in the pre-dawn darkness. I had completed my two or three hour tour with the BAR (Browning Automatic Rifle) and was asleep alone in my dugout. My BAR team ammunition bearer and foxhole buddy had been evacuated with frozen feet. Shells were bursting all around us on both sides of the river. It was certainly by far, the most exciting wake up call I've ever had! At the first lull, I unfastened my sleeping bag, quickly crawled out of the dugout (I slept with my boots on for occasions just like this) grabbed our guide rope and slipped down the slope to my BAR foxhole. Just in time! The shells started coming in again as I cowered at the bottom of the BAR hole with the man who was manning the gun at the time. The Germans obviously had us marked on their target list because they zeroed in on our exact location. When the terrifying storm was over, I crawled out of my hole amazed I was still alive.'
In this initial barrage, the 3rd Battalion lost four men killed in action. At the time of writing, two or three Company L foxholes are still visible off to the right of this small road.

Return to 258 turning left in the direction of Höfen. Upon turning the right hand bend into the village stop with the (now closed) 'Gasthaus Schmiddem' (level with the junction of Wiesengrund Str. and 258) on your left. The German attacks here came mainly from the area off to the left across what were then open fields and the gardens of buildings near the road.

The 3rd Battalion earned itself a Distinguished Unit citation for its defense of Höfen.

The 1st Platoon of Company I, 395th occupied Gasthaus Schmiddem and the surrounding gardens. Thor Ronningen, a member of the 1st Platoon, spoke of his experiences in a tape recording sent to the author several years ago:

'On the night and early morning of 15/16 December 1944, with two other fellows, Roland Saddler and Gus Butterglerry. I was in a position we had dug ten or fifteen metres southeast of Gasthaus Schmiddem in what would be the backyard or garden. I was asleep. We had one fellow on guard and the first indication I had of what had been going on was the incoming rockets. These things screamed and had tremendous concussion when they exploded. I awoke to a ground that was shaking like a bowl of Jello. Needless to say, I was petrified with fear and the first thing that went through my mind was my Sunday school teaching. I started to recite the twenty-third Psalm trying to convince myself that 'Yeah, though I walk through the valley of the shadow of death' I would fear no evil and I was feeling evil tremendously! The artillery and rockets took out our telephone communications and consequently the three of us in the hole decided that we were the last ones left and that we would sell ourselves as dearly as we could.' Ronningen and his buddies eventually heard the sound of enemy small arms fire but as yet, had seen no enemy troops. A heavy screen of friendly artillery and mortar fire gave them protection to their front. Shortly after daylight, wire crews repaired the broken telephone lines and the phones started working again. To their relief, the company executive officer called to tell them that help was available. Ronningen and his buddies contacted the men inside the Gasthaus and told them they were coming inside. They ran in one at a time under small arms fire but nobody was hit. Two days later, Sergeant Thornton 'Moe' Piersall and Private Richard D. Mills both of Company I earned the Distinguished Service Cross for respective acts of combat heroism in the defense of Höfen.

Sergent Thornton 'MOE' Piersall is awarded the DSC for heroism at Höfen.
(Author's collection courtesy 'MOE' Piersall).

Sergeant Piersall's citation reads:

' Sergeant Thornton E. Piersall, 18147913, Company I, 395th Infantry Regiment, 99th Infantry Division, for extraordinary heroism in action against the enemy on 18 December 1944, in Germany. When a strong enemy force threatened to sever a vital supply route to his company's defensive area, Sergeant Piersall occupying a position in the path of the assault, held his ground. Wave after wave of hostile troops attacked him, but he repulsed each attack by his intense fire. In desperation, the enemy brought up a machine-gun and rocket gun in an attempt to eliminate this threat to their advance. With his ammunition supply exhausted, Sergeant Piersall, with complete disregard for his life, courageously crawled from his emplacement, secured a grenade launcher and grenades from the enemy dead in front of him and returned to his position. Taking careful aim, he fired two rounds with devastating accuracy knocking out both the machine-gun and rocket gun. The heroic actions displayed by Sergeant Piersall prevented a heavy penetration into his company's area and reflected the highest traditions of the Armed Forces.'

On foot, cross the road to the large three story house opposite Gasthaus

Schmiddem.This building (called St. Josef's House) is mentioned on page 56 of Ronningen's excellent book Butler's Battlin Bastards.

Ronningen comments,

'In the Company I area, the forward observer team set up shop on the third floor of the highest building in the village where they had a commanding view of the area. This was designated as 'OP-6' (Observation Post) and there were observers for the 81mm mortars here as well. Initially, led by 1st Lieutenant Stanley D. Llewellyn, Captain George W. Looney assumed command of the team on 17 December. In this same building, there were riflemen and machine-gunners on the first and second floors as well as a three-inch gun against the outside wall. '

Ronningen goes on to pay tribute to the artillery that supported the battalion during its defense of Höfen:

'In all, there were thirty-six battalions of artillery that could support the 3rd Battalion. Because of the relatively static situation from 9th November on, artillery pieces were well zeroed in and concentrations mapped for any possible situation. On the 16th, the artillery had been vital in keeping the enemy from penetrating battalion lines as their guns ranged up and down the battalion front as the Germans attacked. In addition to this, the 196th Field Artillery Battalion had also been largely responsible for the capturing of 14 prisoners. The intense fire from their guns not only killed or drove back the enemy it also prevented enemy soldiers in front of the barrage from retreating so these 14 Germans only had the choice of staying in front of the 3rd Battalion lines and being killed or surrendering. They chose to surrender.

The observers directed fire up and down the line in front of the defending troops, often impacting within a few feet of their own men. There was a junkyard across the street (the present day car dealership) from OP-6 and a group of attacking Germans made the mistake of coming through here in an attempt to penetrate the lines. When artillery rounds began exploding among them, the carnage was indescribable. In addition to the shrapnel of the shells, pieces of junk were flying everywhere and they were soon decimated. (When front line soldiers speak of 'artillery', they are including the 60mm mortars from their weapons' platoon and the 81mm mortars of the Heavy Weapons Company.)

Ronningen sums up his tribute to the supporting artillery with comments from two of his 3rd Battalion comrades:

'I cannot say enough good things for American artillery. Those guys were easily the world's best.' John Martin of Company K.

'During the battle there was tremendous artillery, tremendous noise, tremendous firing, tremendous troops all around us.' Thornton Piersall of Company I.

Continue through Höfen passing the church on your left and keeping your eyes open for the occasional thatched roof and tall hedgerows so typical of this region's past. Keep on 258 in the direction of Koblenz. About 8 kilometres further, just before the sign to Malmédy, park in the parking lot to the right of 258.

This is the Wahlerscheid road junction, formerly nicknamed 'Heartbreak Crossroads' by the GIs of Major General Walter M. Robertson's 2nd Infantry Division. The Americans made attacks against Wahlerscheid just four days before the German assault, and came from the south (Malmedy direction) through the forest on both sides of the road. Fourteen German pillboxes ringed the Wahlerscheid road junction along with minefields, barbed wire and infantry

Wahlerscheid or 'Heartbreak Crossroads' as photographed by Sergeant Bernard Cook of the 165th Photo Signal Company on 13 February 1945. Soldiers of the 9th US Infantry Regiment first captured this junction early on the morning of the German attack only to be ordered to withdraw the next day. General Robertson withdrew his entire division in an orderly manner to the Elsenborn Ridge via the twin villages of Krinkelt-Rocherath. The division retook the junction in early February 1945 and by the time Sergeant Cook took this photo it had become a rear area road junction through which traffic passed during the drive into Germany. (US Army Signal Corps).

MALMEDY

fighting positions. On 13 December 1944, the 2nd Infantry Division, supported by the 395th Regimental Combat Team of the 99th Infantry Division attacked Northeast of the twin villages of Krinkelt-Rocherath in the direction of the Roer River Dams. Wahlerscheid constituted a crucial objective within Hitler's Westwall since the heavily fortified junction barred the road that leads Northeast to the dams.

American attack prior to the German offensive

Once Wahlerscheid was captured, Colonel Chester J. Hirschfelder's 9th 'Manchu' Infantry Regiment was to advance astride the road swinging northwest to clear the Germans off the Höfen-Alzen ridge. Following in column as far as Wahlerscheid, Colonel Francis H. Boos 38th Infantry was to deploy to the northeast along the Dreiborn ridge in the direction of the Roer River dams. The sector of the Monschau Forest through which the 9th Infantry first was to push was a kind of no man's land of snow-covered firs, hostile patrols, mines and roadblocks. Though this sector belonged within the 99th Division's defensive responsibilities, that division held such an elongated front that defense of some parts had been left more to patrols than to fixed positions. Not on either side of the forest-cloaked road to Wahlerscheid were there any friendly positions in strength. The gap on the right (east) of the road was of particular concern because the southeastward curve of the 99th Division's line left the sector open to enemy penetration from the east. Approaching along forest trails, the Germans might sever the 2nd Division's lifeline, the lone highway from the Twin Villages (Krinkelt-Rocherath) to Wahlerscheid.

This threat was what had prompted the V Corps commander, Major General Leonard T. Gerow to order a limited objective attack by the 395th Regimental Combat Team of the 99th Infantry Division close alongside the 2nd Division's right flank. Colonel Alexander J. Mackenzie's 395th Combat Team comprised his own 1st and 2nd Battalions and the attached 2nd Battalion, 393rd Infantry under Lieutenant Colonel Ernest C. Peters. The 2nd Battalion, 393rd was to attack to occupy the high ground about a mile and a half Southeast of Wahlerscheid around the junction of the Wies and Olef Creeks in a sector of the forest known as the Hellenthalerwald.

Because the forested no man's land between the Twin Villages and Wahlerscheid was some three miles deep, obtaining accurate intelligence information prior to the attack was difficult. About all the 2nd Division knew was that the junction was held by troops of the 277th Volksgrenadier Division's 991st Regiment. Any real estimate of German strength at Wahlerscheid or any pinpoint locations of German pillboxes and other positions were missing.

Limited observation rendered difficult the planning of artillery fire in support of the attack. The supporting artillery tried to solve the problem by

The difficult terrain of the Belgian-German border made it hard going for the attacking American infantry.

plotting checkpoint concentrations by map, which might be shifted on call from infantry and forward observers as trouble developed.

The Monschau Forest was almost uncannily silent as troops of the 9th Infantry moved forward on foot in approach march formation an hour after daylight, 13 December. Because they knew the Germans had mined the highway, the men had to plough through underbrush and snowdrifts on either side. When a partial thaw set in, branches of fir trees heavy with snow dumped their wet loads upon the men beneath them. In some places, the ground was so marshy that icy water soaked the feet of the attacking GIs. 'A most taxing march' someone noted in a later after action report. Even without the usual combat impediments, it would have proven 'taxing' and these men were carrying more than the norm. So impressed had been their commanders with the misfortunes of the 28th Infantry Division when depending upon one supply road at Schmidt the preceding fall, that they ordered the men to carry enough rations, ammunition and anti-tank mines to last for at least twenty-four hours without re-supply.

At about 13.00, Colonel Hirschfelder ordered the assault against Wahlerscheid by two battalions abreast without artillery preparation.

The 'Manchus' faced a formidable position that in some respects possessed the strength of a small fortress. Grouped compactly about the road junction and sited to provide interlocking fire were machine-gun and rifle positions in and about four pillboxes, six concrete bunkers, a forester's lodge and a former customs house. The forest and deep ravines formed a kind of moat around the entire position. Where trees and underbrush had encroached upon fields of fire, the Germans had cut them away. In some places, rows of barbed wire entanglements stood six to ten deep. The snow hid a veritable quilt of antipersonnel mines.

Within minutes of the attack commencing, the road junction bristled with fire. Mortar and artillery shells burst in the treetops. Exploding mines brought down man after man. One after another, eight men whose job was to clear a narrow path for the 1st Battalion were killed or seriously injured by mines. Bangalore torpedoes set beneath the wire failed to ignite because the fuses were wet. One platoon of the 2nd Battalion nevertheless pressed through the aprons of barbed wire before enemy fire at last forced a halt; yet several more aprons of wire lay ahead.

As night came the weather turned colder. Drenched to the skin, the men were miserable. Their clothing froze stiff. Through the night they tried to keep warm by painfully etching some form of foxhole or slit trench in the frozen earth.

In the forest southwest of Wahlerscheid, the 395th Regimental Combat Team moved northeast in a column of battalions to protect the 9th Infantry's right flank. Shortly after noon and an arduous climb uphill, they struck a line of log bunkers in a sector of the forest known as 'Daubenscheid'. Like the men of the 9th Infantry, they got no further that day and were to spend the night trying to scrape some measure of shelter from the frozen ground.

Throughout the next two days, all attempts to seize Wahlerscheid proved fruitless despite the support of friendly artillery. As darkness fell on 15 December, the 2nd Division after three days of attack could point to no gain against the Wahlerscheid strongpoint. Though the adjacent 395th Regimental Combat Team had achieved considerably more success in the pillbox belt southeast of the road junction, this was a subsidiary action geared in pace to the main attack at Wahlerscheid and offered no real possibility of exploitation to assist the main attack. Both regiments had incurred heavy losses, as much from the cruel elements as from enemy action. Of 737 casualties within the 9th Infantry during these three days, almost 400 were attributable to non-battle casualties.

All might have been gloom that third night except for one thin hope, which stirred the 2nd Battalion commander, Lieutenant Colonel Walter M. Higgins Jr. During the afternoon of the second day of the attack, 14 December, a squad of Company D had slithered, one after another, under the enemy's barbed wire entanglements until all were behind. Another squad had cut the wire so that a narrow four-foot gap existed. Neither squad had yet been in contact with the company headquarters; furthermore, their company commander had been

An American GI examines the steel cupola of a German pillbox in the Daubenscheid area. (US Army Signal Corps Photograph).

wounded and evacuated. As a result, news of the breach had not reached the battalion commander until both squads had withdrawn. When the next night came, Colonel Higgins sent an eleven-man patrol equipped with a sound-powered telephone to pass through the gap and report on German strength and alertness. Though wandering aimlessly until joined by one of the men who had cut the wire the day before, at 21.30 the patrol reported an electrifying development. 'We have surrounded a pillbox' the word came back. The defending Germans apparently were unaware that anything was afoot.

That was all Colonel Higgins was waiting for. Within a matter of minutes, Company F was plodding single file through the gap in the wire. Higgins himself followed with Company E and took such an active part in the fighting that he earned himself the Distinguished Service Cross. By midnight, the 2nd Battalion held a substantial bridgehead within the Wahlerscheid strongpoint and another battalion was filing silently through the gap. One battalion swung northwest, the other northeast. From one position to another, the men moved swiftly, blowing the pillbox doors with beehive charges, killing or capturing the occupants, prodding sleepy Germans from foxholes and capturing seventy-seven at one blow in the customs house. Two hours after daylight on 16 December, even mop-up was completed, and the 38th Infantry was already moving forward to pass through the 9th's positions and push north-eastward along the Dreiborn Ridge toward the Roer River Dams.

Major-General Walter M.Robertson.
(US Army Signal Corps).

By that afternoon, things had taken a decided turn for the worse. Initially, American commanders failed to recognise the German attack for what it was – a major counteroffensive. On his own initiative, the 2nd Infantry Division commander, General Robertson made plans for a withdrawal back down the division's main supply route to the Twin Villages.

At the time of writing, the discerning traveller can still spot traces of the turmoil that reigned supreme here at 'Heartbreak Crossroads'. Here and there sections of the German communications trenches and the occasional shattered chunk of concrete still bear witness to the junction's former strategic importance as part of the Scharnhorst Line.

Continue on 258 as far as Schönesseifen then turn right in the direction of Trier/Hellenthal. In Hellenthal, take first exit at traffic circle onto 265 in the direction of Trier and continue as far as the church in Hollerath.

'Dragon Teeth' anti-tank obstacles run parallel to Rollbahn A, the northernmost attack route for 1st SS Panzerkorps. This photograph shows the eastern edge of the forest as seen from the present day parking lot on the western side of Bundestrasse 265 about a kilometre west of Hollerath.

Alongside the church in Hollerath is the local war memorial featuring the broken church bell, found in the ruined church after the battle. Hollerath, like other villages in the Westwall, had its share of bunkers camouflaged to look like barns or houses. One such bunker, in the western part of the village, served as the forward command post of the 12th SS Hitlerjugend Panzer Division during the initial stages of the German attack. The Daubenscheid pillboxes, objective of the 395th Regimental Combat Team attack, lie just west of Hollerath as do remnants of the 'Dragon Teeth' anti-tank obstacles.

Return to 265 and just before the first major bend to the south (left) about one kilometre west of the village, pull into the parking/picnic

East end of
Rollbahn A

area to the right of the road. As you drive down off the main road note the well-preserved section of Dragon Teeth in the trees to the right. Continue parallel to 265 and park just prior to re-joining it.

Walk along the dirt track that leads into the forest with more Dragon Teeth to your right and stop where the trail and Dragon Teeth bend to the right.

The German offensive

In planning their attack, 1st SS Panzer Korps selected five assault routes code named *Rollbahns* and listed them A to E. Assault route 'Rollbahn A' led west through the forest to the twin villages of Krinkelt-Rocherath, then across the Elsenborn Ridge toward the Meuse River.

The dirt path leading left into the woods is the eastern end of Rollbahn A, the northern most of five major assault routes for Sepp Dietrich's 6th Panzer Army. Attacking German armour drove west of Hollerath to enter the forest here on Rollbahn A.

Please note: *Access on foot only. On certain days, signs in German tell walkers that it is forbidden to enter the forest due to military exercises taking place at nearby Elsenborn. You can walk to Krinkelt from here providing you stick to the trail.*

With its 395th Regimental Combat Team attacking the pillbox line in the forest between here and Wahlerscheid, the 99th Infantry Division's 3rd Battalion, 393rd Infantry and the 324th Engineer Combat Battalion held positions to either side of Rollbahn A. Here, at the eastern end of Rollbahn A, those positions ran more or less south and parallel to 265, which American soldiers nicknamed the 'International Highway'.

The pre-Second World War and present day Belgian-German border lies just inside the forest on the West Side of the 265.

Company K, of the US 393rd Infantry Regiment held positions here at the western end of the forest where Rollbahn A emerged from the trees. Off to its left and rear, Companies L and I were positioned. To the right of Company K, lay the battalion boundary with Captain Henry B. Jones' Company B, 393rd.

Following the opening artillery barrage on 16 December, troops of Grenadier Regiment 989 of *Oberst* Wilhelm Viebig's 277th Volksgrenadier Division struck the Company K position.

Slightly to the south on the battalion boundary, Viebig's Grenadier Regiment 991 attacked Company B. The German artillery barrage played havoc with wire lines, so much so that Company K's 1st Platoon on the right flank was left without communications. Waves of attacking German infantry hit Company K and overran part of Captain Jones' Company B to the south. To the rear of Company K, 'Rollbahn A' descended to the Olef Creek, climbed its West Bank and levelled out for a few hundred yards before descending to a second creek, the Jansbach.

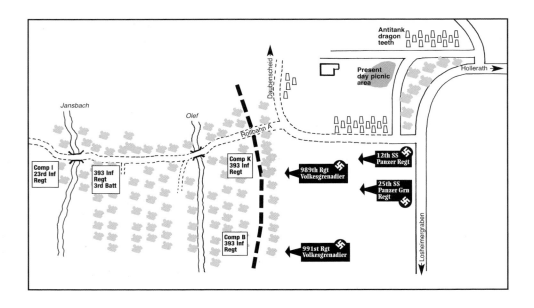

Lieutenant Colonel Jack G. Allen had his 3rd Battalion 393rd command post on the east bank of the Jansbach, to the south side of Rollbahn A. By late morning, given the ferocity of the German attack, Colonel Allen started pulling the remnants of his by then depleted battalion back into a tight all-round defense of his command post on the high ground east of the Jansbach.

Realising that if the Germans managed to break through the 99th Division's front line and exit the forest, they might well cut his main supply route to Wahlerscheid, General Robertson committed his division reserve, Lieutenant Colonel Paul V. Tuttle's 3rd Battalion, 23rd Infantry. They moved to the West Bank of the Jansbach, their initial objective being to move east the next day, team up with Colonel Allen's battalion and push the Germans back out of the forest. As the 16th wore on however, it became obvious to General Robertson that this attack risked cutting the Wahlerscheid road just north of the Twin Villages, thus preventing possible withdrawal of his units at Wahlerscheid. He therefore ordered Colonel Tuttle not to attack and link up with Allen but rather, to 'hold at all costs' on the West Bank of the Jansbach.

During the night of 16th/17th December, two regiments, one armoured and one mechanised infantry, from 12th SS *Hitlerjugend* Panzer Division, reinforced the remnants of Viebig's 277th Volksgrenadier Division.

At 08.00 on 17th, as Colonel Allen's battalion began its counterattack to regain its original positions, they ran smack into the newly committed SS Panzergrenadiers and a heavy firefight broke out. *Sturmbannführer* Siegfried

Müller's *Kampfgruppe* Müller, reinforced by the divisional *Panzerjäger* (tank destroyer) Battalion and a tank battalion had entered the fray, intent on moving west along Rollbahn A.

At the time of writing, most of Rollbahn A is a vast improvement on the dirt trail of December 1944. The extreme eastern end however, gives the visitor an idea of what the rest of it looked like in World War Two. The 3rd Battalion, 393rd Infantry suffered such heavy losses that by noon of the second day, the survivors withdrew across the Jansbach and through Captain Charles B. MacDonald's Company I, 23rd Infantry on the West Bank. Captain Frederick J. Mackintyre and the staff of the 3rd Battalion, 393rd Aid-Station remained behind so as to care for the wounded that couldn't be moved.

Return to your car and resume driving south on 265. As you do so, you are passing positions of Companies K, B and C of the 393rd Infantry in the trees to your right. About 1100 meters before reaching the left turn to Dahlem/Udenbreth; the American foxhole line crossed the highway and continued south on the East Side of 265.

Shortly after passing the left turn to Dahlem/Udenbreth, keep an eye open for the first firebreak to the right, (at the time of writing, barred by a red and white metal gate). Pause here.

The 1st SS Panzerkorps planners designated this trail as Rollbahn B. To their American counterparts of the 2nd Battalion, 394th Infantry, it was known as 'The Corduroy Road' and constituted the main supply route between their front line foxholes and regimental headquarters in Mürringen. An early attempt by a couple of German tanks to move west out of Udenbreth was met by a heavy barrage of American artillery. This had originally been the assigned attack route of *Kampfgruppe* Müller, but given the slow progress made on the first day, *Brigadeführer* Hugo Kraas, the 12th SS *Hitlerjugend* commander, ordered Müller to move north to Rollbahn A. Rex Whitehead, of Company H, 394th Infantry well remembers returning here after spending 15 December at the rest area in Honsfeld:

'We were ready to leave (Honsfeld) when we heard that they were having some trouble on the front, for the 'Jerries' were hitting our lines. This was 16 December 1944. We tried to find out what was going on but that was impossible. There were plenty of bad rumours. They said that we would just have to wait for transportation to get us up there.

Brigadeführer *Hugo Kraas, commanding 12th SS* Hitlerjugend *Panzer Division.*

'It was dark by the time we started back up and on the way there was a lot of anti-aircraft fire, as usual, aimed at buzz bombs. As we neared the battalion headquarters, a medic jeep came by and I saw Ray Gottsacker on a litter. A shell had hit him earlier that day. Captain Legare was at battalion and he told us to get to our companies as soon as possible for they were in need of men. I walked up the 'corduroy road' to the platoon command post at the location where we had first been on line. They said I would have to stay there until morning and then I could go over to my section. I stayed with the 3rd section in their hut and we pulled one hour on guard and two off all night. No one in the platoon had been hit but that morning they had been shelled for two hours. A hut had received a direct hit. They told me of Stan Larson – legs blown off and dead, Zimmerman, dead: Williams had his arm blown off. Only one man was left in that machine-gun squad. The easy life we had been having was over. The guys had not eaten for two days for most of the trucks were knocked out, and the rest were carrying 'ammo'.

'The next morning I went out and looked around the area to find it really torn up by shells – big jobs which left a crater about five feet across. They brought up some C-Rations and we really tore into them. Saw several planes go down and one Jerry landed just in front of Company G. Their outpost got him and they say he had a beautiful watch.'

Shortly after arriving at his platoon location, a phone call told Whitehead and his buddies that they were to pull out in fifteen minutes. Like the rest of the battalion they were to withdraw to the regimental command post location in Mürringen. The 2nd Battalion 394th Infantry vehicles withdrew to Mürringen then Elsenborn followed by the bulk of its infantry.

Continue on 265 and upon arrival at Losheimergraben, park on the south side of the traffic circle by taking the second exit and pausing on the left.

This is the Losheimergraben crossroads from where in December 1944; Rollbahn C led west out of the Losheim Gap. The town of Losheim lies a couple of kilometres to the Southeast on 265. German attacks here came from the east up the road from Losheim and along the railroad tracks.

The 1st Battalion, 394th Infantry under Lieutenant Colonel Robert H. Douglas held this sector of the 99th Infantry Division front line. Company A held positions southeast of the crossroads while Companies B and C occupied the sector to the north and east side of 265. As the major east-west road in the area, Rollbahn C was a primary objective of the initial German attack.

South of Losheimergraben, the road to Lanzerath (N626) crosses the Losheim-Büllingen railroad as does 265 between here and Losheim. In the fall of 1944, retreating Germans blew both bridges over the railroad.

Between the road bridges, a smaller bridge, (unsuitable for heavy traffic), also crossed the railroad. It then led northwest to N626 just south of Losheimergraben. This small bridge remained intact but was of no use to heavy vehicles.

West of the demolished N626 Railroad Bridge, the 3rd Battalion, 394th Infantry constituted the 99th Division Reserve.

On 16th December, despite their determination to do so, the attacking 12th Volksgrenadier Division failed to capture the Losheimergraben crossroads. In a 'friendly fire' incident the opening German artillery barrage hit one of the assembled German battalions causing numerous casualties including the battalion commander, Major Siegfried Moldenhauer. Companies A and B of the 394th lost many men both killed and captured, while the attacking Germans out-flanked an 81mm mortar platoon of Company D in a clearing, (now forested), just southeast of the crossroads. They worked their way west along the railroad cutting then swung back to their right in order to attack the mortar men. As they came under attack, the mortar crews under orders from Staff Sergeant Delbert J. Stumpf swung their mortar tubes around to meet the oncoming infantry. They elevated the tubes to an angle approaching 89 degrees and removed some of the increment used to propel the mortar rounds. The resulting fire stopped the German attack dead in its tracks.

At 11.00 on the morning of 16th December, men of the 394th Regimental antitank company spotted an enemy *Sturmgeschütz* assault gun about six hundred yards Southeast of the crossroads and heading towards them on 265. This vehicle had moved along a forest trail from the village of Frauenkron and reached 265 without having to cross the railroad. With their first shot, the anti-tank gunners disabled the vehicle by knocking off a track. Hardly had the smoke cleared, when with a second well-aimed shot, they set the assault gun alight. The anti-tank gun crew ammunition bearers shot and killed the crew as they tried to exit the burning vehicle. By nightfall of the 16th, the attacking 12th Volksgrenadier Division had increased pressure on all elements of the 1st Battalion. Under cover of darkness, remnants of Companies B and C along with two anti-tank platoons pulled back to the then customs houses on the south side of 265 about 200 yards Southeast of the crossroads.

Captain Jim Graham of Company C, sent his 2nd and 3rd Platoons to support Company B at the crossroads and his 1st and 4th Platoons north to support the 2nd Battalion, 394th.

Two non-commissioned officers, Staff Sergeant John W. Hilliard and Technical Sergeant John C. Trent, took the 2nd and 3rd Platoons of Company C and occupied the house that stands immediately to the east of the traffic island on the right (south) side of 265. A few years ago, the owners of this house stripped away all external rendering to reveal numerous bullet holes and other war damage. They then completely restored the building to its more modern appearance. (This house is visible on both a painting by Harrison Standley and the crossroads aerial photo from the Hatlem collection). From

International Highway

Büllingen

Hilliard and Trent

Sgts Kirkbride and Weidner

Losheim

Büllingen

Knocked out German assault gun StuG

An aerial view of the Losheimergraben cross roads. On the left is the house defended by Sergeants Hilliard and Trent and their men. (Hatlem collection).

this house the defenders were able to cover a wooded draw that the Germans might use to approach the crossroads. Twenty survivors from Company B who had escaped the vicious attack on their position earlier that morning joined Hilliard and Trent's men around dusk on the 16th.

On 17 December, *Oberstleutnant* Wilhelm Osterhold's 48th Grenadier Regiment continued its costly frontal attack while *Oberstleutnant* Georg Lemm's 27th Fusilier Regiment managed to flank the crossroads to the west bringing the road to Büllingen under fire.

The bulk of the 1st Battalion moved across country to the Regimental Headquarters location in Mürringen whilst the crossroads defenders remained in place.

In the closing stages of the battle for Losheimergraben, the Germans threw in all they could. German artillery pounded the position as Me-109 fighters strafed and bombed the buildings. Three additional self-propelled assault guns drove up the 265 to join in the final assault.

From the central of the three customs houses closest to 265, Staff Sergeant Mel Weidner of Company C and Staff Sergeant William P. Kirkbride of Anti-tank Company used a bazooka to knock out one of these assault guns. The attacking Volksgrenadiers threw in their trump card by withdrawing slightly as their artillery and fighters bombarded the immediate vicinity of the crossroads.

Once more the attacking German infantry moved in to try and capture the position. *Oberstleutnant* Osterhold supervised the assault on the customs houses alongside 265. From the rear of the easternmost house, Osterhold's men were within sight and earshot of Sergeant Kirkbride and his buddies in the middle house. Bill Kirkbride recalls the moment of capture as he and his fellow GIs experienced it:

'We could see enemy troops moving closer. Just before darkness, we decided to give up as we did not know what else to do. We did not want to go through the night with them close enough to throw grenades into our basement windows.

'When we decided to surrender, no one wanted to face the Germans. We stuck a white flag out of the south window and an officer (I presume it was Osterhold) immediately came forward towards the house and asked if we wanted to surrender. When I saw him leave cover and come out towards our flag, I immediately surmised that he trusted us not to shoot him, therefore I also knew that he wouldn't shoot us. I volunteered to go out and talk to him. He was of average size, wearing a light tan trench coat, very neat and cleanly dressed. I seem to recall a cap type hat and even have a vision of a light coloured scarf around his neck. He was clean-shaven and seemed to speak excellent English.'

(**Author's note:** In conversation with the author, *Oberstleutnant* Osterhold confirmed his having worn such a scarf, in order to help his men recognise their commander in the heat of battle.)

Bill Kirkbride continues:

' His first words were, 'Do you wish to surrender?' I told him 'Yes' and he instructed me to go inside and tell the others to come out quickly. We had already decided that if they had any type of flame-thrower or rockets, we were not going to try to fight them. Our people were all very leery of being burned.

'When I reported back to the basement, everyone started getting ready to come out. We disassembled our guns etc. and somehow must have taken too long because he reappeared and told us he would burn/blow the house down. That did it, we hurried out.'

Unknown to Kirkbride and his buddies, Osterhold intended ordering his men

Central Customs House from which Sergeants Bill Kirkbride and Mel Weidner knocked out an enemy assault gun.

Hilliard and Trent

To Losheim

Losheimergraben looking towards Losheim. The now restored white house on the right was held by soldiers led by two intrepid non-commissioned officers named Trent and Hilliard.

to pile mines up against the wall of the house and to detonate them, destroying the house if necessary. In conversation with the author in June of 1989, Osterhold explained his reluctance to kill more people that day:

'We were behind schedule and it would have taken us far less time to blow all these houses to pieces without caring what had become of the defenders. Today, I am happy that the Americans noted the pleading tone in my voice otherwise I would have had to do what I hated to do, kill human beings when it was not necessary. My opponents at Losheimergraben were brave soldiers and it is the obligation of their former enemy to say so.'

Prior to the German capture of Losheimergraben, early that second morning, the attacking Germans had already cut Rollbahn C when *Kampfgruppe* Peiper advanced from Lanzerath, south of the railroad via Honsfeld to capture Büllingen. With the capture of Losheimergraben later in the day, the Germans effectively closed a major withdrawal route for the 99th and elements of the 2nd Division.

At the time of writing, visitors to Losheimergraben can still see the emplacements where the 81mm mortars of Company D were positioned. From where you are parked walk down the dirt trail to the left of the monument to the 1st Battalion, 394 Infantry Regiment and attached units of the 99th Infantry Division. On the left, is the old house that served as the mortar platoon command post. Swing right in front of the small white vacation home (named 'Pax') and about 50 metres further down the trail, the emplacements are located in the trees off to your left. During the battle, this was a clearing, which is now forested. Return to your car and drive south on N626 stopping on the Railroad Bridge.

German engineers demolished this bridge in the fall of 1944. About 1400 meters west of here Major Norman D. Moore's 3rd Battalion, 394th Infantry served as 99th Division Reserve positioned around Buchholz Station. Oberstleutnant Heinz Georg Lemm's 27th Fusilier Regiment used this deep railroad cut to attack towards Buchholz on the morning of the 16th.

Continue south on N626 past the right turn sign posted 'Buchholz' and into the village of Lanzerath. As you enter the village, note the wooded hill to your front right (known as the 'Schirmbusch'). Drive just past the first small street on the right and park by the former school (now a night-club) on the right. Walk up that small street just north of the club and follow it around to the right. Continue up the dirt road to your front then cross the field to your left up to the top of the wooded hill. Here stands a memorial to the men of I&R Platoon of the 394th Infantry.

Young, bright and good-looking, First lieutenant Lyle Joseph Bouck commanded the southernmost element of the 99th Infantry Division, the Intelligence and Reconnaissance Platoon (I+R) of the 394th Infantry. Bouck enlisted in the National Guard aged fourteen in 1938 and upon mobilisation ended up in the Aleutian Islands. He applied for airborne training and received his commission, aged eighteen at Fort Benning. The I+R Platoon consisted of eighteen soldiers with sports or college backgrounds and in the words of the Regimental Intelligence Officer, Major Robert L. Kriz, comprised 'One of the sharpest platoons I ever had the privilege of knowing.' A few days prior to the German attack, Major Kriz gave the I+R Platoon the mission of moving to the Schirmbusch, right on the division south flank. They were to be the eyes and ears of the 99th Division and maintain contact with Task Force X, an element of the 14th Cavalry Group attached to the newly deployed 106th Infantry Division.

Their valiant stand and ultimate capture by the German 3rd Parachute Division is well documented and their unit citation reads:

'The Intelligence and Reconnaissance platoon, 394th Infantry Regiment, 99th Infantry Division, distinguished itself by extraordinary heroism in action against enemy forces on 16 December 1944 near Lanzerath, Belgium. The German Ardennes Offensive, which began the Battle of the Bulge, was directed initially against a small sector defended by the Intelligence and Reconnaissance Platoon. Following a two-hour artillery barrage, enemy forces of at least battalion strength launched three

Dr. Lyle J. Bouck, former commander of the I+R Platoon, revisits Lanzerath in August of 1989 and stands outside the former Café Scholzen. (Author's collection).

separate attacks against the small Intelligence and Reconnaissance platoon of 18 men. Each attack was successfully repelled by the platoon. The platoon position was becoming untenable as casualties mounted and ammunition was nearly exhausted. Plans were made to break contact with the enemy and withdraw under cover of darkness. Before this could be accomplished, a fourth enemy attack finally overran the position and the platoon was captured at bayonet point. Although greatly outnumbered, through numerous feats of valor and an aggressive and deceptive defense of their position, the platoon inflicted heavy casualties on the enemy forces and successfully delayed for nearly twenty-four hours, a major spearhead of the attacking German forces. Their valorous actions provided crucial time for the other American forces to prepare to defend against the massive German offensive. The extraordinary gallantry, determination and esprit de corps of the Intelligence and Reconnaissance Platoon in close combat against a numerically superior enemy force, are in keeping with the highest traditions of the United States Army and reflect great credit upon the unit and the Armed Forces of the United States.'

(**Author's note:** Lieutenant Warren P. Springer and three men of Battery C, 371st Field Artillery Battalion, joined and supported the I+R Platoon in its defense of the Schirmbusch.)

Return to the village and walk past your vehicle and the Calypso night-club. Stop in front of the next building on the right. In 1944, this building was known as Café Scholzen.

Upon capture by the enemy, the Schirmbusch defenders marched down the hill into captivity. Café Scholzen served as a joint aid-station/command post for the parachute battalion that had captured the Americans. At midnight on 16 December, as Bouck and his fellow prisoners tried to get what rest they could, the front door burst open and several seemingly impatient Germans entered the building.

The captured soldiers of the I+R Platoon, 394th Infantry and Battery C, 371st Field Service Artillery were initially held in the Café Scholzen on main street Lanzerath by their German captors.

Bouck noticed that the new arrivals wore different uniforms to those of their captors. Although he didn't know it at the time, many years later, he established beyond doubt that the newcomers' short-tempered commander was none other than *Obersturmbannführer* Jochen Peiper commander of *Kampfgruppe* Peiper. Angered by the paratroops' failure to exploit the capture of Lanzerath, Peiper took charge of the proceedings.

Drive back out of the village in the direction from which you came and turn left in the direction of Buchholz/Honsfeld. In Buchholz, pause by the first two houses on your left.

Major Norman D. Moore's 3rd Battalion, 394th Infantry held positions around Buchholz in its mission as 99th Division Reserve. The actual station building, now demolished, stood off to your right across the field and atop the railroad embankment.

On 16 December 1944, distant German artillery fire served to awaken the men of the 3rd Battalion. They nonetheless continued to line up for breakfast outside the station building, one platoon at a time. At 07:05, First Lieutenant Neil Brown, commanding officer of Company I, looked out of the station window to see men walking along the track from the east. Lieutenant Brown and Sergeant Elmer P. Klug instantly recognised the on-coming men as German infantry. In conversation with the author, Lieutenant Brown described Klug as an 'enormous man, near six feet tall, a superb athlete, barrel-chested and bull-necked'.

Sergeant Klug grabbed an M-1 carbine and raced out of the station and along the track in the direction of the approaching Germans. At a distance of about seventy-five yards, Klug roared for them to halt whereupon one of them began shouting orders to his men. Klug shot him and the others scattered to seek refuge behind a couple of empty railroad cars on a nearby siding.

Sergeant Klug returned to the station and told Lieutenant Brown that he estimated that between twenty-five and fifty Germans were hiding either in or behind the railroad cars. He then dispersed the men in the chow line and mustered the platoon that was eating in position close to the station building. An attempt by these men to advance upon the railroad cars met with heavy artillery and automatic weapon fire.

The artillery lasted for about an hour and two Americans tried unsuccessfully to dislodge the Germans from the boxcars. Soon thereafter, Staff Sergeant Savino Travalini and two other men drove into the area behind the station in a jeep towing an anti-tank gun. They unhooked the gun and immediately set about firing several rounds directly into the boxcars killing or wounding many of the Germans in the process.

During a subsequent lull in the fighting, Sergeant Klug discovered a dead German who'd been carrying a briefcase containing a copy of an inspirational general field order issued by *Feldmarschall* Gerd von Rundstedt and aimed at motivating the attacking infantry. This order was the first printed indication of German intentions to fall into American hands.

Little by little, as the situation elsewhere in the 99th sector deteriorated, the

99th Division commander, General Lauer, committed his division reserve. By the end of the first day, the 3rd Battalion's presence at Buchholz was down to two rifle platoons and a three-man observation team from Battery C, 371st Field Artillery Battalion.

Sergeant Elmer P. Klug was to die in tragic circumstances. Prior to the battalion withdrawal from Buchholz, he dove headlong into a hole to escape incoming artillery fire and landed on his head and shoulders breaking his neck. Medics placed him in a truck alongside other wounded for evacuation to Elsenborn via Krinkelt. Unidentified machine-gunners knocked out the truck on the outskirts of Krinkelt killing its occupants including the valiant sergeant.

Continue your journey entering Honsfeld, turning right and passing under the Railroad Bridge in the direction of Losheimergraben. At the junction with N632 (Rollbahn C) turn left (west) and take another left into Hünningen stopping with the church steeple just to the right of your car. In the church steeple is a small window through which First Lieutenant Charles Stockell, a forward observer with the 37th Field Artillery Battalion called fire down upon Germans attacking from the woods across the fields east of the village.

Given the severity of the attacks against the 99th Division on the first day, General Lauer asked for a rifle battalion to man a position on the east/southeast edge of Hünningen. Lieutenant Colonel John M. Hightower's 1st Battalion, 23rd Infantry of the 2nd Division assumed the mission of defending Hünningen, late on the afternoon of the 16 December and moved from Elsenborn to take up position as ordered. Hightower's men were in position before daylight on 17 December. They found themselves in an exposed and difficult position, so Colonel Hightower deployed his main strength to counter German pressure from the Buchholz/Honsfeld area facing east/southeast. By daylight 17 December, First Lieutenant William D. Amorello of the 1st Battalion could clearly see *Kampfgruppe* Peiper's column moving between Buchholz and Honsfeld on its way to Büllingen and his battalion's rear.

The first assault at Hünningen came at 16:00, preceded by six minutes of furious shelling. When the artillery stopped firing, *Oberstleutnant* Gerhard Lemm's Fusilier Regiment 89 began moving through a neck of woods just southeast of the village. First Lieutenant Charles W. Stockell, a forward observer with the 37th Field Artillery Battalion was with Company B facing the woods. He and his radio operator dashed into the church and climbed a set of rickety wooden ladders to a small window in the steeple (still visible) from where they directed fire on the attacking Volksgrenadiers until they were within a hundred yards of the Company B foxhole line. A number of the attackers did break through, but the attack evaporated when machine-gunners just to the Company B rear killed about fifty of them. Lemm's soldiers made a

Lieutenant Colonel John M. Hightower (front left) commanding 1st Battalion 23rd Infantry and his staff, stand outside of their command post. (Author's collection-courtesy of William D. Amorello).

further seven attacks that afternoon and evening but at no time, despite numerous penetrations in the 1st Battalion line, was the enemy able to capture Hünningen.

At 23.30, Colonel Chester J. Hirschfelder, the 9th Infantry regimental commander, reached Hightower by radio and informed him that his battalion and the nearby 394th Infantry in Mürringen were almost surrounded and that if the battalion expected to withdraw, it must move at once.

He also informed Hightower that the 1st Battalion was now attached to the 9th Infantry and that Hightower should use his own judgement as to the timing of any

Private First Class Hugh Burger, the yougest soldier in Company I of the 23rd Infantry.
(Author's collection, courtesy of Hugh Burger).

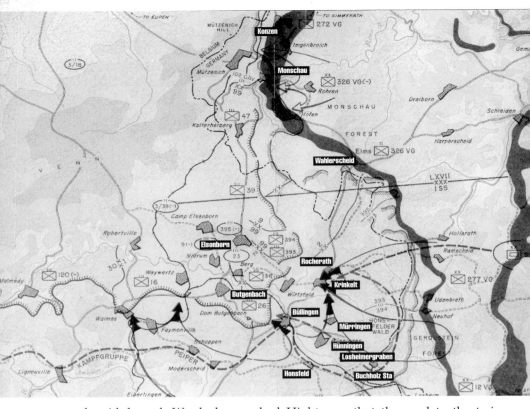

such withdrawal. Word also reached Hightower that the road to the twin villages of Krinkelt-Rocherath was still open. Shortly after midnight, the German attack against Hünningen lost its impetus and Colonel Hightower called together his company commanders to examine tentative plans to begin withdrawal at 02:00 on 18 December. Upon withdrawing from the village, the 1st Battalion left 250 enemy dead in front of the Company B position alone. The vehicles left the village first and Colonel Hightower led the men out on foot, their withdrawal protected by a small, heavily armed rearguard.

> Drive away from the church and leaving it to your right rear follow the sign for Büllingen (on your left). Upon reaching N632 (Rollbahn C), cross it in the direction of Mürringen. Upon entering the village, turn left at a black stone cross and keep left at the top of the hill following signs for Rocherath. Stop after the last house in the village with the valley of the Holzwarche Creek to your front and the houses of Krinkelt-Rocherath across the valley on the far slope.

East of German-held Büllingen, the American troops in Mürringen faced being surrounded, occupying as they did, a precarious jutting angle between the defense forming around the twin villages and the southern part of the sector forming at Bütgenbach. The sole remaining withdrawal road to the Elsenborn Ridge assembly area ran back west through Krinkelt whose tenure by friendly troops was none too certain on the night of 17 December. The chances of a successful withdrawal from Mürringen were dwindling by the hour. Shortly after midnight, the remnants of the 394th Infantry at Mürringen formed two columns, one composed of foot troops, the other made up of the remaining vehicles. Colonel Don Riley, commanding the 394th, started the motor column, including Hightower's vehicles, along this road toward Krinkelt at 02:15 under hostile shellfire. On the outskirts of Krinkelt, scouts reported seeing German tanks on the streets and someone ordered the vehicles abandoned while the men moved west on foot to Elsenborn. (These vehicles were later recovered).

The Infantry column, including Sergeant Stumpff and the mortar men of Company D, 394th Infantry who'd defended Losheimergraben, set out from Mürringen minutes after the vehicles.

They marched quietly towards Krinkelt across the fields and through the trees to the east (right) of the Mürringen-Krinkelt road.

Sturmbannführer *Schulze-Kossens commander 2nd Battalion, 25th SS Panzergrenadier Regiment, the unit that attacked 3rd Battalion, 23rd Infantry.* (Author's collection, couresty of Richard Schulze-Kossens).

Continue driving toward Krinkelt and downhill to the Holzwarche Creek, pausing at the bottom of the draw with a large sawmill off to your right.

Emerging here at the bottom of the draw on your right, the foot column from Mürringen found the road lined with deserted trucks and jeeps. After some indecision, the infantry manned some of the vehicles and edged their way through Krinkelt via Wirtzfeld to Elsenborn. Elements of the 1st Battalion, 393rd Infantry and 2nd Battalion, 394th had become separated from neighboring units during the withdrawal toward the twin villages from the International Highway. These units joined forces and at daylight on 18 December had entered Mürringen only to find it in enemy hands. They withdrew from the village and by the time it started getting dark, they emerged from the forest here at the junction of the Enkelberg Draw and the road to Krinkelt. An artillery observer at the edge of Krinkelt, spotted the column as it moved out of the draw and presuming it to be German, called down artillery fire, which resulted in numerous casualties. When the shelling stopped, the survivors either made their way uphill to the village or crossed the road and moved along the draw in the direction of Wirtzfeld.

Drive uphill into Krinkelt taking the first left and next right then on the main street park opposite the imposing village church.

During close quarter fighting in the twin villages from 17-19 December, the wartime church suffered major damage and as a result, the present building replaced the original. It stands on the same site as its predecessor and marks the boundary between the villages. Everything south of the church is Krinkelt and to the north Rocherath. Numerous tanks, both German and American, littered the streets after the battle, along with wrecked tank destroyers, trucks, jeeps and other vehicles.

In the small park opposite the church, there are two monuments, one commemorating the exploits of the 99th Infantry Division and the other those of the 2nd Infantry Division.

Drive north up the main street in the direction of Wahlerscheid. About 450 metres further on, at the Y junction where the main street continues to the front left, take the road to your front right. Pass a large concrete water tower on the left and turn right at the next junction. Follow this road, passing minor roads both left and right, then after passing a set of stone farm buildings across a field off to the left, keep front right at the next Y junction. Continue to the edge of the forest, parking in front of the wooden gates. <u>Access to the forest is limited. Only forestry and agricultural vehicles are permitted on the forest roads.</u> Access is restricted to walkers who must remain on the paved trails. At the time of writing during the hunting season (15 September-31 December) it is absolutely forbidden (as well as dangerous) to enter the forest before 09:00 and after 15:00.

This is Ruppenvenn, the point at which Rollbahn A emerged from the western edge of the forest. Facing the trees, Rollbahn A was the black topped road leading to your front left. In 1944, a section of forest shaped like a bird's beak, jutted out into the field to your left.

Late afternoon on 16 December 1944, Lieutenant Colonel Paul V. Tuttle's 3rd Battalion, 23rd Infantry drove east of Rocherath through snow-covered fields that were pock marked with shell holes. The vehicles stopped just short of Ruppenvenn, enabling the occupants to get out. Initially, the 3rd Battalion was to act as a counterattack force to push the Germans back through the forest. The hard-hitting attack against Colonel Allen's 3rd Battalion, 393rd Infantry, as well as events elsewhere, forced a drastic change in Colonel Tuttle's mission. His new orders were 'To hold at all costs!' The 3rd Battalion was none too well prepared for such a defense, having arrived with no mines and very little ammunition. 'Ammo' trucks bringing forward ammunition found the road between Büllingen and Krinkelt barred by the enemy and couldn't reach the battalion in its new position.

Incoming artillery and rocket fire, prompted Captain Charles B. MacDonald and the men of Company I to move east into the forest through the trees on the left side of Rollbahn A. They moved to a point about 1100 yards east of Ruppenvenn on the West Bank of the Jansbach creek and dug in on either side

Prior to the battle two soldiers of Antitank Company, 393rd Infantry, wash up outside number 85 Krinkelt. (Author's collection-courtesy Harry Parker).

The 393rd Infantry Regiment Command post in Krinkelt pictured in November 1944. Today this is number 129 Krinkelt about two blocks southwest of the present-day church. (393rd History John Rogers).

of the trail. Companies K and L of the 3rd Battalion were off to MacDonald's right and rear. That first night First Lieutenant Victor L. Miller's medium tank platoon from Company C, 741st Tank Battalion, joined Colonel Tuttle's men in the woods east of the twin villages. The 3rd Battalion flanks were wide open, since by virtue of necessity, the unit was operating on its own. On the 17th, shortly after withdrawing troops of the 3rd Battalion, 393rd Infantry passed through the Company I position, SS Panzergrenadiers launched seven successive infantry assaults out of the Jansbach draw directly against Company I. Lieutenant Miller's tanks withdrew to the rear to assume positions at Ruppenvenn thereby covering both trails as they exited the forest.

At 15:30 that afternoon, things took a serious turn for the worse when Panther tanks of SS *Oberststurmbannführer* Siegfried Muller's *Kampfgruppe* appeared on the scene. The preceding night, these fresh troops from the 12th SS *Hitlerjugend* Panzer Division, in the shape of a reinforced battle group, moved forward to reinforce the attack west along Rollbahn A.

These tanks and marching SS Panzergrenadiers struck the Company I left flank rolling forward till their machine-guns enfiladed the foxholes in which the defenders crouched. Company I held until its ammunition was nearly gone, then tried to withdraw to a nearby firebreak but went to pieces under fire raking in from all sides. Private Richard E. Cowan and Sergeant José M. Lopez both earned their Medals of Honor in separate actions supporting Company I, during its withdrawal.

Here at Ruppenvenn, in a duel at close quarters, Lieutenant Miller's tanks destroyed the first Panther at the forest edge. A second Panther then appeared alongside the first and succeeded in knocking out the two Shermans, killing Lieutenant Miller and two of his men in the process. The two survivors from Miller's tank and the crew of the other Sherman escaped.

Colonel Tuttle's battalion received a Distinguished Unit Citation for its role in this crucial delaying action.

Retrace your route stopping at the junction just before the stone farmhouse and outbuildings. This is Lausdell, the scene of what the late Charles B. MacDonald considered as one of the most significant actions in the entire Battle of the Bulge.

On the afternoon of the 17 December, General Robertson met Lieutenant Colonel William D. McKinley and the advance party of his 1st Battalion, 9th Infantry at a place called Baracken on the Rocherath-Wahlerscheid road about 800 yards north of the twin villages. He ordered McKinley to rush his battalion here to Lausdell and to hold the position 'until ordered to withdraw'. By dusk, the 1st Battalion, and the attached Company K, were deployed here at Lausdell overlooking the road from the Ruppenvenn junction on the edge of the woods to the east.

A thick fog lay close to the snow-covered ground as McKinley's men dug in

Lieutenant Miller's tank (left) knocked out at Ruppenvenn on 17 December 1944 by the spearhead of 12th SS Panzer Division as it emerged from the western edge of the forest, Miller and two of his crew were killed.

The view toward the Twin Villages from Ruppenenvenn at the western edge of the Krinkelterwald. The attacking Germans nicknamed this corner 'Sherman Ecke', a soldierly tribute to the crewmen of Lieutenant Victor Miller's tank platoon who died here, when their two Shermans were knocked out by the advance guard of 12th SS Panzer Regiment close to where the small tree now stands on the left of the photograph.

around the road junction in front of the farm buildings. Around them was a scene of wild confusion, stragglers with and without arms hurried along the road and across nearby fields to the sound and flash of gunfire coming from the forest to the east. Company K was dug in around the farmhouse and its outbuildings backed up by three tank destroyers from the 644th Tank Destroyer Battalion. The 1st Battalion occupied positions just east and south of the farm buildings. Colonel McKinley's command post was in an abandoned artillery dugout halfway between the then Palm farmstead and the Baracken crossroads on the road to Wahlerscheid.

The battalion had not picked up its mines during the hasty disengagement from the Wahlerscheid area, but managed to get some from the supporting tank destroyer crews for use on the road. They had an ample supply of bazookas along with the required ammunition. First Lieutenant John G. Granville, a forward observer with the supporting 15th Field Artillery Battalion, was on hand and frantically working to establish communications with Major Herron N. Maples at the battalion Fire Direction Center.

At 19.30 three unidentified tanks and a platoon of infantry came along the road from Ruppenvenn and pulled into a field behind Company A. Minutes later, they machine-gunned the farm buildings setting alight a wooden barn that stood just left of the farmhouse. (Today a large stone structure occupies the spot where the barn stood). Captain MacDonald of Company I, 23rd Infantry and several of his men had sought refuge here and vacated the burning building post haste. In subsequent heavy fighting around the Palm farm buildings at Lausdell, the defenders knocked out a number of enemy tanks. Private William A. Soderman of Company K personally knocked out three enemy tanks with bazooka rockets and was seriously wounded in this action which earned him the Medal of Honor. Supporting artillery proved instrumental in stopping the attacking Germans although a few tanks and some infantry did get through to the twin villages during that first night, only to be taken care of by the men of Colonel Francis Boos' 38th Infantry Regiment of the 2nd Division. At one point, two of McKinley's men, Sergeant Odis Bone of Company B and Corporal Charles Roberts of Company D climbed aboard an immobilised Panther to set it alight using gasoline and a thermite grenade.

Just prior to dawn, the following day, 18 December, German infantry and tanks renewed their attack at Lausdell. Supporting friendly artillery shelled the approach road and a confused firefight broke out the length of the American foxhole line. The morning fog was heavy and visibility almost nil. The American infantry let the tanks roll past then turned to tail them with bazookas or turned to meet attacking infantry with grenades and even bayonets and knives. They beat off the first assault but as the fog lifted, at about 08.30, three enemy tanks rolled right along the Company A foxhole line firing their machine-guns as the German infantry rushed forward. First Lieutenant Stephen K. Truppner of Company A radioed that his company had

Lieutenant Colonel William D. McKinley and members of his staff from 1st Battalion, 9th Infantry confer outside a westwall bunker on the Schnee Eifel prior to the Battle of the Bulge. (Author's collection, courtesy Colonel James McKinley.)

been overrun and requested that artillery fire on his own position. For thirty minutes, supporting artillery did so and only twelve men escaped. Four tanks from Company A, 741st Tank Battalion counter-attacked just before noon on 18 December. This allowed the 1st Battalion to begin disengaging at 13.00. They withdrew via Baracken then passed through elements of the 2nd Battalion, 38th Infantry at the northern end of Rocherath.

The 2nd Battalion journal for 18 December read: 'Colonel McKinley's group (Index Red) has withdrawn completely and Colonel McKinley arrived CP'.

On 30 December 1944, the *New York Times* ran an article by Harold Denny in which he heaped praise upon McKinley and his men.

In a tape recorded message to the author, Colonel William F. Hancock, who as a major, served as McKinley's Executive Officer said of his former commander: 'As a commander, he was the best. He was a strong, deep thinker, all the men liked him'

Turn right and pass the farm buildings to your left and left rear. Pause just before the first left turn. The corner of the field on your left was the location of Colonel McKinley's command post, which overlooked the rear of the Palm farmhouse and outbuildings. Continue straight ahead until you reach the main road just north of Rocherath at Baracken. Stop before joining the main road.

This is Baracken, the junction through which the bulk of the 2nd Division passed on its way south of Wahlerscheid to the twin villages. It was to the first house on your right upon reaching the junction, that Captain Macdonald reported to Colonel Tuttle after he and his men vacated the burning barn at Lausdell. Major General Walter M. Robertson, commander of the 2nd Infantry Division, came here to supervise the division's withdrawal south of Wahlerscheid and its subsequent deployment in and around Krinkelt-Rocherath.

Turn left towards Rocherath. Continue south through Krinkelt turning right in the direction of Wirtzfeld/Elsenborn. At the western edge of Krinkelt, pause where the first minor road joins from the right.

The first Germans entered the Twin Villages in the early evening of 17 December. The tenacious defenders had held onto Krinkelt/Rocherath in hand-to-hand fighting that bought precious time for withdrawing troops to pass through on their way to reserve positions on top of Elsenborn Ridge. In the closing stages of the battle here, Technician Grade 4 Truman Kimbro earned himself a posthumous Medal of Honor.

Disengagement from the villages was made from left to right along the line from Rocherath to Wirtzfeld. Lieutenant Colonel Jack K. Norris pulled his 2nd Battalion, 38th Infantry, back first from the northern end of Rocherath. Lieutenant Colonel Frank T. Mildren's 1st Battalion, 38th Infantry followed. Lieutenant Colonel Olinto. M. Barsanti's 3rd Battalion, 38th Infantry supported by men of Company C, 2nd Engineer Combat Battalion and two M-10 Tank Destroyers from Lieutenant Charlie Coates' 3rd Platoon, Company C, 644th Tank Destroyer Battalion acted as a rearguard.

The battle for the Twin Villages was over, its outcome favouring the Americans. By 20 December, they were firmly entrenched atop Elsenborn Ridge against which all further German attacks would prove futile. Such attacks lacked adequate tank and artillery support like that which had enabled the Germans to reach Krinkelt-Rocherath.

The small stone cross to your right commemorates Arnold Schroeder, a local man killed here on 14 April 1945 while removing mines from the roadside.

Continue into Wirtzfeld past its church and following the sign for Elsenborn. The schoolhouse in Wirtzfeld was the command post for 2nd Division Artillery

Soldiers of the 38th Infantry Regiment enter their former command post in Rocherath upon its recapture by the 2nd Infantry Division early February 1945. (Cavanagh collection courtesy Colonel Tom C. Morris).

Joseph Goebbels promised the German people "Total War". This must be what he meant! The scene outside the church in Krinkelt. (Author's collection, courtesy Colonel James W. Love).

Major-General Walter M. Robertson presents Lieutenant Colonel Frank T. Mildren with the Silver Star for his part in the defense of the Twin Villages. (Author's collection, courtesy General Frank T. Mildren).

while the division command post was a farmhouse at the northern extremity of the village. Upon climbing the forward slope of the Elsenborn Ridge and reaching its crest, the land to the right side of the road is a restricted area forming part of Camp Elsenborn. This is an active Belgian Army training area. After passing the wind turbines and the small trees on the right side of the road at the top of the ridge, pause with the rolling open landscape off to your right. This is the impact area for the firing of live ammunition of every calibre.

Upon their withdrawal to Elsenborn Ridge, troops of the 2nd Infantry Division occupied positions off to your left as far as and including the village of Berg. The 99th and 9th Infantry Divisions occupied the area off to your right and as far as Kalterherberg. In spite of their attempts to do so, the Germans never set foot on this high ground. Their American counterparts spent the next 6 weeks in snow-covered foxholes, here on the highest ground in Belgium. All attempts to move around in daylight resulted in drawing German artillery fire.

Extracts from the journal of First Lieutenant Kendall M. Ogilvie of Battery A, 17th Field Artillery Observation Battalion, reveal the daily temperatures at specific times on certain dates to have been as follows:

Date	Time	Temp (°F)
12.16.44	01:40	27
12.16.44	11:40	34
12.16.44	23:35	38
12.27.44	01:45	14
12.27.44	13:50	25
12.27.44	23:40	17
01.1.45	03:40	20
01.1.45	11:45	23
01.1.45	21:40	13

Continue into Elsenborn turning left at the church toward Bütgenbach on N632. Pass under the railroad viaduct. In Bütgenbach, take the second minor road to the right then the first left passing a large stone building off to your right. This retirement home, served as the 99th Division Message Center from 11/11/44 – 12/17/44 and was occupied by the Division Signal Company.

Pass the first house on the right and pause outside the large White House then the home of the Kirsch family. This house served as General Lauer's Division

An M-10 Tank Destroyer crew from Company C, 644th Tank Destroyer Battalion, load shells onto their vehicle in Wirtzfeld, under the watchful eye of their Platoon Leader 1st Lieutenant Owen R. McDermott. From left to right: Private John Grimaldi, Corporal Henry McVeigh, Sergeant George Holiday, Private Ed Kummer, Private Henry Bragg and at right, Lieutenant McDermott.
(Author's collection, courtesy Owen R. McDermott).

One of the six Sturmgeschütz (Stug) from 3rd Panzer Grenadier Division knocked out by supporting artillery fire called down by Lieutenant Colonel Justice Neale commander of the 324th Engineer Combat Battalion. They tried but failed in their attack against the boundary of the 393rd and 394th Infantry Regiments north of Wirtzfeld on 12/28/44. (Courtesy Colonel "Bob" Neale).

German POW's line up for inspection in Sourbrodt. (National Archives Collection).

Headquarters during the same aforementioned period. On the garden wall is a plaque commemorating a visit made to the house by the Supreme Allied Commander, General Dwight. D. Eisenhower in November of 1944 when the building served as headquarters for the 9th Infantry Division.

Continue on N632 in the direction of Büllingen and park just to the right of the traffic island sign posted 'St. Vith'. Pause to inspect the obelisk in the centre of the traffic island.

Nicknamed 'The Big Red One', the 1st Infantry Division saw its first Second World War action in late 1942 during the North African landings. Along with the 29th Infantry Division, it led the V Corps assault on Omaha Beach on 6 June 1944. In the 'Bulge' its 2nd Battalion 26th Infantry stopped all German attempts to move west of Büllingen on Rollbahn C and Corporal Henry F. Warner, of Captain Donald P. Rivette's Anti-tank Company, earned himself a posthumous Medal of Honor during hard fighting here at Dom Bütgenbach. The obelisk commemorates the men of the division killed in the 'Bulge' The 1st Infantry Division held the Bütgenbach-Waimes

Deep in the forest, northeast of Elsenborn on 22 September 1950, a Polish refugee named Toni Jajesnica, who'd settled in Belgium, died when his horse struck a mine left over from the battle.

(Author's collection).

Signal personnel of the 1st Infantry Division. (US Army Signal Corps).

On the left-Lieutenant Colonel Rex Rowie, commander 5th Field Artillery Battalion, centre; Major W.V. Ledley Executive Officer and on the right; Captain N. H. Barnhart Fire Direction Officer in the vicinity of Bütgenbach during the battle. (Author's collection, courtesy Colonel Rex Rowie).

Medics of the 393rd Infantry evacuate wounded atop Elsenborn Ridge. (John Rogers, 99th Division collection, Army War College).

The graves of German engineers killed north of the Twin Villages. (Author's collection, courtesy Colonel Tom C. Morris).

PFC Hugh Brady of Company I, 23rd Infantry is awarded the DSC for action in the Krinkelterwald.

Troops and vehicles of the 1st Infantry Division enter Bütgenbach.
(US Army Signal Corps).

sector throughout the battle, rounded up German paratroops and participated in the re-capture of ground lost to the Germans during the attack.

Suggested Reading:

MacDonald: *'Company Commander'* Chapters 10-12

MacDonald: *'A Time For Trumpets'* Chapters 8,10,18.

Cavanagh: *'Krinkelt-Rocherath, The Battle for the Twin Villages'* .

Cole: *'The Ardennes – Battle of the Bulge'* Chapters 5-6.

Former Sergeant Richard H. Byers rides 'Shotgun' over Elsenborn Ridge on 17 December 1994 in a jeep restored and owned by Pierre Dullier. Pierrre named his jeep 'Chiquita' after the one in which Byers rode during his time in Belgium as an artillery observer with 'C' Battery in the 371st Field Artillery Battalion.
(Author's collection).

CHAPTER 2

KAMPFGRUPPE PEIPER-LOSHEIM TO LA GLEIZE

<u>STARTING POINT: THE SCHEID RAILROAD BRIDGE-CARRYING
BUNDESTRASSE 421 OVER THE RAILROAD JUST EAST OF LOSHEIM,
GERMANY (+/- 25 KM SOUTHEAST OF MALMÉDY, BELGIUM) FACING
WEST TOWARD LOSHEIM.</u>

The strongest fighting unit in 6th Panzer Army, *SS-Oberführer* Wilhelm Mohnke's 1st SS *Leibstandarte* Panzer Division, was to spearhead the German attack over the Meuse River and onto Antwerp. Mohnke divided his division into four battle groups, *(Kampfgruppen)* the most important of which carried the name of its commander, twenty-nine year old *SS-Obersturmbannführer* Jochen Peiper.

The strength of *Kampfgruppe* Peiper's was one hundred and seventeen tanks, one hundred and forty-nine halftracks, eighteen 105mm guns, six 150mm guns, thirty to forty anti-aircraft weapon systems, four thousand eight hundred men.

When Peiper reached the Scheid railroad bridge he found that it had been destroyed. He swung down the dirt track to the right crossing the tracks less than a hundred yards to the north.

SS-Oberführer *Wilhelm Mohnke, commander of 1st SS* Leibstandarte *Panzer Division.*

Elements of *SS-Obersturmbann-führer* Otto Skorzeny's 150th Panzer Brigade included a tank company with five disguised Panthers and a single captured Sherman, two infantry companies each with approximately 120 men and a heavy company with mortar, anti tank, pioneer and panzer grenadier platoons, in all about five hundred men.

Mohnke called Peiper to his headquarters in the village of Tondorf, Germany on 14 December to inform him of his unit's mission in the coming attack. On the following day, Peiper briefed his subordinates and they in turn, informed their company and platoon leaders.

SS-Obersturmbannführe* Jochen Peiper, commander of Kampfgruppe Peiper.*

On 16 December, after the opening artillery barrage, elements belonging to Generalmajor Gerhard Engel's 12th Volksgrenadier Division began their attack, their mission being to break through the front line positions of the 394th Infantry Regiment. Peiper himself, went to the 12th Volksgrenadier headquarters near Hallschlag to monitor the progress of this infantry attack and was disappointed to learn that things were not going as quickly as planned. That afternoon, therefore, he re-joined his unit and by 17.00 his lead elements reached the Scheid railroad bridge only to find that retreating Germans had blown it the previous September. He quickly solved this problem by taking the dirt trail to the right of the bridge and crossing the line to the northwest. Accompanying *Kampfgruppe* Peiper was at least one *Kriegsberichte* (combat photographer) whose film subsequently fell into American hands.

Drive west on 421 in the direction of Losheim passing a large sawmill on the left. At the junction with 265 turn right then first left in the direction of 'St. Vith-Belgien'.

Between here and the Our River valley, Kampfgruppe Peiper encountered mines that slowed its progress until cleared by engineers. Continue into Belgium downhill then turn right in the direction of Hullscheid, where you keep left turning up hill and in the direction of Merlscheid. In Merlscheid, pause by the small white chapel on the right side of the road.

Continue on the same road and at the junction with N626, turn right in the direction of Lanzerath (2km). In Lanzerath, pause at the building on the left just before the old schoolhouse today known as the 'Calypso' night-club.

This building, then known as 'Café Scholzen' served as temporary headquarters of the German airborne battalion which had earlier captured the Intelligence and Reconnaissance Platoon, 394th Infantry on the high ground overlooking the village. The Germans held their prisoners here in Café Scholzen prior to moving them into Germany. At midnight on 16/17 December, SS-*Obersturmbannführer* Jochen Peiper arrived here and immediately set about moving his column out of Losheim. Accompanied by men of the parachute battalion, Peiper's column began its advance in the direction of Buchholz Station.

TSCHTO ETO TAKÓJE?
deutsch: was ist das?

Unsere Soldaten können Alles,
sie sprechen auch sofort etwas **Russisch!**

Wichtig! Die Betonung ist unbedingt auf die Silben mit dem Zeichen zu legen.

Notwendige Worte.

Halt !...sstoi !	wer da....kto tamm
Freund....prijátelj	Feind....njáprijátelj
Hände hoch !........	ruki wwerch !
was ist das ?.......	tschtó éto takóje ?
wo.....gdjé	wohin....kudá
woher....otkúda	warum.....potschemú
ja.....da	nein......njät
auf.....na	in.......w
links....ljáwyi	rechts....práwyi
ich.....ja	du.......ty
er.....onn	sie......oná
wir.....my	essen....jestj
schlafen.spátj	trinken..pitj
schlecht.njácharoscho	gut......chárascho
süss.....sel´ádko	salzig...ssóljno
sauer....kisslo	bitter...górjko
gross....boljschói	klein....máljenki
weit.....daljóko	nah......blíssko
vorwärts.wperjód	zurück...nasát
wieviel.kostet....	sskóljko sstóit
schön....krassíwyi	hässlich..njákrassíwyi
Farben....krásski	rot.......krássnyi
grün.....seljónyi	blau......gólubói
schwarz..tschórnyi	grau......ssjáryi
Pinsel...kistj	kl.Pinsel.kístotschka
dahin....tudá	Dummkopf..durák
Schuft...sswólotsch	Teufel....tschort
Gott.....bog	Engel.....ángel
Heilige..sswjatói	Pfarrer...sswjäschts
	chénnik

An unidentified SS man left this Russian front dictionary in Lanzerath. (Author's collection, courtesy Sany and Nicholas Schugens).

Drive just past the 'Calypso' stopping by the steel railings on the left. At the end of the railings where a minor road leads left, note the small house on the corner to your front left. This house was the home of Christoph Schur and family.

The larger building slightly north and across N626 from the Schur home is the Café Palm. It took most of the second day for the bulk of Peiper's 800 vehicles and men to pass through the rural backwater village of Lanzerath. About mid-morning, a group of American prisoners of war captured in Honsfeld a few

The Schur family house in the winter of 1943, a year before the battle. (Courtesy Adolf Schur).

The Schur family outside their home. (Courtesy Adolf Schur).

hours earlier marched down N626 into the village. Among the prisoners were men of Headquarters Company, 3rd Battalion 394th Infantry, including Technical Sergeant Luther C. Symons. After interrogating Symons and his buddies in Honsfeld, the Germans marched them back down the advancing column along with two Belgian civilians; a man called Peter Müller from Hasenvenn and his fifteen-year-old nephew Johann Brodel from Krewinkel. The Belgians had tried to escape from the Manderfeld area at the start of the attack and found themselves in Honsfeld as *Kampfgruppe* Peiper captured the village. As the column of prisoners marched past Café Palm, an SS man standing by a tank outside the building presumed them to be 'partisans' and pulled them from the group. He took them into a wooden shed at the south side of the building and shot them both with a pistol. The boy died instantly but his uncle, shot behind one ear, fell to the ground and played dead. Sometime later, when things had calmed down somewhat, Müller rose to his feet and dashed across the darkened street to Christoph Schur's front door. Inside, Christoph Schur and his wife cleaned Müller's head wound as more than a score of sleeping German paratroopers slept on, regardless of the activity among them. Suddenly, the door flew open and several SS men entered intent on killing the wounded Belgian. In the First World War, Christoph Schur had served in the Kaiser's army, he bravely told the newcomers that this was no manner in which to treat a civilian while referring to his service for the Kaiser and showing them a photo of himself in WW1 uniform. Apparently respectful of his status as a veteran, the SS men left the house as quickly as they'd entered. Müller survived but has since passed away as has Christoph Schur. Today, the photograph of the WW1 German *Landsers,* hangs proudly in the home of Christoph's son, who still lives in the village.

Circled; the young Christophe Schur as a German soldier in World War One.
(Courtesy Adolf Schur).

Continue north on N626 turning left in the direction of Buchholz/Honsfeld. Upon reaching Buchholz, drive on until you reach a bend where the road continues to Honsfeld or turns right in the direction of Losheimergraben. Keep left and pause just upon turning this bend. The forester's home off to your left existed in 1944.

By the time *Kampfgruppe* Peiper got here, men of the 1st and 2nd Platoons,

Company K, 394th lightly held Buchholz, the bulk of their battalion committed elsewhere in its role as the 99th Division reserve. In addition to the few sleeping Company K riflemen, three soldiers of Battery C, 371st Field Artillery Battalion, Lieutenant Harold R. Mayer, Sergeant Richard H. Byers and Sergeant Curtis Fletcher had spent the night in this house. As Peiper's column entered Buchholz, the infantry put up a token defence. Determined to escape, the artillerymen attempted to reach their jeep, which they'd parked the previous night by the stone outbuilding to your left. Seeing the Germans had already turned the bend towards Honsfeld, they couldn't retrieve their jeep. Mayer and his men turned back intending to go through the building in the hope of making their escape on foot. German paratroops captured Fletcher but Mayer and Byers made good their escape. Working their way through the trees in the dark, they managed to crouch beneath some low-hanging branches at the roadside just in front of where you are presently parked. As a gap occurred in the German column, they raced over the road and through the trees eventually reaching friendly lines in Hünningen, still held by the 1st Battalion, 23rd Infantry blocking Rollbahn C.

First Lieutenant Harold R. Mayer of 'C' Battery 371st Field Artillery Battalion. (Author's collection, courtesy of Harold and Marie Mayer).

Continue west and a little further on at a 'Y' junction keep right in the direction of Honsfeld. Drive into the village stopping after the school at the Eifelerhof guesthouse by a bus stop on the right.

American prisoners captured here, along with some captured later in Büllingen, were assembled in the bar of the guesthouse for interrogation. Private First Class Roger V. Foehringer of Service Battery, 924th Field Artillery Battalion, captured in Büllingen early on the morning of 17 December has vivid memories of what happened:

'We were taken to a building that reminded me of a big dance hall of some kind. Our troops had been using it as a rest centre where they could get hot food and warmed up. I would say there were about two hundred American prisoners sitting on chairs in this theatre-like room with a stage in front. In a short time, a German officer got up on this stage and told us in perfect English that they were going to interrogate some of us. A young

German soldier walked down the aisle by me. I gave him 'the glare', he gave me 'the finger' and I joined him as he pointed a Luger at me. We went into the wings of a room opposite the stage. He spoke very good English and the first thing he did was to push the pistol in my stomach as he pulled the dogtags off my neck. He was wearing some American clothing and upon examining my dogtags became concerned upon reading that my next of kin was Mrs. William Foehringer. He couldn't figure out the grammatical connection between a 'Mrs' and the name William.'

Private Roger V. Foehringer, Service Battery, 924th Field Artillery Battalion. (Author's collection courtesy Roger and Ruth Foehringer).

Shortly after Foehringer's interrogation, American fighter-bombers strafed and bombed *Kampfgruppe* Peiper so Foehringer and his fellow prisoners sought refuge in the cellar of the dance hall.

Continue past the old church on your right and pause just around the next bend to the right, opposite a water trough. Note the memorial to the 612th - 801st TD Battalions and attached units of the 99th Infantry Division.

Some of the most well-known photographs taken during the battle are those showing three dead GI's lying face down in the mud in front of this trough as German soldiers try on the dead men's boots. Roger Foehringer well remembers passing those dead Americans:

'There were several [three] bodies lying in the road, it was hard to visualise that these were bodies because so many German vehicles had run over them. We tried to avoid walking on them, they were like pancakes, but the Germans made us walk over them.'

Continue up the hill towards Bullingen and after approximately 200 yards stop by the village cemetery on your right.

Here and in the yard of the house just before the cemetery, soldiers of the *Kampfgruppe* Peiper murdered Americans they'd already taken prisoner. One of the SS men (not

Honsfeld. The spot where young men once died.

The bodies of American dead lie by the water trough in Honsfeld. They were later flattened under the wheels and tracks of German vehicles.   (US Army Signal Corps).

identified) involved in killing the men as they exited the farmhouse, bragged about it later in front of a local teenager who later testified of hearing this when called to the post-war trial of surviving members of the *Kampfgruppe* Peiper. Unknown SS men also murdered a teenage girl named Erna Collas.

Exit Honsfeld following the same road north in the direction of Büllingen. Upon reentering Bullingen pause by the bus stop on your left. Ahead of you the road branches front left and right, you will ultimately keep front left.

Sergeant Grant Yager of Service Battery 924th Field Artillery Battalion, disabled Peiper's lead tank as it entered Büllingen early on the morning of 17 December 1944.
(Author's collection, courtesy Grant and Helen Yager).

As *Kampfgruppe* Peiper approached Büllingen, ten of eleven Piper Cub observation planes, belonging to 99th Division Artillery, managed to take off right under the noses of approaching German tanks as they headed for the improvised airstrip off to the distant left. Over to the right, pilots of 2nd Division Artillery, who couldn't reach their planes, called friendly fire down upon their aircraft before making good their escape on foot. Captain James W. Cobb of Service Battery, 924th Field Artillery Battalion based in Büllingen, sent a lightly armed platoon under Lieutenant Jack Varner to block this road into town. Varner positioned his men along the hedgerow across the field immediately off to your left. In their role as bazooka team, Sergeant Grant Yager along with Privates Arthur Romaker and Santos Maldanado took up position behind a small rise in the ground which then existed on the spot today occupied by the

Men of Service Battery, 924th Artillery Battalion held a roadblock here on the morning of 17 December as Kampfgruppe *Peiper entered Büllingen from the direction of Honsfeld. Private Bernard J. Pappel, a machine gunner, was wounded where the small sign is now located. After his capture an SS-Sturmbahnführer shot him in the garden to the right.*

Grant Yager's Bazooka team

Bernard J Pappel's .30 calibre Browning machine gun position

Bernard J Pappel murdered in this garden

thatched roofed house off to your front left. Private Bernard Pappel Jr., a 50-calibre machine gunner, placed his machine gun in the hedge to your front where the road splits left and right. Sergeant Yager well recalls that winter's morning 56 years ago:

'About 07.00, on Sunday 17 December, Staff Sergeant Zoller, our ammunition sergeant, had us set up what he said was to be a roadblock out of town. Besides our carbines, we carried a number of grenades, one bazooka and a number of bazooka rockets. About 07.30, while the three of us were off to the side of the road, a German tank came over the hill following the road into Büllingen. In just a minute or two, a second tank came over the hill, by which time I'd decided I could fire the weapon without sights just by aiming alongside the barrel. When it was directly in front of us, at about 100 feet, I fired the bazooka. The round hit somewhere on the side and the tank turned part way around in the road. As the crewmen left the disabled tank, I fired my carbine hitting the first two but as I went to shoot a third, my carbine failed.

'By this time, the rest of the column had come to a halt directly in front of us, only a hundred feet distant. The front vehicle was a halftrack loaded with Panzergrenadiers, this is the group that took us prisoner. At this time, we noticed one of our men, Bernard Pappel, had been wounded and was lying near the side of the road where he had been manning a 30-caliber machine gun. The German soldiers that were there allowed Romaker. Maldanado and myself to give Pappel first aid, using our first aid kits and sulphur powder. A German officer, in a cream-coloured jacket, approached me talking fast in German and poking me with his pistol. I couldn't understand him and he apparently spoke no English. He walked away, leaving me standing by the halftrack and in a few minutes, the column was ready to move on. They made the three of us sit on the hood of the German halftrack, me in front by the radiator and Romaker and Maldanado behind me nearer the windshield. I heard a single pistol shot and Romaker spluttered "My God! They shot Pappel in the head".'

Bernard Pappel is buried in Henri Chapelle U.S. Military Cemetery, (Plot C, Row 10, Grave 60) close to Joseph Browzowski (Plot C, Row 8, Grave 38) killed in the 'Malmedy' Massacre a few hours after Pappel died here in Büllingen).

Taking the left fork of the road drive on into Büllingen and as you descend into the village, pause at the bend in the road with a stone house ahead of you on the left and a grassy bank to the right.

As the lead tank of *Kampfgruppe* Peiper began its descent into the village, Privates First Class Roger V. Foehringer and Alfred Goldstein of Service Battery 924th Field Artillery Battalion were walking up this hill carrying a box of grenades. Upon reaching this bend in the road they came face to face with

Büllingen church pathway after the battle. (US Army Signal Corps).

Peiper's lead tank. Dropping the grenades, they ran off to the front left as machine-gun bullets cracked all around them. Foehringer lay still as a second tank and a halftrack carrying ten or twelve SS-Panzergrenadiers sped down into the village following the first tank. From the garden/yard of the red brick house, just up from the bend, the two GIs could clearly see the vehicles moving down the hill past a stone house on the left (now demolished and replaced by a post-war structure on the same spot). Goldstein spotted two Service Battery cooks who were trying to load a bazooka from the wrong end. Rushing up to them he seized the weapon, loaded it and fired downhill at one of the tanks, the rocket detonating as it hit the side of the house. He and Foehringer then joined other Service Battery soldiers inside the red brick house and for a short while they and other soldiers fired carbines and rifles at the German vehicles moving downhill into the village. Eventually, SS-Panzergrenadiers captured the troublesome 'Amis' and after relieving them of watches etc. marched them south in the direction of Honsfeld.

Continue down then uphill straight ahead of you and upon reaching the junction with N632 turn right (East) on the main street. A little further on, take the first left and then keeping right with the church to your left, drive downhill and under the former Railroad Bridge. Pause at the left-hand bend beyond the bridge.

While the bulk of *Kampfgruppe* Peiper turned left at the junction of N632 with the road from Honsfeld, a small group of tanks and halftracks turned right and downhill in the direction of Wirtzfeld. Just prior to this a mixed bag of American vehicles tried to escape from Büllingen via Wirtzfeld to Elsenborn. Sergeant Roger D. Phillips and other men from the 2nd Platoon, Company C, 254th Engineer Combat Battalion, marched this same route and upon turning left at this bend, started uphill out of town behind the fleeing vehicles. As they did so, the approaching German armour began firing shells past the engineers at the American vehicles hitting a weapons carrier and setting it alight before it reached the top of the hill.

Phillips and his buddies hastily left the road in a field off to the right as machine-gunners on enemy halftracks took them under fire. With no possibility of concealment, Phillips' platoon leader, a lieutenant named Anderson, ordered his men to throw down their weapons and surrender. Panzergrenadiers marched the engineers back down to Büllingen and assembled them atop the Railroad Bridge. As a young SS-man relieved Phillips of his watch, American fighter-planes swooped down and began circling Büllingen a couple of times. The Germans quickly herded their prisoners down off the railroad and obliged them to stand around tanks and other vehicles as the planes circled above. The fighters swooped down and upon spotting khaki-clad troops assembled around the vehicles, the pilots refrained from strafing or bombing this part of the German column. The tanks and halftracks, which had earlier captured the engineers, attacked Wirtzfeld, then defended by men of 2nd Division Artillery Headquarters, the 2nd platoon of Company C, 644th Tank Destroyer Battalion and a 155mm howitzer of Battery C, 372nd Field Artillery Battalion under the command of First Lieutenant Charles Biggio. Together, these American defenders stopped this attack on Wirtzfeld, knocking out at least two enemy tanks in the process.

Turn around and head back the way you came turning right upon reaching the main street just past the church. At the West End of Büllingen, turn front left off N632 in the direction of St. Vith. Pause by the trees on the left just before the 'Gendarmerie' (Polizei). To your left is the former cattle market, which in 1944 was an American fuel depot.

Some of Peiper's halftracks and tanks were able to re-fuel here and at 09.00, the column continued its advance in the direction of Möderscheid. A number of books erroneously suggest that Peiper's men murdered American prisoners here having forced them to load jerrycans onto the German vehicles. No such massacre ever occurred in Büllingen.

Continue west until you reach the first traffic circle. Here you continue straight ahead before taking a minor concrete road through the woods to your front passing sawmills off to your left and right on the way to Möderscheid. Upon entering the village, you take the first right turn and drive downhill past the

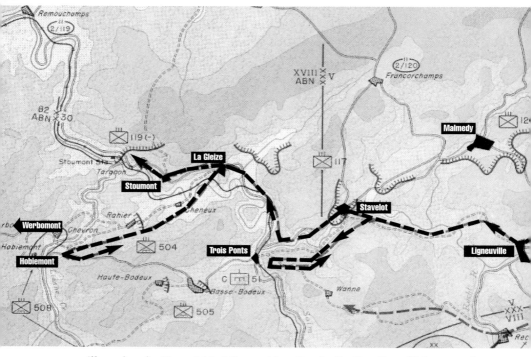

village church. Turn right at the next junction in the direction of Schoppen where you take a left turn sign posted 'Amel'. At the next junction turn right in the direction of Faymonville then at the western end of the village just before the sign for 'Schoppen' (with a red bar through the name) turn left on a minor road. Follow this road through the fields past a couple of small factories (on the right), a kilometre further on, the road turns sharply to the right. At this point take the minor road straight ahead. At the next 'T' junction, turn left. The first building on the left of this road is a large farmhouse called 'Stephanshof'. Pass a second farmhouse (on the right) and take the next right, pausing immediately after turning the corner. The woods to your left are where Captain Charles B. MacDonald of Company I, 23rd Infantry was wounded in a night attack aimed at outflanking a German roadblock on 18 January 1945. The roadblock was across the Ondenval to Amel road and MacDonald and four of his men were wounded in a north-south firebreak close to the far side of the woods and overlooking the road.

Drive downhill and past an old farm on the right then turn second left downhill into Ondenval. In Ondenval turn right on N676 then turn first left in the direction of Thirimont, continue uphill, passing the village cemetery on your right (outside the village) and in Thirimont keep on the main road passing the modern village church on the right. At the western edge of the village where the road takes a major bend to the right, pause. Note the small lane to your left.

Shortly before noon on 17 December 1944, Kampfgruppe Peiper reached this point in its dash to the Meuse River. Here Peiper intended taking the shortest

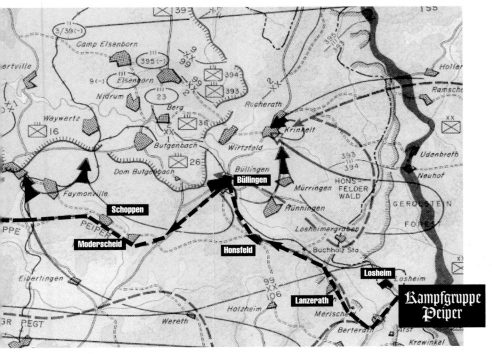

Labels on map: Camp Elsenborn, Waywertz, Nidrum, Berg, Butgenbach, Dom Butgenbach, Faymonville, Eibertingen, Wereth, Holzheim, Krinkelt, Rocherath, Wirtzfeld, Udenbreth, Neuhof, HONSFELDER WALD, Mürringen, Hünningen, GEROLSTEIN FOREST, Losheimergraben, Buchholz Sta., Merlscheid, Berterath, Krewinkel, Lanzerath, Krinkelt

Schoppen
Büllingen
Moderscheid
Honsfeld
Losheim
Lanzerath

Kampfgruppe Peiper

A German combat photographer took this shot of men from the 1st SS Panzer Division off to Peiper's south flank at Kaiserbaracke and the film was later captured by the Americans. (US Army Signal Corps captured film).

American troops Evacuate Civilians in Malmedy in front of the Cathedral. (US Army Signal Corps).

An American MP directs traffic through Malmedy after its mistaken destruction by US bombers. (US Army Signal Corps).

route to Ligneuville, which meant sending elements of his spearhead down this lane. Unfortunately for them, these vehicles got bogged down between here and the Baugnez-Ligneuville road. The bulk of the column therefore kept to the main road leading north/northwest of Thirimont.

Continue out of the village on the main road, passing through a small patch of woods and pausing about 150 metres further on.

Upon reaching this point, across the open field to their front left, the spearhead Panzergrenadiers and tankers of *Kampfgruppe* Peiper could clearly see the Baugnez road junction and American vehicles turning south in the direction of Ligneuville. Today, the view has changed considerably given the amount of construction in the immediate vicinity of the crossroads. From where you are parked, the crossroads is hidden by a large blue metallic building, whereas in 1944 only a few buildings existed, today the area is largely built up. To give the reader the view on the American side, this itinerary takes you down into Malmedy prior to visiting Baugnez, the junction where the 'Malmedy Massacre' occurred.

Carry on until you reach the 'T' junction, with the main road (N632) where you turn left in the direction of Malmedy. Continue downhill a couple of kilometres, crossing over the railroad and passing the Carrefour supermarket on the right. Pause at a convenient place on your left approximately 90 metres before reaching the next traffic circle.

Around 12:30 on 17 December 1944, a column of trucks and jeeps belonging to Battery B, 285th Field Artillery Observation Battalion, pulled up here outside the (now demolished) command post of Lieutenant Colonel David E. Pergrin's 291st Engineer Combat Battalion. Pergrin advised Captain Mills, the Battery B commander against continuing on to St. Vith via Baugnez since he had reports of German armour approaching Malmedy from the east and felt it would be safer for them to take an alternative route to St. Vith. They chose to ignore his advice and the column set off towards its fateful encounter with 'Hitler's Own' – SS *Leibstandarte*.

Move on into Malmedy and park in the town centre.

In three 'friendly fire' incidents American aircraft completely destroyed the town centre (except for the cathedral and an obelisk in the main square) killing American soldiers and Belgian civilians alike. In the grassed area to the right rear of the cathedral are four large black stones commemorating the civilian victims of the bombing and listing their ages and respective names. Around the other side of the cathedral is a large stone bearing the names of all the American units that spent time in Malmedy either at the liberation in September 1944 or later during the 'Bulge'. The stone mason obviously didn't realise that the 99th Infantry Battalion (Separate) and 'Hansen's Norwegians' are one and the same, neither could he or she spell 'Engineer' or '740th'!

Return to Baugnez following road signs for Waimes. Turn right on N62 in the direction of St. Vith and park in front of the large blue garages to your left, just past the monument.
Note the 'Baugnez 44 Historical Center'. (www.baugnez44.be)

The incident most often referred to as the 'Malmedy Massacre' occurred on the right side of N62 in the field directly outside the stone farmhouse across the road from the prefabricated blue building. In 1944 this was an open field, the red brick house and its driveway having been built post-war. The Battery B column of trucks and jeeps came under fire after the point turned due south in the direction of Ligneuville. The men exited their vehicles to be marched back up to the field opposite you by their German captors.

At the request of the author, Danny S. Parker, himself the author of *Hitler's Warrior*, a book on Jochen Peiper and 'Fatal Crossroads' has kindly summarized the massacre:

'The massacre was neither a premeditated slaughter, nor a complete battlefield accident. There were elements of both, primarily brought on by the actions of Max Beutner or Eric Rumpf (which, is not completely clear). Suffice it to say that the battlegroup commander, *Obersturmbannführer* Jochen Peiper was not there. However, Werner Poetschke was present and fuming after a particularly testy encounter with Peiper regarding the lack of progress of the tank group and the missing nature of Werner Sternebeck's spearhead (unknown to them it had already motored on ahead). Peiper was also annoyed that the firing would alert the American forces in Ligneuville nearby. He had learned that an American general, (General Edward Timberlake) was there and having never captured one before, was intent on that prospect!

A post-war house now stands just right of the location of the Malmedy Massacre. Prisoners from Battery B, 285th Field Artillery Observation Battalion were murdered just left of where the house now stands.

The grim discovery under the snow – the body of a victim with an identification marker. (US Army Signal Corps).

In any case, Peiper gave Poetschke an earful about having shot up the trucks, suggested that he impress them into the column and drove on. His exact words to Poetschke were 'What is the meaning of this sitting around! The little there is to be done here can be taken care of by the infantry!' With that, Peiper in a jeep driven by Paul Zwigart, zoomed off. On the radio. Peiper immediately ordered Arndt Fischer to proceed to Ligneuville at maximum speed. Peiper drove right behind him. Peiper gone, Poetschke then dismounted from his tank to approch the prisoners walking up to the crossroads. His blood must have boiled when he found that the surrendered Americans ignored his request in broken English (Chauffeur? Chauffeur !) that some of the Americans volunteer to drive the trucks for his column. They kept walking and completely ignored him. They did not even turn their heads! Ignoring an angry SS officer may have sealed their fate. After that, Poetschke gave Rumpf an earful and prepared to leave himself. What he said is unclear as Beutner died at Stoumont a few days later and Rumpf appears never to have been completely honest regarding his involvement. That is the way command works--negative admonishment flows downhill. By the time, the shooting began, it appears that Poetschke, too, was headed south. A few tanks of the 7th Panzerkompanie were parked by the prisoners. (Hans Siptrott, Roman Clotten and Pilarsek further back). Several halftracks from 9th Panzer Pioniere Kompanie were also present. In his original deposition (later retracted at Landsberg), Siptrott indicated that he was ordered to fire on the prisoners, but refused claiming inadequate ammuntion. However, a Romanian SS volunteer in his tank, Georg Fleps, popped out of one tank hatch, produced a pistol and fired. As if on signal, several machine-guns on the nearby halftracks opened fire. Most of the GIs were stood in the field when the shooting started (first pistol shots), but not all. At least two Americans bolted for the rear at the first shot. The rest stood when the firing began, but there was a good amount of shouting. Such is understandable; men were dying. It is notable that Siptrott had never denied the shooting that ensued, and has always maintained that his first reaction to the above was to kick Georg Fleps and throw his Mark IV in gear to get away from this mess. A detailed map shows the position of each body in the field by the crossroads. It makes it clear that a mass shooting did happen to men standing there although with a number shot as they ran. A number ran at the first shots. Later, in Ligneuville, an angry Siptrott reported on Flep's actions, knowing that this whole incident would create a lot of trouble. He was right.

After the initial shooting, members of the *pioniere* battalion moved through the mass of Americans lying in the field and shot anyone who appeared to remain alive. Amazingly, after the Germans departed the scene later that afternoon, some thirty Americans, who were still alive and feigning death, rose suddenly from the field and ran towards friendly lines. Many would escape and report an incident that would haunt Peiper and his men for the rest of their days.

Continue down N62 in the direction of Ligneuville. As the road begins to descend and you approach the first major bend to the right, note the narrow dirt road that joins you from the left. This is the place at which Kampfgruppe *Peiper would have joined the main road, had its lead vehicles not gotten bogged down upon leaving Thirimont.*

Drive down into Ligneuville stopping at the monument on the right, just before the Hotel du Moulin.

Situated several kilometres west of the front lines on 16 December, Ligneuville had been considered relatively 'safe and secure' by GIs of Combat Command B, 9th Armored Division and the staff of Brigadier General Edward W. Timberlake's 49th Anti-aircraft Artillery Brigade. The Service Companies of the 14th Tank, 16th Field Artillery and 27th Armored Infantry Battalions were scattered about the village. Two companies were across the Amblève River to the south and that of the 14th Tank Battalion in the vicinity of where you are now parked. The Hotel Du Moulin, reputed for its fine cuisine, served as General Timberlake's headquarters.

Early that morning, General Timberlake learned of the breakthrough in the 99th Division sector via a radio message from one of his front line firing batteries near Bütgenbach and prepared his headquarters to evacuate Ligneuville at short notice. Shortly after 13:00, Timberlake and his staff hurriedly departed.

Tanks and halftracks of SS-*Obersturmführer* Werner Sternebeck's spearhead led the rest of the *Kampfgruppe* down into the village. Here, the German column encountered its first American armour in the shape of tanks of the 14th Tank Battalion. As Sternebeck's vehicles moved down into the village they came under fire from an American tank-dozer (A Sherman tank with a bulldozer blade attached) positioned in a barn on the high ground to your right rear. The American tank knocked out the third tank in the column, a Panther commanded by SS-*Untersturmführer* Arndt Fischer, as it passed the Hotel Du Moulin on the right and then the village church off to its left. The tank-dozer then hit a follow-up halftrack which burst into flames outside a small house about 75 yards up the hill to your left rear.

Another German halftrack subsequently knocked out this troublesome tank-dozer which Peiper himself is reputed to have gone stalking with a Panzerfaust, having left his command vehicle, a halftrack, by the church.

The monument to your right commemorates several GIs murdered by an SS sergeant. At least one American survived this incident and later fled the scene only to be re-captured elsewhere in the village.

In a sworn statement made after the war, SS-*Oberscharführer* Paul Ochmann stated that he and SS-*Sturmmann* Suess of *Kampfgruppe* Peiper murdered these prisoners:

'Suess stepped from his vehicle (a halftrack) after having previously taken a weapon from the vehicle. I no longer know what kind of weapon it

SS panzergrenadier belonging to the 1 SS Leibstandarte Panzer Division *enjoys a cigerette 'captured' from the Americans during the drive to the Meuse.*

85

Reverand Francois Emes officiates at the temporary burial of civilians killed by the Waffen-SS in Stavelot. (US Army Signal Corps).

was. Together with Seuss, I led the prisoners past the SPW (halftrack) of SS-*Unterstrumführer* Hering over to the other side of the road. I cannot tell any longer exactly how far I led the prisoner (sic) but it was hardly more than a hundred metres, probably even less.

'Thereby I again went back a short distance on the road on which we came, therefore north in the direction toward Malmedy.

'In the vicinity of the cemetery at a place where the terrain descends on the right of the street, I stopped the prisoners, who were marching one behind the other. (If I now say 'right', I mean right as one goes in the direction toward Malmedy). I formed them right at the edge of the road for I selected this location intentionally because there the bodies could drop right down the steep terrain without lying in our way.

I then indicated to the prisoners with my hand that they should place themselves with their backs towards me and therefore with the face towards the slope, as I intended to kill them by a shot in the neck. I know that by a shot in the neck the victim falls forward.

Thereupon, I first shot the first American prisoner of war from a distance of about 20cm. I shot him with a shot into the neck from the rear because I know from my service with the *'Totenkopf Einheit'* that this is the customary way to shoot people. All told, I myself shot and killed with my pistol in this manner four or five of these American prisoners of war. SS-*Sturmmann* Suess of the 9th Panzer Company shot the other prisoners in my presence. About 500 metres north of the place where SS-*Sturmmann* Suess and I shot the prisoners stood another eight prisoners of war. I believe an officer was among them. I brought these prisoners into a hotel located in the village because I was of the opinion that enough prisoners of war were already bumped off. These eight prisoners whom I brought to the hotel were still together with some other wounded American prisoners of war when I left the hotel around noon on 18 December 1944.'

Ochmann later retracted this statement.

Marie Lochen, a then resident of Ligneuville witnessed this incident and testified to the effect of having seen two Germans shoot these prisoners.

At about 17:00, the *Kampfgruppe* Peiper began leaving Ligneuville.

Continue through the village crossing the Amblève River Bridge and at the top of the hill turn right in the direction of Vielsalm/Pont on N660. Pass through Pont and under the viaduct carrying E42. Take the next right in the direction of Stavelot and keeping off E42. Drive six kilometres to Vau Richard and here watch out on the right for a house with a (false) red brick finish. Past this house, keep your eyes peeled for a small road leading uphill to your left rear. Turn up this road sign posted as a 'dead end' and park where the road takes a sharp bend uphill to the right. Walk up the dirt trail leading past a single storey house on the left and into the woods. Just as you enter the trees note the monument to your right.

Here where the monument stands, unknown SS men took twelve American prisoners and three local civilians and murdered them in cold blood. Later, as the battle wound to a close, local villagers searching for the missing civilians discovered the bodies. The GIs lay where the monument now stands and the civilians across the trail where a wooden bench marks the spot.

The murdered soldiers were men of Company A, 27th Armored Infantry Battalion of the 9th Armored Division. This unit would earn itself a place in history a few months later when, under Captain Karl Timmermann, it captured the Ludendorf Bridge over the Rhine River at Remagen.

SS-Sturmbannführer Knittel (right) commander of 1 SS Leibstandarte *Panzer Division' s Reconnaissance Battalion, confers with his adjutant, SS-*Obersturmführer *Leidreiter, during the fighting around Stavelot.*

Return to the main road turning left in the direction of Stavelot. At the West End of the village (Vau Richard) note a narrow lane leading to the front left between two houses. The house between the lane and the main road was that of Albert Petit and his family.

A photograph taken by a German *Kriegsberichter* on 18th December 1944 shows SS-*Sturmbannführer* Gustav Knittel commander of the Reconnaissance Battalion of 1st SS and the commander of his 3rd Company *Obersturmführer* Walter Leidreiter studying a map.

Continue a few hundred metres in the direction of Stavelot and as the road begins to descend prior to reaching the rock outcrop note a small moss-covered stone foundation just left of the road. Pause here.

Locally, this spot is known as 'La Corniche' and this stone foundation is all that remains of a pre-war Belgian army guard hut built for sentries guarding the road from Ligneuville.

At about 1830 on 17 December 1944, Sergeant Charles Hensel and his twelve-man squad from Company C, 291st Engineer Combat Battalion placed mines across the road and a bazooka team and .30- calibre machine gun a little further downhill. Hensel sent one man, Private Bernie Goldstein beyond the roadblock to the guardhouse to keep watch for the approaching Germans.

About 21.00, Peiper's spearhead reached the engineer roadblock and after a brief exchange of fire during which Goldstein escaped up a path through the trees above the road, Peiper ordered the column to bivouac overnight. Hensel's men climbed into their truck and freewheeled silently down into Stavelot.

Continue downhill and stop just past the last bend on the high ground overlooking the ancient town of Stavelot to your front right.

The high wooded hill on the far side of town was the location of U.S. First Army Fuel Dump number 3, a massive fuel depot, which fortunately, for the Americans, Peiper's column never spotted.

In Stavelot, a large red brick building, clearly visible from where you are parked, served as a shelter for civilians during the battle given the thickness of its walls and an extensive network of cellars. This building features prominently in the story of Marcel Ozer, a local man and Tony Calvanese, an American soldier.

Marcel Ozer with his wife Julia just after the war. (Courtesy Marcel and Julia Ozer).

Continue downhill and upon reaching the brick houses on the right, the more sharp-eyed traveller can still spot traces of gunfire in the brickwork. Bullet holes bear now silent witness to the passage of Kampfgruppe *Peiper. Closer to the bottom of the hill (opposite house number 13) keep an eye out for a small monument on the left side of the street. Pause here.*

Marcel Ozer, a 'Stavelotain' erected this and other memorials on his own initiative. It commemorates the men of the 825th Tank Destroyer Battalion, 291st Engineer Combat Battalion and 526th Armored Infantry Battalion killed here in Stavelot and on the road to Trois Ponts.

At about 06.00 on 18 December, four halftracks of Company A, 526th Armored

Soldiers of 1st Platoon, Company A of the 825th Tank Destroyer Battalion inspect the wreckage of two of their guns and halftracks knocked out by Kampfgruppe *Peiper early on the morning of 18 December 1944.*
(Courtesy Mrs. Frances W. Doherty).

Infantry Battalion and two towed 3″ anti-tank guns of Lieutenant Jack Doherty's 1st Platoon, Company A, 825th Tank Destroyer Battalion, crossed the Amblève River bridge. Second Lieutenant James Evans positioned his 3rd Platoon, Company A, 526th Armored Infantry Battalion just Southeast of the bridge. Sergeants Jonas Whaley and John G. Armstrong the two tank-destroyer commanders turned their halftracks sharp left upon crossing the bridge and found themselves up a dead-end street. They quickly turned around and began moving uphill on La rue du Vieux Château in the direction of the advancing German column. In the lead tank, SS-*Rottenführer* Eugen Zimmermann's gunner spotted Armstrong's halftrack and set it alight with his first shot killing some of its crew (Sergeant Armstrong and five other soldiers of Company A would die in this action). The survivors sought refuge in nearby houses or fled back across the river. The Germans then hit the 1st and 3rd Platoons of Company A, 526th Armored Infantry and Sergeant Jack Ellery commanding a machine gun squad was killed on the bridge. The surviving infantrymen withdrew across the bridge taking up position in houses on the far bank.

Corporal 'Bob' Hammons a survivor from Sergeant Whaley's halftrack sought refuge in a shed and later a basement potato bin before successfully wading the icy waters of the Amblève and reaching friendly lines in nearby Malmedy.

Private Tony Calvanese, shot in the left thigh, managed to find shelter in, what today is, house number 13. Later that morning when a passing SS officer shot at him through a window, Tony climbed out of a large hole at the rear of the property and crawled to a nearby dairy to find it full of terrified civilians. Among them were Marcel Ozer and Louis van Lancker, two young men in their mid-twenties. Earlier that morning, in the dark, the two Belgians had tried to escape from Stavelot but ran into SS *Panzergrenadiers* on the bend downhill from your present position. These Germans apparently chose not to shoot the intrepid pair thus risking alerting nearby American troops and told them to 'get lost'. Hurrying away, the Belgians went straight to a dairy in the street behind these houses and were present later that morning when Tony Calvanese showed up.

Continue downhill pausing by the monument under a copper beech tree on the left as you turn right toward the bridge. This plaque commemorates the civilian men, women and children murdered by the Waffen-SS in and around Stavelot.

Private Tony Calvanese of Agawam Massachussetts after his rescue by the citizens of Stavelot. (Author's collection, courtesy Tony Calvanese).

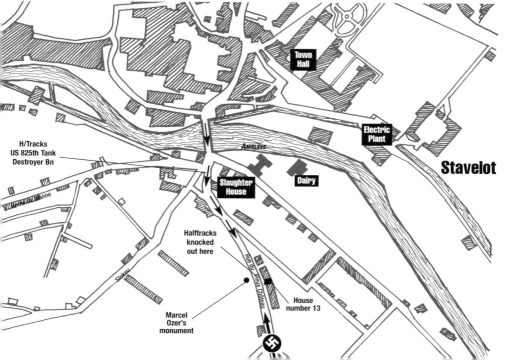

Königstiger

Stavelot after heavy shelling by the Americans. This vital bridge over the River Amblève was heavily contested for the best part of two days. A Königstiger *can be seen on the far side of the bridge.*

>   *Prior to crossing the bridge, park on the right side of the road.*
>   *The halftrack to your left, honours the men both American and Belgian who kept Peiper's main supply route closed after the Americans blew the bridge behind him on 19 December. The dairy to which Tony Calvanese escaped was along the street to your right when facing the bridge.*

At 08.00 on 18 December, German mortar and artillery fire hit Stavelot as tanks of SS-Panzer Regiment 1 crossed the then narrower stone bridge over the Amblève.

At about 10.00, it became obvious to the civilians in the dairy that if SS men discovered Calvanese in their midst, they may well vent their anger on all present. Marcel Ozer volunteered to wade over the river in order to try and get help from the Americans on the far bank. Setting foot in the icy water, the current proved too strong and swept him off his feet and a short distance downstream. He nonetheless struggled free of its grasp and climbed up the riverbank soaked to the skin. He rushed home to change his clothes then returned to the dairy, where he and other townspeople decided to evacuate the injured GI. A local Red Cross worker, Madamoiselle Berthe Beaupain said she could get a stretcher from a nearby Red Cross building and promptly set off to collect it and her nurse's uniform. Arriving at the house in question, she found it occupied by twenty local people and Father Antoine Bernard, a priest from the German speaking village of Amel. Together, she and Father Bernard made their perilous way through advancing SS Panzergrenadiers and gunfire, back over the bridge to the dairy with the much-needed stretcher.

Quickly, the courageous Belgians decided to evacuate Calvanese across the bridge then being crossed by the bulk of Peiper's column. Marcel Ozer and Louis van Lancker volunteered to carry the injured American across the river accompanied by Berthe Beaupain, her brother Gustav and Father Bernard. Upon reaching your present location they paused as a Panther tank rounded the bend and began crossing the bridge. Marcel Ozer then seized the initiative and urged the group into the depths of hell. Walking behind the tank, they passed the crushed remains of Sergeant Ellery while further on a dead SS officer sat with his back propped up against the bridge parapet with his legs turned sideways in order to prevent the tanks from running over him. Both small and larger calibre gunfire raked the bridge as the Belgians raced across the river.

On the evening of 19 December 1944, American Engineers blew the bridge span nearest the far bank, effectively cutting Peiper's link with the rest of 1st SS.

Cross the bridge and upon doing so, pause on the far side.

Across the Amblève, Marcel Ozer and his companions turned right along a narrow street and made their way unhindered to the large red brick building you saw from the top of the hill.

Continue up the street keeping front right at the 'Y' junction and pausing by the archway on the right.

Here in the present day city hall, the group separated after placing Tony Calvanese in part of the extensive cellar system beneath the building. While the others returned across the bridge, Marcel Ozer stayed behind with Calvanese until soldiers of the 117th Infantry regained possession of the buildings facing the river and evacuated the wounded American.

Continue up the same road turning right at the first major junction. Drive straight ahead past a mini traffic island to the next traffic circle where you join the N68 (second exit) in the direction of Trois Ponts. Pause at the western edge of town just past the right turn marked 'Parfondruy'. Peiper's column drove up the old main street of Stavelot but present day traffic signs won't permit today's traffic to do likewise.

After 19 December, the Germans made numerous attempts to recapture the Amblève River Bridge head on from the south bank of the river; they also attacked in strength from the direction of Trois Ponts. Here at the western edge of town, SS-*Obersturmführer* Manfred Coblenz led his attacking 2nd SS Reconnaissance Company under heavy fire up the Trois Ponts road to capture the very first few houses in town but got no further. In his command post just west of Stavelot, SS-*Sturmbannführer* Gustav Knittel ordered elements of his Reconnaissance Battalion to move east and north of the main road to capture Parfondruy and hit Stavelot from the north. Upon clearing Parfondruy, SS-*Obersturmführer* Heinrich Goltz and his men ran into American opposition at

Medics of the 82nd Airborne Division load a wounded SS man onto a stretcher. He was aged 20 and had been in the service for four years at the time the Americans captured him in Erria. (US Army Signal Corps).

Renardmont and therefore joined Coblenz in further attempts to take Stavelot from the west.

Civilians in Parfondruy and other hamlets west and northwest of Stavelot suffered the wrath of the attacking Waffen-SS when Goltz's men massacred men, women and children alike.

Bitter fighting at the western edge of town and in the villages to the right (north) side of the road to Trois Ponts continued unabated until dusk on Sunday 24 December.

Continue west in the direction of Trois Ponts pausing after one kilometre opposite a large red brick farmhouse on the left. This is the Antoine Farm, SS-Sturmbannführer Gustav Knittel's command post during the attacks toward the western edge of Stavelot. Knittel and his staff shared their basement refuge with numerous terrified civilians. The east gable of the house still supports its hard-earned battle scars in the shape of gunfire damage.

Continue in the direction of Trois Ponts and 2.2 kilometres further on note the Petit Spai Bridge to the left of the road. Pause here.

On Thursday 21 December 1944, infantry elements of the 1st SS Panzergrenadier Battalion, crossed the swollen Amblève River here at Petit Spai, then moved up the high ground to your right on their way to the fighting in and around Parfondruy. Soon after these infantrymen crossed the bridge their commander sent his Jagdpanzers (tank destroyers) in their wake. Under the weight of the lead Jagdpanzer, the Petit Spai Bridge collapsed into the turbulent waters of the Amblève. All further attempts by the 1st SS Pioneer Battalion to bridge the river during daylight failed but that night they managed to put in an infantry footbridge. Ultimately on Christmas Eve Gustav Knittel ordered his remaining men to withdraw across the river using the twisted remains of this infantry bridge.

Continue in the direction of Trois Ponts stopping just before the two railroad tunnels.

In 1944, the building off to your left just before the tunnels was known as the Hotel Lifrange. Recognising the importance of stopping Peiper from moving through Trois Ponts, a mixed bag of American defenders set about blocking the road at this point while men of the 51st Engineer Combat Battalion wired the nearby Amblève River Bridge for possible demolition.

Lieutenant Richard Green commanding the 3rd Platoon of Company C, 51st Engineer Combat Battalion, had orders to defend east of the railroad tunnels near Trois Ponts, supported by a 57mm anti-tank gun crew of the 526th Armored Infantry Battalion. Two other men of the 526th, Corporal Bruce Frazier and Private First Class Ralph J. Bieker positioned themselves 250 yards east of the anti-tank gun with the intention of pulling a 'daisy chain' of mines in front of the lead German tank as it approached from the direction of Stavelot. The job done, the two GIs were to run back to the anti-tank gun just east of the hotel.

Shortly before noon on the 18th December the lead tank nosed around a bend towards the 57mm anti-tank gun. Frazier and Bieker fired several rifle shots at the approaching Germans as the tank and others behind it stopped at the daisy chain. Other engineers came back down the road to Lieutenant Green's position to warn him of the Germans' approach. By this time the anti-tank gunners and engineers in the vicinity of the gun could see the lead tanks and heard others moving down the road through the trees. The gun crew had to make every round count since they only had a total of seven rounds available. As they pondered when to open fire, the third tank in the column fired four rounds in quick succession. One shell skipped over the river to their backs and a second no more than six inches above their heads. Another hit a tree behind the anti-tank gun; felling the tree and showering fragments in the area. The anti-tank gunners opened fire and one of their first rounds caused the lead tank to start smoking. There was some difficulty initially with ammunition for the anti-tank gun since seven rounds would not suffice to stop the attacking enemy armour. Captain Robert N. Jewitt, Supply Officer of the 1111th Engineer Group headquarters in Trois Ponts started throwing shells across the road to Lieutenant Green, who passed them to another man who in turn handed them to the gun crew. The defenders clearly heard the detonation as their buddies in town blew two of the three bridges behind them effectively cutting them off from Trois Ponts. The 1111th Engineer Group commander, Colonel H. Wallis Anderson observing with binoculars from across the river, counted a total of nineteen tanks that came through the position and then turned right in the direction of Coo. Back at the anti-tank gun the German shells got closer and closer until one hit the base of the gun killing the gun crew. Their position now hopeless, the remaining engineers piled into a halftrack and a 2½ ton truck and proceeded by their only escape route – the road to Stoumont. The sacrifice made by this anti-tank gun crew is commemorated on Marcel Ozer's monument on La rue du Vieux Château in Stavelot. Shortly after this action, between the tunnels, men of the Headquarters Company, 1st SS Panzer Reconnaissance Battalion murdered brothers Gustave and Oscar Job of Stavelot.

By the church in Trois Ponts a stone marks the passage of the 505th Parachute Infantry Regiment.
(Author's collection).

Continue through the tunnels and turn left in the direction of Hamoir/Vielsalm. Cross the bridge then turn around and drive back over it stopping on the north side. Note the plaque on the wall of the bridge commemorating the role of Captain Sam Scheuber's Company C, 51st Engineer Combat Battalion in the defense of Trois Ponts.

As Peiper's tanks made their way through the tunnels men of Company C blew the Amblève River Bridge effectively stopping Peiper from taking the direct road to Werbomont and forcing him to take the alternative road in the direction of Coo. Men of the 51st and 291st Engineer Combat Battalions defended Trois Ponts until relieved by incoming soldiers of the 505th Parachute Infantry of the 82nd Airborne Division. Major Robert B. Yates, Executive Officer of the 51st, witnessed SS men chasing a young boy, thirteen year-old Michel Nicolay between the houses on this side of the blown bridge. From across the river, Major Yates fired his Colt 45 in a vain attempt to help the unfortunate boy whom the pursuing SS men caught and later murdered.

Colonel Anderson, the Engineer Group Commander, sent his Motor Pool Officer, Captain A.P. Lundberg to warn First Army Headquarters in Spa of the approach of *Kampfgruppe* Peiper. Captain Lundberg and his driver were to run smack into Peiper's spearhead as it neared the Neufmoulin Bridge

In the small park in front of the Trois Ponts parish church is a monument to the 504th Parachute Infantry Regiment.

Continue on N63 in the direction of Liege/Remouchamps passing through Coo and ultimately entering La Gleize. Upon

SS-Obersturmbannführer *Peiper wearing his Knight's Crossed with Oakleaves and Cross Swords.*

97

reaching the village take the second road to the left driving down a narrow lane marked 'Rahier 7.' At the time of writing there is also a sign saying 'Descente de L'Amblève en Kayak arrive Cheneux.' Pause at the bottom of this short lane before turning right. Note the impressive Château Froidcour in the trees to your front. This castle, ancestral home to the De Harenne family, figured prominently in the battle since a stone farmhouse in its grounds served as Peiper's command post while in the vicinity of Stoumont. The Germans also used the castle bedrooms to hold American prisoners captured in the La Gleize/Stoumont area.

Turn right in the direction of Cheneux/Rahier following the winding road down to the Amblève River Bridge at Cheneux where you pause.

At about 13.30 on 18 December, the spearhead of *Kampfgruppe* Peiper began its descent toward the river at Cheneux. Spotting movement in the vicinity of the bridge, the machine gunner on the lead Panther opened fire fully expecting the bridge to be blown before the column reached it. Unfortunately, the five people spotted near the bridge were civilians, a man and four women. One woman died instantly and a second shortly afterwards. The man and a third woman were less seriously wounded.

Continue uphill toward the village pausing at the first bend to the right.

Minutes later, as Peiper's lead vehicles crossed the bridge, American fighter-bombers strafed and bombed the column wrecking three tanks and five halftracks in the process. Peiper and Gustav Knittel sought temporary shelter in the pre-war Belgian pillbox to your left and overlooking the bridge. During this attack, a bomb exploded knocking out a panther tank and blowing out the gable end wall of the Dumont house to your front right.

Continue uphill into Cheneux noting the splendid view of the Château Froidcour to your front right. Continue through Cheneux and the next villages of Rahier and Froidville to the junction with N66 turning right and pausing immediately upon joining the main road.

At approximately 16:15 on 18 December, as Peiper's lead tank turned right onto N66 in the direction of the Neufmoulin Bridge, the jeep carrying Captain A.P. Lundberg Motor Officer of the 1111th Engineer Group and his driver ran smack into it. One American died instantly while the Germans shot the other at the roadside.

Continue downhill in the direction of E25 crossing the Lienne Creek at the Neufmoulin Bridge. Pause on the left side of the road on the far bank.

At about 15.00 on 18 December, Sergeants Edwin L. Pigg and Robert C. Billington of the 2nd Platoon, Company A, 291st Engineer Combat Battalion arrived here at the bridge to prepare the structure for demolition. Lieutenant Alvin Edelstein, their platoon leader, joined them shortly afterwards and by 16.00 the 180 foot-timber trestle bridge was ready to be blown. At about 16.45, as the lead Panther turned the bend, Corporal Fred Chapin turned the key and blew the bridge sky-high. The engineers subsequently made good their escape. Note the monument to the 291st, again erected by Emile la Croix and the members of the C-47 club.

Turn around and return back in the direction of Rahier/Froidville taking the second turning to the left marked 'Chauveheid'. Stop at the small stone bridge in Chauveheid.

When the Americans blew the Neufmoulin Bridge in his face, Peiper ordered halftracks of the 11th Panzer Grenadier Company across the then timber trestle bridge here at Chauveheid. The structure was capable of supporting halftracks but not tanks. Other halftracks of the 10th SS Panzergrenadier Company crossed another wooden bridge at nearby Moulin Rahier.

Carry on to the junction with the main road turning left then as far as the junction with N66. At this junction turn right and drive about 100 yards uphill pausing at the Belgian Touring Club marker on the right side of the road.

At the Neufmoulin Bridge a monument commemorates the role of the 291st Engineer Combat Battalion in stopping Kampfgruppe Peiper. (Author's collection).

Upon crossing the Lienne Creek at Chauveheid, the 11th Panzer Grenadier Company halftracks eventually drove uphill to where you are now where soldiers of the 2nd Battalion, 119th Infantry supported by four M-10 tank destroyers and three 57mm anti-tank guns knocked them out. In radio contact with his Panzergrenadiers, Peiper ordered them back across the Lienne then turned his entire column back through Cheneux to the grounds of the Château Froidcour.

Continue a couple of kilometres further to the village of Werbomont where on the right side of the road in the centre of the village, stands a monument to the 'All American' 82nd Airborne Division. Return across the Neufmoulin Bridge and via Froidville and Rahier to the bend by the church in Cheneux. Here on the right side of the road stands a monument to Colonel Reuben H. Tucker's 504th Parachute Infantry Regiment of the 82nd Airborne.

Königstiger *213 was abandoned by* Kampfgruppe *Peiper in La Gleize.*

Upon his withdrawal back through Cheneux, Peiper left fourteen flak guns here in Cheneux to cover his rear. These flak gun crews were later joined by the battered remnants of the 11th SS Panzergrenadier Company after it suffered heavy losses near Stoumont Station. Also in Cheneux were five 105mm guns of the 5th SS Panzer Artillery Battery along with reinforcements of the 6th Panzergrenadier Company of 2nd SS Panzer Regiment who crossed the Petit Spai Bridge and moved to Cheneux in the early morning darkness of 20 December. At midday that same day, Colonel Reuben H. Tucker of the 504th Parachute Infantry ordered Companies A and B of his 1st Battalion to launch a night attack against Peiper's rearguard in Cheneux.

By 23:00, the defending SS men still held onto the main part of the village having inflicted tremendous losses upon the attacking paratroopers.

At 03:00 on Thursday 21 December, Company G of the 504th attacked Cheneux but made no headway.

At 17:00 that same day, Peiper ordered a withdrawal toward La Gleize and Tucker renewed his attack by the 1st Battalion and Company G.

At 18:30, company G supported by two tank destroyers moved into the main part of Cheneux against light resistance, since by then most of the defending Germans had left the village.

Exit Cheneux in the direction of La Gleize and 1.6 kilometres further on turn left at the crossroads and uphill through the trees. On a bend in the trees, note the stone farmhouse off to your left that served as Peiper's command post during the attack towards Stoumont. Many of Peiper's vehicles spent the night here on the grounds of the De Harenne estate. At the junction with the main road (N633) turn left in the direction of Stoumont (not sign posted). A few hundred metres along the road where the Château Froidcour driveway joins N633 from the left note the gatekeeper's lodge that served as the command post of Sturmbannführer Werner Poetschke's 1st SS Panzer Battalion during the battle for Stoumont.

As N633 bends to the right leading into Stoumont, keep an eye out for the brick 'Gendarmerie' (Polizei) on the left. The half-timbered house after the Gendarmerie existed in 1944 and features prominently in film and photographs taken by German combat photographers during the battle for Stoumont. In this film, German paratroops are clearly seen setting up a machine-gun in the then small field where the Gendarmerie now stands. In that same film, SS-Sturmbannführer Werner Poetschke can be seen turning around to pick up a discarded Panzerfaust anti-tank weapon.

Continue to the church in Stoumont.

On Tuesday, 19 December 1944, a mixed bag of American troops defended Stoumont. They included ten tanks of the 743rd Tank Battalion, elements of the 1st and 3rd Battalions, 119th Infantry and eight tank destroyers of Company A, 823rd Tank Destroyer Battalion as well as three 57mm anti-tank guns in nearby Roua.

At 08.30am, eight or nine German tanks drove straight down the main street into the village as SS Panzergrenadiers, pioneers and paratroopers, moved around the south edge of Stoumont on foot. Reduced visibility enabled

Panthers approaching the village of Stoumont. The leading tank has received a direct hit.

SS-Sturmbannführer *Poetschke commanding the action in Stoumont.*

German infantry to get in among the tank destroyers and overrun them before they could fire a shot. American tanks were able to evacuate some of the infantrymen while others fled through the woods north of town. Many never escaped and the Germans captured them. Throughout the fighting, many civilians sought refuge in the basement of the 'Préventorium St. Edouard', an imposing stone building at the western edge of Stoumont.

Continue west on N633 noting the former 'Préventorium' off to your right as the road exits the village. Continue downhill out of Stoumont driving through the next village of Targnon, then passing a hotel on the left and pausing at the bottom of the hill with Stoumont Station and the railroad track on your left.

On Tuesday 19 December at around midday, seven Panthers began their descent from Stoumont and after passing through Targnon, withdrew quickly when they came under artillery fire. At the bend several hundred metres past the station, twelve tanks of the US 743rd Tank Battalion, four tank destroyers, a 90mm anti-aircraft gun of Battery C, 143rd AAA Gun Battalion and troops of the 3rd Battalion, 119th Infantry lay in wait for the approaching German column.

The village of Stoumont falls and its defenders, men of the 119th Infantry Regiment, 30 Infantry Division, surrender. They were eventually released when the Kampfgruppe withdrew a few days later.

Soldiers of the 82nd Airborne Division assemble German prisoners on a forest road. (US Army Signal Corp).

> *Drive toward the bend west of the station and keep an eye out for a Belgian Touring Club stone marker on the left side of N633. Pause here.*
>
> *Around 14.30 on 19 December, the defending Americans knocked out Peiper's three lead tanks whereupon Peiper ordered a withdrawal to Stoumont.*
>
> *Turn around and drive back to Stoumont stopping at the entrance to the village by the driveway to the 'Préventorium St. Edouard.'*

On Thursday/Friday 21/22 December 1944 during vicious fighting in and around St. Edouard, children (including Josette Sarlette an aunt of the author), nuns and l'Abbé C. Hanlet, a Catholic priest, huddled in the basements of the main building as fighting raged around them. By the night of the 21 December, it had become evident to Peiper that he must withdraw from Stoumont and concentrate the remnants of his depleted *Kampfgruppe* in and around La Gleize. Before first light on 22 December, he ordered the withdrawal taking out his walking wounded but leaving about eighty badly wounded men and several American prisoners in the care of a German medical NCO and two American medics. With tank support and a tremendous artillery barrage, men of the 119th Infantry recaptured Stoumont from a small SS rearguard later that day.

> *Return to La Gleize and once in the village turn right driving with the church wall to the right of you. Note the 'December 1944' museum (www.december44.com) and next to it indisputable evidence of the presence of Kampfgruppe Peiper in the now sleepy village during those turbulent days of late 1944!*
>
> *This is* SS-Obersturmführer *Dollinger's Tiger 213 of the 501st Heavy SS Panzer Battalion, undoubtedly the most impressive relic on the battlefield today.*

American GI's look over two Germans killed in the fighting for Ligneuville. (US Army Signal Corps).

Hopelessly surrounded, out of fuel and low on ammunition, after heavy American shelling on 22/23 December, one of Nazi Germany's most decorated tank commanders decided the game was up. Peiper requested and was given permission to withdraw; the ambitious attack had failed!

On Sunday, 24 December, he and about 800 of his heavily armed SS men walked out of '*Festung* La Gleize' in the early morning darkness leaving some 300 more seriously wounded comrades behind in the care of an SS doctor. The withdrawing men, battle weary and exhausted, set out across the icy waters of the Amblève and over the high wooded terrain south of the village. On Christmas Day 1944, the battered survivors of this once powerful fighting unit reached their division command post in Wanne just south of Stavelot.

Suggested Reading:
MacDonald: Chapters 10,11,21 and 22.
Cole: Pages 334-352,359-377, 599-600
Grégoire Gerard: *'Les Panzers de Peiper Face À L' U. S. Army'*
Reynolds Michael: *'The Devil's Adjutant- Jochen Peiper, Panzer-Leader'*

Soldiers of the 463rd Ordnance Evacuation Company load Königstiger 332 onto a tank trailer for eventual transportation stateside as a war trophy.
(Courtesy William C Warnock)

CHAPTER 3

THE LOSHEIM GAP-SCHNEE EIFEL-SCHOENBERG ST VITH-VIELSALM

STARTING POINT: LOSHEIM, GERMANY ON PRUMER STRASSE 265, ABOUT 24 KILOMETRES EAST/SOUTHEAST OF MALMEDY, BELGIUM. PARK NEAR THE CHURCH IN VILLAGE CENTRE.

Losheim gives its name to the Losheim Gap, a broad valley that cuts through the Schnee Eifel Ridge, i.e. the high ground, just east of the Belgian – German border. The Losheim Gap constituted the boundary between the United States V and VIII Corps as well as an important route for the planned German attack into eastern Belgium. According to Dr. Hugh M. Cole 'The Losheim Gap is no pleasant pastoral valley but is cluttered by abrupt hills, some bare, others covered by fir trees and thick undergrowth. Most of the little villages here are found in the draws and potholes which further scoop out the main valley'.

A reinforced Cavalry Squadron of Colonel Mark Devine's 14th Cavalry Group occupied the Losheim Gap prior to the German attack. To the left of the Cavalry Group ran the corps' boundary and the right flank of the 99th Infantry Division. The newly arrived 106th Infantry Division, commanded by Major-General Alan W. Jones, to which the cavalry were attached, occupied the central and southern sections of the heavily forested Schnee Eifel.

Major General Alan W. Jones commanding general 106th Infantry Division. (Author's collection courtesy Mrs Alan W Jones).

As you exit Losheim, heading south, running parallel to 265 and to your left is a long stretch of 'Dragon Teeth anti-tank obstacles of the once vaunted Siegfried Line, often referred to as the 'Westwall'.

Continue driving south on 265 and in village of Kehr, about 100 metres past the church, take the minor road to the right marked 'Ausser Anlieger' (Level with Garage Scholzen). Continue downhill until you reach the village of Krewinkel and upon passing the new church on your left, turn left and drive around the steeple of the old church to your front right. Keep driving until you can turn right again and stop with the old church to your right rear.

Krewinkel typifies the small rural villages of the Losheim Gap. The village was occupied by the 2nd platoon of Troop C, 18th Cavalry Reconnaissance Squadron and a Reconnaissance Platoon of Company A, 820th Tank Destroyer Battalion. Positioned here in the centre of the village, the defenders occupied the various buildings from which excellent observation and good fields of fire covered all approaches to Krewinkel from the east. In the early morning dark under the beams of searchlights reflected off low-hanging clouds to create 'artificial moonlight', an assault company of the German's 3rd Fallschirmjäger Division boldly approached the village in columns of four. The troopers held their fire until the enemy infantry were within twenty yards of the outer strands of defensive wire – then cut loose. The column quickly disintegrated, but the Germans quickly resumed the attack in more open order and were shortly in the village streets. At one point, half the village was in German hands, but eventually the defenders got the upper hand and the enemy withdrew.

Fallschirmjäger *(paratroopers) machine gun team. They were used as ordinary infantry after they suffered heavy casualties in the invasion of Crete in May 1941.*

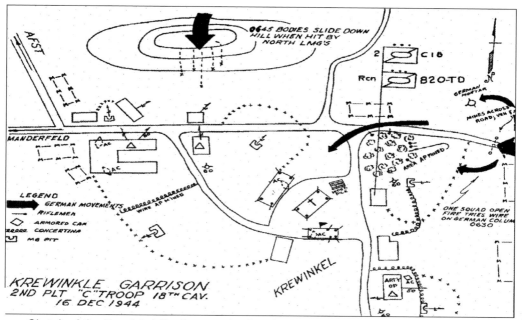

Sketch of the Krewinkel Garrison made after the battle and held in the US National Archives.

One of the last to leave shouted in English 'Take a ten minute break, we'll be back!' An exasperated trooper yelled out in reply '—— you! We'll still be here'. At 06.45, an attack from the bald hill (at the time of writing forested) to your left, was met and stopped by heavy fire from the light machine-guns positioned on the northern edge of town. A most welcome re-supply of much needed ammunition arrived on the scene when Troop C's executive officer arrived in a halftrack, only to be killed on his way back to the nearby village of Afst.

By the time the Germans made their next assault on the village the defenders were well prepared. A few enemy paratroopers made it into the eastern edge of Krewinkel but made no further progress. By late morning, group headquarters informed the cavalrymen in front of Manderfeld that they should withdraw to the ridge line marked by that village and if necessary, to a second ridge two miles behind Manderfeld. The defenders of Afst and Krewinkel made a perilous escape under fire from Germans to either side of the road while other cavalrymen elsewhere were unable to withdraw.

Continue straight-ahead then take the first right returning in direction of Kehr. (At the time of writing after you pass the new church, a barn and farmhouse on

The house marked 'ARTY OP' on sketch.

the left still bear evidence of gunfire on one gable end. This is the building marked 'Arty OP' at the bottom right hand corner of the sketch). In Kehr, turn right onto 265 and continue in the direction of Prum. At Mooshaus turn right in the direction of 'Roth bei Prum 1km'. Pause briefly prior to reaching Roth.

The forested high ground running parallel to the left side of the road is the central section of the Schnee Eifel along which all three battalions of the 422nd Infantry of the 106th Infantry Division were positioned. The regimental commander, Colonel George Descheneaux, located his regimental command post in the village of Schlausenbach, about midway between the Schnee Eifel and the road you are travelling on. This road leads from Roth, via Auw to connect with the Bleialf-Schönberg road just northwest of Bleialf. In Auw, a minor road branches west to Andler then follows the Our River to Schönberg. If the Germans captured either road this would enable them to envelop the Schnee Eifel defenders. Colonel Charles C. Cavender's 423rd Infantry had one battalion in the Westwall atop the Schnee Eifel, another bending around the

110

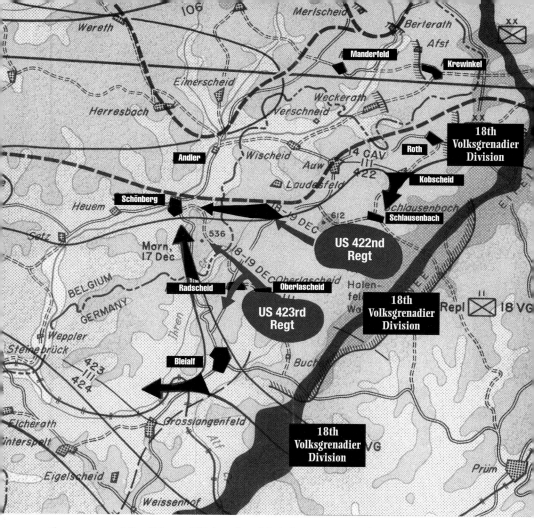

southern nose of the Schnee Eifel and a third, its remaining battalion, back to the west acting as division reserve near Born, north of St. Vith. The regimental command post was in Buchet, a small village on the West Side of the Schnee Eifel and north of the road leading into Bleialf from the east. This road circumvents the south end of the Schnee Eifel then passes through Bleialf toward Schönberg thus permitting envelopment from the south.

Continue into Roth and head for the village church in the centre.

Captain Stanley E. Porche' and a few men of Troop A, 18th Cavalry Reconnaissance Squadron, supported by two towed tank destroyers, found

Volkesgrenadiers advancing during the Battle of the Bulge.   (Roland Gaul)

themselves under attack here in Roth by elements of the 18th Volksgrenadier Division. The attack came along the road from Mooshaus and initially, the cavalrymen held their ground, but the attacking *Volksgrenadiers* persisted in their attempts to capture the village and the road via Auw to the Our River. About 11.00, Captain Porché radioed Troop A headquarters in nearby Kobsched to inform them that the troops of the 106th Infantry Division farther south were moving back and that the Roth garrison would attempt withdrawal and that Kobscheid should do likewise. Unfortunately, the German grip on Roth proved too strong and later on the afternoon of the 16th the cavalrymen surrendered.

Return to 265 turning right and climbing the reverse slope of the Schnee Eifel. Upon reaching the crest turn right, following the sign for 'Brandscheid'. As you travel along this road keep an eye open on bends for the remains of concrete bunkers of the Westwall. At the third such bend, (just prior to reaching firebreaks to both left and right) to your left are some of the more obvious remains of such a bunker. Make a pause here.

In the early morning hours of 16 December 1944, here, high in the centre of the Schnee Eifel, the 422nd Infantry missed the first rude shock of the pre-dawn attack. It was not part of the German attack plan to engage the 422nd by frontal assault. The enemy penetration just north of Roth during the hours of darkness, quickly brought the assault troops of the 294th Regiment of the 18th Volksgrenadier Division down the road to Auw and onto the American Regiment's flank and rear. At daylight, small groups of Germans began pressure against the forward battalions of the 422nd in an attempt to fix American attention to their front. Company L, 422nd rushed to the defence of the regimental command post located in a Schlausenbach 'Gasthaus'.

Resume your journey travelling the length of the 422nd Infantry front line as well as that of a battalion of the 423rd. Continue driving for ten kilometres until you reach the junction with the Prum – Bleialf road where you turn right in the direction of Bleialf. Stop prior to entering the village.

Intense artillery fire laid on the 423rd Infantry at the start of the attack had disrupted telephone communications, but the radio net functioned well. By 06.00, Colonel Cavender had word that his anti-tank company was under small arms attack in Bleialf, the key to the southern route around the Schnee Eifel. When shock troops of the 18th Volksgrenadier Division's 293rd Regiment struck the 423rd Regimental Anti-tank Company in Bleialf, one group filtered into the village. Another, marching along the railroad, cut between Bleialf and Troop B of the 18th Cavalry Squadron, blocking the latter and destroying the right platoon of Anti-tank Company.

Continue into Bleialf and in the village follow the sign 'Leidenborn' to the southern edge of Bleialf. Passing roads to Pronsfeld and Urb respectively. At the 'Zum Bahnhof' guesthouse pull over on the left side of the road.
To your front left stands a modern pre-fabricated factory building behind which are the remains of the wartime railroad which at the time had a station (to your front left). Troop B of the 18th Cavalry under Captain Robert G. Fossland was attached to the 423rd Infantry and southwest of the rest of the squadron.

At 06.00 on 16 December 1944, artillery of every calibre and in heavy concentration fell on the forward areas. From their position in Winterscheid, the men of the troop headquarters could see it falling up and down the front line positions. A few rounds fell in the town of Winterscheid, but it was mostly of harassing nature and Captain Fossland made the observation that it did not seem to be concentrated on places, which the enemy would suspect of having American troops in position.

Following the barrage, which seemed to last about an hour, an armoured car patrol of three men, volunteers, attempted to contact the forward platoon positions and supply them with SCR 536 radios. All wire communications with these platoons had been cut, and as yet, the platoons had not opened the emergency SCR 508 radio channels that they held open for such an emergency.

The three volunteers bumped into an enemy patrol of about twelve men in the vicinity of the northern outlet of the Bleialf railroad tunnel and tangled with this group in a brisk fire fight. The Germans took off, but the patrol was skeptical of its chances of getting the radios through in view of indications that there were other German troops in the area.

Daylight came at about 07.15 and with it came the first strong pressure from enemy rifle troops. At about the same time the 508 radio channels to the platoon positions overcame enemy jamming and the Winterscheid headquarters was able to determine the progress and development of the fight to its front. The first attacks to be felt came in the vicinity of the 3rd Platoon, five hundred metres Northeast of Grosslangenfeld, a town one thousand metres south of Winterscheid held by soldiers of the 106th Infantry Division's Cavalry Reconnaissance Troop.

The next pressure, and seemingly more intense, came against the 1st and 2nd Platoons here in position near the Bleialf railroad tunnel. Defensive artillery and the cavalrymen's many automatic weapons took a heavy toll on the attacking Germans. The defenders held their position securely, although they were running low on ammunition. During a brief lull in the fighting, Sergeant Wade Bankston and four of his men managed to drive an armoured car from Winterscheid to Bleialf bringing with them some much needed ammunition. Again the Germans attacked and this time no further ammunition reached the beleaguered Americans from troop headquarters in Winterscheid. Captain Fossland called Colonel Cavender to inform him of the situation in Bleialf and Cavender gave him permission to withdraw his three platoons to Winterscheid.

Return in the direction of the centre of Bleialf turning left at the sign for 'Urb' and stopping in Winterscheid.

The Troop B withdrawal to Winterscheid was effected under cover of mobile support provided by three armoured cars under the command of 1st Lieutenant Richard Winkler. The withdrawal was made with no additional casualties and the 2nd and 3rd Platoons brought out all their equipment.

Here at Winterscheid, by darkness, the cavalrymen established an all-round defence of the village. Throughout the night of 16/17 December, intermittent rocket and artillery fire struck the village as Captain Fossland's men struggled to establish a new main line resistance. The 423rd Infantry informed Troop B of the presence of friendly engineers in Bleialf but patrols sent to establish contact failed to find any such friendly troops.

Renewed attempts to establish contact with friendly troops to the north failed on the morning of the 17th and at 10.00 the 423rd Infantry ordered Troop B to withdraw to Mützenich just west of the Bleialf – Schönberg road to set up flank security for the regiment.

Return to Bleialf church and turn left in the direction of Schönberg. Stop at the road junction about one kilometre north of Bleialf.

The road to your right leads Northeast from here via Auw and Roth to the Losheim Gap. Back to your right rear the high-forested ground were the Schnee Eifel positions of the 422nd and 423rd Infantry. From here it is clear that by capturing both ends of this road, the Germans would be in position to spring shut the jaws of a pincer movement west of the Schnee Eifel defenders.

Prior to the battle, American vehicles passing this junction were quite often subjected to incoming German artillery fire and therefore nicknamed this junction '88 Corner'. In order to permit the free movement of vehicles between Schönberg and Bleialf, men of the 168th Engineer Combat Battalion built a 'corduroy' road bypassing '88 Corner' and known as 'The Engineer Cut-Off'.

Insignia of the US 106th Infantry Division – the Golden Lions

Continue in the direction of Schönberg and upon reaching the second sharp bend in the road (about 1,200 metres) a dirt track joins you from the right. At the time of writing, it is marked 'Anlieger Frei' and bears a sign (Land und Forst Wirtsch Verkehr Frei) limiting access to vehicles less than 3.5 tons. Make a brief stop here.

This track to your right was nicknamed 'The Engineer Cut-Off'. Engineers of the 168th Engineer Combat Battalion improved this trail so vehicles could avoid coming under fire. On the evening of 16/17 December, Major General Alan W. Jones of the 106th Infantry Division ordered his division reserve, Lieutenant Colonel Joseph F. Puett's 2nd Battalion, 423rd Infantry forward from St. Vith to help the 589th and 592nd Field Artillery Battalions displace further west.

Colonel Puett ordered 2nd Lieutenant Oliver B. Patton to take a jeep with three men and drive from Schönberg via the corduroy road to locate the artillery battalions, then return to act as guides for the rest of the battalion to move forward.

As Lieutenant Patton, his driver and the other two men negotiated the log road in the inky dark, suddenly they heard the unmistakable sound of a tracked vehicle and shouts in German. Running their jeep into the roadside they sought refuge in the dense undergrowth as several German assault guns and infantrymen passed by.

The danger gone, Lieutenant Patton's party got their jeep back onto the road and resumed their journey. Upon locating the artillery men and taking one of them as a guide for their return with the rest of the battalion, they drove back to Schönberg without incident. In his book, *A Time For Trumpets*, Charles MacDonald presumed: 'The German vehicles and soldiers Patton and his men encountered on the Engineer Cut-Off apparently constituted a patrol and may have subsequently established a roadblock at 88 Corner'.

Continue downhill a short distance, until you reach Ihrenbruck where a minor road to the left leads to Mützenich. Follow this road to the village (about 1km).

Here, at Mützenich, Captain Fossland's Troop B, 18th Cavalry, joined forces with four officers, forty-three enlisted men and fourteen vehicles of the 106th Infantry Division's Reconnaissance Troop and six men of the 423rd Infantry. They promptly established positions around the village and prepared to defend it. Cavalrymen often referred to such a position as a 'sugar bowl'. It lay in the middle of a three-sided depression, commanding the only approach from the east and as such, constituted a veritable 'sugar bowl' for the attacking enemy who could take advantage of the high ground and covered approaches that stood on three sides of the position.

Shortly before 14.00, the cavalrymen spotted their first Germans moving northwest toward Schönberg on the Bleialf- Schönberg road. At about 14.00, a German enlisted man from this column came into town from the east under a flag of truce. In fluent English, he spoke with one of Captain Fossland's lieutenants offering the troopers the chance to surrender, they refused his offer and the German returned from whence he came.

The enemy column continued passing off to the northwest and out of range so Captain Fossland sent three armoured cars to determine the extent and power of the enemy forces on the Bleialf-Schönberg road and stated that Mützenich was no position from which to fight a delaying action. The 423rd responded by asking the cavalrymen to join them in Buchet but Fossland told them the area between them was full of German troops. He requested and was granted permission to move to the vicinity of Schönberg then start a delaying action back toward St. Vith. The 423rd Infantry told Troop B that Schönberg was reported as being in German hands but the cavalrymen nonetheless moved out. The 3rd Platoon took the lead followed by the 1st, headquarters, the 2nd and with elements of the 106th Reconnaissance Troop bringing up the rear.

Return to the Bleialf-Schönberg road and pause prior to turning left toward Schönberg.

As the withdrawing Americans reached this spot on the road, a jeep cut into the column between the 1st Platoon and the Headquarters group. Fossland's men couldn't believe their eyes, the jeep's occupants were four or five enemy soldiers armed with Panzerschrecks and MP 40 machine pistols. Immediately, an armoured car of the 1st Platoon fired several 37mm high explosive rounds at the captured vehicle which rolled off the road into the ditch killing the passengers.

Continue in the direction of Schönberg and stop about 1,200 metres further on where you reach a major bend in the road.

The forested area off to the right is known as Lindscheid and is where the retreating troops of the 422nd and 423rd Infantry ended up surrounded prior to their surrender on 19 December 1944.

Continue downhill passing a builder's yard named 'Leufgen' on the left and stopping at a small religious shrine on the right.

Arriving on the outskirts of Schönberg, which had earlier been reported as being in German hands, Captain Fossland halted his column here on the edge of town and ordered Lieutenant Elmo J. Johnston and his leading 3rd Platoon to enter town and determine the situation. Lieutenant Johnston led the platoon in his armoured car followed by two more armoured cars and trailed by the platoon's six jeeps. They entered town and crossed the Our River bridge turning left in the direction of St. Vith. Upon doing so they spotted a column of American 6 x 6 trucks lined up on the road ahead of them and facing west toward St. Vith. At first glimpse, in the growing dusk, Lieutenant Johnston and

The intrepid Sergeant (later Lieutenant) Donald L. Rubendall of Troop B, 18th Cavalry Reconnaissance Squadron. (Author's collection, courtesy of Donald L Rubendall).

117

his men believed the occupants of the trucks to be American troops but closer examination revealed them to be German. The cavalrymen initially presumed this to be a large group of prisoners awaiting transport to the rear but soon changed their minds when they saw the 'prisoners' were armed.

The armoured car crewmen immediately realised what lay before them and sprang into action driving along the left side of the column and blasting the loaded trucks with canister shells at a range of five to six feet!

Enemy soldiers leapt in panic from the trucks and tried in vain to scurry to safety, as they scrambled, without weapons for cover. Lieutenant Johnson's armoured car led the way closely followed by those of Sergeant James R. Hartstock and Sergeant Donald L. Rubendall.

Back on the hill, leading into town, Captain Fossland heard the first reports of contact and the crackle of gunfire over Lieutenant Johnston's radio just before the Germans knocked out the lead armoured car killing Lieutenant Johnston's driver, Bennie O. Webb and seriously wounding the Lieutenant. Sergeant Hartstock radioed to say he was stuck, and after this message, Fossland heard nothing more of those two armoured cars.

Meanwhile, Sergeant Rubendall and his crew followed in the wake of the other two, shooting at everything in sight. What Rubendall later described as a 'Mark IV' tank lumbered out of a side road from the right and blocked the progress of Rubendall's vehicle. So sudden was the appearance of this enemy tank that the M-8 armoured car was within five or six feet of the tank when it screeched to a halt. Immediately, Rubendall's gunner began firing armour-piercing shells point blank at the Mark IV setting fire to the engine compartment.

Slowly, the long 75mm cannon on the tank started to traverse toward the American armoured car. Sergeant Rubendall noticed that the enemy vehicle's turret was open and threw a grenade at the open hatch in an attempt to get it inside. He missed but noticed that as he threw a second grenade, the turret's traversing halted as each grenade clanged against the hull. Evidently the enemy tankers were flinching as each grenade hit the outside of their steel monster threatening to pop inside the open hatch. This helped stop traversing of the turret. The intrepid sergeant threw five or six such grenades until he ran out and in desperation grabbed the nearest thing at hand, an empty shell casing, ejected from his 37mm cannon. He hurled it blindly at the tank and as it clanged against the side of the tank Rubendall noticed that once again, the enemy gun barrel stopped its slow traversing toward his M-8 armoured car. Maintaining a steady stream of brass shell casings hurling at the enemy, he covered the actions of his crew as they bailed out and raced back to where they had left the six jeeps only to find the jeep crewmen engaged in a fire fight of their own. Only one of the jeeps made it back out of the village to rejoin Captain Fossland here on the road above town. All the other men in the column scattered and started off toward the south and west in an attempt to

Panzerkampfwagen *MkIV. This type remained in production throughout the war and became the mainstay tank of the German Army.*

reach friendly lines. Rubendall, Jack Borge, Gerald Hurnee, Warren Varner and a medic from the 106th eventually made their way out and participated in the defense of St. Vith rejoining their squadron on New Year's Day 1945.

After disabling their vehicles by removing or breaking critical parts, Captain Fossland and his men 'shorted' their radios and booby-trapped demolished equipment before splitting up into small groups and making their way out on foot.

Author's note: Broad consensus states that the 18th Volksgrenadier Division only had assault guns and not tanks, in Schönberg that morning. Sergeant Rubendall's description of the 'tank' as having an open hatch on a revolving turret would seem to indicate the presence of at least one German tank in Schönberg – German assault guns did not have revolving turrets. Despite the inability of many WW2 GIs to accurately identify enemy armoured vehicles, and their tendency to refer to all tanks as being 'Tigers', it is likely that an NCO in a cavalry reconnaissance unit would be able to differentiate between the two. Rubendall's description, at a range of a few feet, leaves little doubt as to the true identification of the vehicle in question. It was a tank.

Continue into Schönberg and opposite the church at the traffic circle take the first exit in the direction of Manderfeld. Pass a car dealership on the right and take the third minor road to the right (about 1,500 metres after the 'T' junction). At the time of writing, this road is directly after the last house on the right (#55) and just before a bus stop sign (#216).

Upon turning right continue up the incline then stop at the first junction.

It was on the high ground to your right, between here and the Skyline Drive that the remnants of the withdrawing 422nd and 423rd Infantry Regiments were ultimately surrounded.

Attempts to enter Schönberg drew heavy fire from half track mounted flak and assault guns. As elements of the 1st Battalion, 422nd Infantry attempted to cross the road on the West Side of the Schnee Eifel; they came under heavy machine-gun and assault gunfire, which inflicted large numbers of casualties. Ultimately, by early afternoon on 19 December, Colonel Descheneaux and his 2nd and 3rd Battalions reached the high ground overlooking the Schönberg – Andler road. Below them (and to your left) they spotted a column of vehicles lined up bumper to bumper. No sooner did they begin walking downhill, than they came under a hail of machine-gun and assault gunfire from the Germans on the road that forced them back into the forest.

Oberst *Otto Ernst Remer commander of the Führer Escort Brigade.* (Author's collection, courtesy Otto Remer).

When enemy tanks of *Oberst* Otto Remer's *Führer Begleit* Brigade appeared to his rear, Colonel Descheneaux realised that he and his men were completely surrounded. Colonel Puett of the 2nd Battalion, 423rd Infantry, unable to contact Colonel Cavender of the 422nd decided to head for the Andler – Schönberg road only to come under friendly fire when they ran into Descheneaux's 3rd Battalion. When this firing stopped Puett and his men joined forces with the 422nd.

By this time, the effects of three days of fighting and a severe shortage of food, water and ammunition simply added to the misery of the surrounded Americans.

Colonel Descheneaux decided that the time had come to surrender although a few men decided to try and escape. Colonel Puett's executive officer, Major

Men of the US 106th Infantry Division after their surrender to elements of the 18th Volksgrenadier Division.

William Cody Garlow, a grandson of the famous Buffalo Bill, volunteered to meet the Germans to arrange the surrender. Nearby, Colonel Cavender had reached the same decision. As Major Garlow walked down toward the road between Schönberg and Andler, the surrounded Americans began destroying their weapons.

Close to where you are stopped, Major Garlow met with the Germans and agreed the surrender terms. German *Kriegsberichter* camera crews made a point of filming the masses of prisoners in a field in nearby Andler as German tanks rolled by on the road, one even sporting a black teddy-bear on its gun barrel.

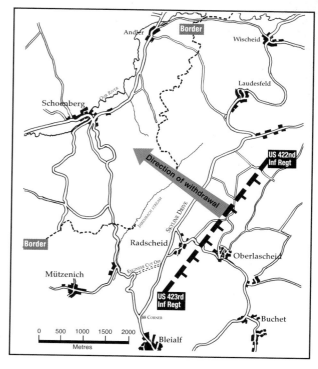

Return to Schönberg pausing on the far bank of the Our River.

Lieutenant Johnston and the men of the 3rd platoon, 18th Cavalry Squadron were not the only Americans to enter Schönberg only to find the village in German hands. The executive officer of Battery A, 589th Field Artillery Battalion, 1st Lieutenant Eric Fisher Wood and the commanding officer of Battery B, Captain Arthur C. Brown both had similar encounters with the Germans in those trucks. Captain Brown eventually escaped with a small group of men and the help of a Belgian farmer named Edmond Klein in the village of Houvegnez near Stavelot. Lieutenant Wood, less fortunate, died in the forest just north of the road to St. Vith.

Proceed in the direction of St. Vith and after about 1.5 kilometres stop near the bend as you enter the village of Heuem.

As reinforcements brought in to bolster the 14th Cavalry Group defense, the men of Troop B, 32nd Cavalry were positioned in Andler astride the main German approach road to both Schönberg and St. Vith. At daybreak on 17 December, two of the troop's reconnaissance teams, about twenty men, were suddenly engulfed by enemy tanks and infantry of the 506th Panzer Battalion, thrown in by Sixth Panzer Army to reinforce its advance toward Vielsalm. This force had detoured south of the inter-army boundary in search of a passable road. Contact was momentary and Troop B hastily withdrew to Schönberg while the enemy tanks went lumbering off to the northwest. In Schönberg, Troop B was hit again, this time by elements of the 294th Regiment, 18th Volksgrenadier Division led in person by the division commander Generalmajor Hoffmann-Schönborn. The cavalrymen headed west toward St. Vith, looking for a defile or cut which would afford an effective delaying position.

They finally reached a favourable point at this sharp bend near Heuem. Here while other troops streamed through from the east, the troop commander, Captain Franklin B. Lindsay, Jr. deployed his six armoured cars and fifteen jeep-carried machine-guns and mortars. For almost two hours Troop B repelled every attempt by the pursuing Volksgrenadiers and enemy armour to pass through Heuem.

Finally at 10:50 the 14th Cavalry Group sent orders by radio for Troop B to withdraw through St. Vith and rejoin the rest of the 32nd Cavalry Squadron northeast of the city.

Continue west along N626 and upon reaching Eiterbach take the first minor road to the right where small wooden signs indicate 'Eric F. Wood U.S. Monument 2.1 km'. At this distance from the main road on an uphill stretch of road and on the left stands a small stone cross, erected on the spot where Lt.

Wood's body was found in late January 1945.

In numerous accounts of the battle, a number of authors have subscribed to the theory that Lieutenant Wood teamed up with other American 'stragglers' to form some sort of guerrilla band which harassed the Germans in the forest around Meyerode continually over the next few weeks. On page 99 of his book *Decision at St. Vith*, the author Charles Whiting indicates that two local civilian men, discovered Lieutenant Wood's body and those of 'several Germans' on 23 January 1945. Neither Whiting nor any other author who has written about Wood has ever identified or located any dead or surviving Americans supposed to have been in Wood's group. Whiting goes on to state that 'the villagers buried him where he had died in the woods' and goes on to tell his readers that 'the grave is still there, a quarter of a century later'. Lieutenant Eric Fisher Wood's grave is in the Henri Chapelle U.S.

The stone cross marking the place where local people from Meyerode found the body of Lieutenant Eric Fisher Wood. (Author's collection).

Military cemetery and the location is G-3-46. Captain Arthur C. Brown, Sergeant Rubendall and the scores of other Americans who found themselves separated from their units had but one goal in mind, that of reaching friendly lines. In 1983, Staff Sergeant Francis H. Aspinwall of Battery A, 589th Field Artillery Battalion wrote:

'On December 17, I was part of that 'rabble' fleeing for safety behind American lines. Let me say, in all honesty, if on that day, had I met Eric Wood, and he had asked, or ordered, me to join his wolf pack, I would have told him he was suffering from battle fatigue and promptly reported the incident to my superiors!'

No one has ever attempted to discover the supply source of this 'roving wolf pack', who would, given their supposed guerrilla activity spanning a few weeks, have used up considerable amounts of food and ammunition.

In his book *A Time for Trumpets* Charles B. MacDonald sums up the Eric Wood legend as follows:

'For the Belgian civilians, at any rate, there were no doubts. Whether Lieutenant Wood died on December 17 while trying to reach St. Vith or whether he did indeed fight on with a small band of men, the Belgians erected a monument to him in the forest where, they say, he for long continued to fight. Set at the edge of a patch of fir trees along almost eerily silent gravel [now a tarmac trail], it is a touching memorial'.

Turn around and return to Eiterbach turning right onto the main road in the direction of St. Vith. You will climb a hill on which the left side of the road is forested while the right side is open fields. At the top, you pass a minor road leading right to the village of Wallerode. Stop near this junction.

This hill is called the Prummerberg and dominated not only the road from Schönberg to St. Vith but also a minor road from the Our River via Schlierbach to St. Vith. A combined force of engineers from the 81st and 168th Engineer Combat Battalions defended the Prummerberg. The 168th Engineer Combat Battalion command post was located in the schoolhouse at Wallerode. In their attacks toward St. Vith the Germans would use both roads over the Prummerberg as well as the road from Winterspelt via Steinbrück to St. Vith. General von Manteuffel himself placed great importance upon the capture of St. Vith and intended to make his main attack against the town in strength across the open fields between it and Wallerode. Problems of traffic congestion hampered the German advance to the extent that both von Manteuffel and the Army Group B commander, Field Marshall Model took a personal hand in trying to sort out the traffic jam at Schönberg. Lieutenant Colonels William L. Nungesser and Thomas J. Riggs of the 168th and 81st Engineer Combat Battalions respectively, decided that this high ground, about a mile outside of St. Vith, must be defended in order to prevent the attacking Germans from firing directly into the town.

As the engineers began digging in on either side of the road an artillery observation plane flying above the road spotted a German column of infantry led by an assault gun about two miles east of the Prummerberg. Gunners of the 592nd Field Artillery Battalion fired a volley of 155mm shells setting alight the assault gun and dispersing the accompanying infantry. This enemy column would be further delayed by the appearance of three P-47 fighter-bombers, which strafed it repeatedly inflicting heavy casualties. At no time that day did the Germans use more than three assault guns and one or two platoons of infantry in their piecemeal attacks west of Schönberg. The successive concentrations laid by the American artillery on Schönberg and both sides of the road west from 09.00 must have affected enemy movement considerably.

Brigadier General William M. Hoge commander CCB 9th Armored Division at St Vith. General Hoge had led the 5th and 6th Engineer Special Brigades on Omaha Beach on D-Day. His combat command captured the Ludendorf Bridge over the Rhine at Remagen on 7 March 1945. (US Army Signal Corps).

The original German plan of advance called for the mobile battalion of the 18th Volksgrenadier Division to advance upon St. Vith from Wallerode. The bulk of its advance guard toiled through the woods toward Wallerode, arriving there in the early morning. At about 08.00 on the morning of 18 December, the Germans launched a reconnaissance in force northeast of St. Vith, advancing from Wallerode toward Hünningen. Here, only 2,000 yards from St. Vith, two troops of the 87th Cavalry Reconnaissance Squadron and a few anti-aircraft half-tracks were forced back toward St. Vith. As the cavalry commenced its delaying action, a hurried call went out for CCB 9th Armored Division to send tanks and anti-tank guns to the rescue. Two companies of the 14th Tank Battalion and one from the 811th Tank Destroyer Battalion joined the fight knocking out six armoured vehicles and effectively stopping the German attack.

Late on the afternoon of 17 December, the Prummerberg defenders were joined by men of the 38th Armored Infantry Battalion and Troop B of the 87th Cavalry Reconnaissance Squadron astride the Schönberg road. On 18 December, the attacking Germans tried three times to rush their way through the foxhole line occupied by the 38th Armored Infantry and Troop B but, aided by engineers and supporting artillery, the Americans drove back these attacks.

Continue in the direction of St. Vith and on the downhill stretch at a sharp bend to the right turn left and back uphill in the direction of Schlierbach. Upon reaching the crest of the Prummerberg, on the left-hand side of the road, you will see the monument to the 168th Engineer Combat Battalion (signposted US Monument). Stop at the monument. When facing it at the time of writing, in the

Veterans of the 168th Engineer Combat Battalion at the Dedication of their memorial atop the Prummerberg. (Author's collection).

trees to left side of the dirt trail off to your left, a number of slit trenches dug by Company B of the 168th can still be seen.

First Lieutenant William E. Holland, commanding officer of Company B, 168th Engineer Combat Battalion participated in the defense of the Prummerberg. Initially, Lieutenant Holland found himself in the woods overlooking the road to Schönberg where he earned himself a Silver Star for his part in stopping a combined attack by infantry and an assault gun of the 18th Volksgrenadier Division. Upon the arrival of reinforcements from General Robert W. Hasbrouck's 7th Armored Division, the 168th commander Lieutenant Colonel Nungesser informed his company commanders that they were to re-align their front lines with Company B occupying the crest of the Prummerberg.

At one stage in the fighting here, Lieutenant Holland was briefing a Lieutenant in command of two tanks from the 14th Tank Battalion when four German assault guns burst out of the trees about 1,200 yards down the road to Schlierbach. Retired Colonel Bill Holland recalled that incident in a letter to the author:

'About 14.00, two Shermans with 76mm guns came up the road behind us. The lead tank under the command of a 1st Lieutenant stopped right beside our main line of defense. I jumped up on the tank and was briefing him on the situation when what we thought were four tanks (assault guns) broke from the woods to our front left coming straight down the road towards us. The lieutenant asked me if I was sure they were German and I replied "Hell Yes! Shoot the sons of bitches!" At the time I was not sure if they were friendly or not. He gave his gunner a fire order and I jumped off the tank. He hit the lead "tank" with his first shot, spun it sideways and set it alight. Some crewmembers jumped out and fled while the other three vehicles turned to their left behind a house and back into the woods at full speed. The lieutenant then backed downhill slightly so they couldn't be hit by direct fire.

'Things quietened down and I couldn't help but wonder if we had knocked out a German or American tank. I took a couple of my men with me and we worked our way several hundred yards to the front of the Company B main line of resistance where I could see the knocked out vehicle clearly with my field glasses. There was the prettiest black and white cross on the assault gun that I had ever seen'.

Colonel Holland also recalled the approach of a lone enemy infantryman later in the battle:

'A single German soldier walked from the woods toward a house [the first house along the Schlierbach road] past the 168th with his rifle at sling arms. I'm not sure if we first yelled at him to surrender, but he ignored us and kept walking toward the house. When he was about 25 yards from the house and about 250 yards from us, I told a small group of men near me to 'get him'. At least four or five men in prone position with M-1 rifles shot him; I also shot him with my M-1 carbine. There must have been at least eight shots fired but we only hit him once in the leg. He lay there crying, while our medics pressured me into letting them go get him. After five minutes, I relented and told them to do so. I was afraid the Germans would kill them out in the open. They went out and got him without being fired upon. I later learned that he was hungry like many of the attacking troops and was going to the house in search of food'.

On the night of 21 December, at 21.30, the defenders of the Prummerberg received orders from Brigadier General Bruce C. Clarke, then commanding the troops defending St. Vith, to withdraw behind the town. This order proved impossible to execute, so individually, or in small groups the Prummerberg defenders tried to make their way out on foot. Given the then ferocious German attack along the Schönberg road, Lieutenant Holland and the men with him took a small path through the woods (still visible at the time of writing directly opposite the monument) hoping to reach the Steinebrück – St. Vith road.

> *Continue in the direction of Schlierbach and on the far left side of the village turn right in the direction of Alfersteg on the Our River. Upon reaching the river, turn right just before the bridge passing through Weppeler and past a sign for St. Vith on your way to Steinebrück. In Steinebrück, stop at the 'T' junction with the N646 (Prum – St. Vith road).*

On 17 December, *Generalmajor* Friederich Kittel's 62nd Volksgrenadier Division attacked and by daybreak captured the village of Winterspelt, three miles to the Southeast of Steinebrück. The commander of LXVI Panzercorps *General der Artillerie* Walther Lucht came to Winterspelt in person to supervise the attack on the bridge at Steinebrück. The 62nd Volksgrenadier Division had suffered heavy losses in its attacks near Heckhuscheid and the division on its left, now pulled out and left the 62nd to go it alone. This seriously damaged Lucht's ability to exploit the dent hammered into the American lines at Winterspelt. The right regiment of the 62nd advanced almost unopposed north of Winterspelt while the division centre, now composed of *Oberst* Arthur Jüttner's 164th Regiment, reinforced by assault guns and engineers, continued beyond Winterspelt to occupy the saddle which overlooked the approaches to Steinbrück.

Brigadier General William M. Hoge's CCB, 9th Armored Division arrived in St. Vith before dawn on 17 December then began moving forward to the west bank of the Our River.

By 09.30, elements of CCB had crossed the Our at Steinbrück and attacked German infantry dug in on high ground overlooking the village of Elcherath. In subsequent fighting that day, CCB captured Elcherath only to be told by

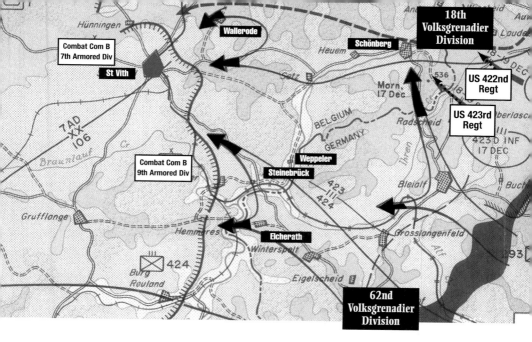

General Jones of the 106th Infantry Division to withdraw back across the Our that night of 17/18 December. The withdrawal completed CCB and the 424th Infantry occupied a seven thousand-yard line from Weppeler to Burg Reuland along with Troop D of the 89th Cavalry Reconnaissance Squadron, the latter holding the three thousand-yard sector between Steinebrück and Weppeler.

On 18 December as elements of the cavalry contingent began moving out of the area on their way to help stem the threat developing north of St. Vith, General Hoge cancelled the movement order due to increased enemy pressure here at Steinebrück. As the morning wore on, the Germans increased in number, slipping into positions on the south bank under the cover of exploding smoke shells. To counter this threat the light tank platoon moved into Steinebrück, leaving the American left uncovered. A provisional rifle company from the 424th Infantry west of Steinebrück took off and one of the cavalry platoons had to be switched hastily to cover this gap.

Thus far, the all-important bridge had been left intact, in the hope that part of the 423rd Infantry might free itself from the Schnee Eifel trap.

By noon, the situation was such that the little group of troopers dare delay no longer. On General Hoge's orders, a platoon of armoured engineers went down and blew the bridge – almost in the teeth of the Volksgrenadiers on the far bank.

An hour later, the platoon west of the village saw an enemy column of horse-drawn artillery moving into position. American gunners west of Lommersweiler answered the cavalry call for aid. An hour later however, some twenty-two enemy guns opened fire in support of an attack across the river, crossing the Our and passing through unoccupied Weppeler to hit the cavalry left flank. Only five Americans escaped. Two or more enemy companies crossed near the blasted bridge and despite the pounding delivered by the 16th Field Artillery Battalion, and the rapid fire from the cavalry tanks, assault and machine-guns, had nearly encircled Troop D. A cavalry request from medium tanks couldn't be met; General Hoge had no reserve. A Company of the 27th Armored Infantry Battalion, however, came in to cover the cavalry left flank. With German infantry now inside Steinebrück and their artillery knocking out the American vehicles one by one, the cavalry withdrew toward St. Vith.

His line no longer tenable, General Hoge consulted General Jones and the two decided that the combat should withdraw from the river to higher ground. Commencing at dark, the move went off unhindered and CCB took up positions two and a half miles southeast of St. Vith blocking the Winterspelt – St. Vith road and the valley of the Braunlauf Creek.

Continue in the direction of St. Vith and upon passing under the viaduct proceed through Wiesenbach, stop with the wooded Volmersberg hill off to the right of the road.

Upon reaching the wooded hill to your right and overlooking the Steinebrück road, the American engineers who'd escaped from the Prummerberg, split into smaller groups. Lieutenant Bill Holland of Company B, 168th Engineer Combat Battalion, took eight of his own men and an artillery observer in an attempt to cross the road only to find that the Germans had posted guards every two to three hundred yards along the road. By then, totally exhausted, the engineers made their way to a house near the highway and surrendered to a group of Germans, that Holland later estimated to number seventy.

The Germans loaded and locked their prisoners in a closed van with wire mesh over its windows and drove out into the woods where the van stopped as the two Germans in the cab argued for minutes, Holland supposed over the fate of their prisoners. The matter apparently resolved, they returned to the road and drove several miles before unloading the Americans at what appeared to be a Regimental Command post for interrogation. The prisoners received no food over the next couple of days.

Continue towards St. Vith and upon entering St. Vith take the third exit at the main traffic circle heading down Klosterstrasse. Go as far as the school and note the monument to the 106th Infantry Division. Return to the traffic circle and take the third exit following signs for Stavelot/Malmedy down the town main street. At the far edge of town across the road from the town cemetery off to your right is a black marble monument to the 2nd Infantry Division.

Prior to the arrival of the 106th, the 2nd occupied positions in the Schnee Eifel east of St. Vith. On 11 December 1944, incoming troops of the 106th replaced those of the 2nd who then moved north to take part in the attack toward the Roer Dams.

Continue in the direction of Stavelot/Malmedy and at the traffic circle in the village of Hünningen, take the third exit following signs for Vielsalm/E-42. Pass under E-42; continue through Rodt to Poteau where you turn left and stop on the left. The large stone house across the street from the road from Rodt served as the temporary command post of the 14th Cavalry Group during its brief time here.

On 22 December, the overall ground commander in the area, Field Marshall Sir Bernard L. Montgomery, informed the 7th Armored Division commander, Brigadier General Robert W. Hasbrouck that his division had done what was expected of it and was hereby ordered to withdraw from St. Vith. The initial plan called for the withdrawing Americans to form an oval-shaped defensive position to be known as the 'Fortified Goose Egg' in front of and encompassing Vielsalm. Later, the decision was made for this withdrawal to be made as far as the west bank of the Salm River at Vielsalm. Three roads lent themselves to this withdrawal. This one, the main St. Vith to Vielsalm route through Poteau, a gravel road leading through a forested area called the 'Grand Bois' and General Clarke's headquarters location of Commanster to Vielsalm, and lastly the road leading along the Salm valley into Salmchâteau from the south.

Upon falling back from the Manderfeld area, the 14th Cavalry Group established its command post here in the building diagonally opposite the

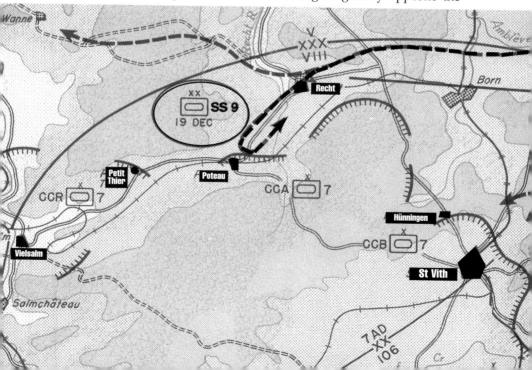

road from Rodt. Early on 18 December, in keeping with orders from 106th Division, the acting Group commander, Lieutenant Colonel Augustine Duggan intercepted elements of the 18th Cavalry, Troop C of the 32nd and the one remaining platoon of towed 3-inch guns of the 820th Tank Destroyer Battalion. He placed them under the command of Major J. L. Mayes as a task force to comply with orders from the 106th to return to Born, which they had just evacuated, and occupy the high ground.

Task Force Mayes moved out toward Recht at first light on 18 December but had only gone some two hundred yards when German bazooka fire set the leading tank and armoured car on fire. The glare of the burning vehicles silhouetted the figures of enemy infantrymen advancing toward the Poteau crossroads. The cavalrymen pulled back into the village and hastily prepared to defend the dozen or so houses there, while to the north a small cavalry patrol dug in on a hill overlooking the hamlet and made a fight of it. By this time, the remnants of traffic, including vehicles of CCR, 7th Armored Division, milling around the village were leaving.

All through the morning the Germans pressed in on Poteau, moving their

US Army Artist Harrison Standley painted this picture of the Poteau road junction after the battle. (US Army collection The Pentagon).

machine-guns, mortars, and assault guns closer and closer. At noon the situation was critical, the village was raked by fire, and the task force was no longer in communication with any other Americans. Colonel Duggan finally gave the order to retire down the road to Vielsalm. Three armoured cars, two jeeps, and one light tank were able to disengage and carried the wounded out; apparently a major part of the force was able to make its way to Vielsalm on foot.

What are definitely among the most well-known photographs and film taken during the battle by either side, are the series of shots taken by German cameramen and cleverly analysed by Jean Paul Pallud on pages 209-224 of his monumental *Battle Of The Bulge – Then And Now*. These widely published shots were taken on a curve a few hundred yards along the road from Poteau in the direction of Recht.

The German units attacking Poteau on 18 December were elements of the 1st SS *Leibstandarte*, which, by that evening had left the area. In a counterattack, Colonel Dwight A. Rosebaum's CCA, 7th Armored Division regained Poteau and deployed around the village with CCR on its right flank.

Poteau lends itself well to defensive action. It stands at the entrance to the valley road that leads to Vielsalm, and mechanised attack from either Recht or

American convoy caught on the road from Recht to Poteau and destroyed.

Rodt had to funnel through the narrow neck at this crossroads, vehicle manoeuvre off either of the two approaches being almost impossible. Away from the crossroads the ground rises sharply and is cluttered with thick stands of timber. The formation adopted by CCA was based on a semi-circle of ten medium tanks fronting from northwest to east, backed by tank destroyers with riflemen in a foxhole line well to the front. About 10.45 the blocking troops left by the 9th SS *Hohenstaufen* Panzer Division made an attack. Tank and artillery fire stopped the Germans just as it had on previous days. Perhaps the enemy would have returned to the fray and made the final withdrawal hazardous. However, shortly after noon, some P-38's of the 370th Fighter Group, unable to make contact with the 82nd Airborne Division control, to which they were assigned, went to work for the 7th Armored Division, bombing and strafing along the road to Recht. The enemy recovery was slow.

At 13.45 General Hasbrouck sent the signal for CCA to pull out. In an hour the armoured infantry were out of their holes and their half-tracks were clanking down the road to Vielsalm. Forty minutes later the tanks left Poteau, moving fast and exchanging shots with German tanks, while the 275th Field Artillery Battalion fired a few final salvos to discourage pursuit. When the last vehicle of CCA roared over the Vielsalm Bridge (at 16.20) the remaining artillery followed; then came the little force from CCR, which had held the road open while CCA made its withdrawal. Darkness descended over the Salm valley as CCR sped across the Vielsalm Bridge.

Continue in the direction of Vielsalm and on reaching Petit Thier take the first minor road to the left passing through the nearby village of Blanchefontaine. Continue on the same blacktopped road into the woods (bearing left at a white wooden cross) as far as the small white chapel of Tinseux Bois on the right side of the road. Turn around and stop by the large house opposite the chapel.

After abandoning their remaining vehicles and escaping from the village of La Gleize, SS-*Obersturmbannführer* Jochen Peiper and the remnants of his once strong *Kampfgruppe* Peiper came to Petit Thier for a few days rest and refit. In 1969, the wartime Catholic priest, Curé Cahay sent the author extracts of the parish records covering Peiper's arrival in Petit Thier and his having lodged in this house:

'On the evening of 24 December SS troops arrived in Petit Thier and occupied the more comfortable houses in the village. They said they were waiting for replacement vehicles (which never arrived). Their commander,

With the road blocked with burning American vehicles these SS Panzergrenadiers take to the field alongside the road.

Peiper, was at Tinseux and after they left, the bodies of some executed Americans were discovered there.'

The Tool and Weapons Sergeant of Peiper's Headquarters' Company, SS-*Unterscharführer* Otto Wichmann in a post-war statement made of his own free will, spoke of the killing of one such American prisoner here at Tinseux Bois. The man in question had emerged from the woods and surrendered to the Germans whereupon they took him into the house where Peiper, the unit surgeon Dr. Kurt Sickel, and an unidentified *Sturmbannführer* examined his papers. In his statement, Wichmann describes the prisoner's fate:

'*Sturmbannführer* Sickel motioned with his thumb to me and said in a sharp loud voice, 'Get the swine out and bump him off'. I then went into the nearby chapel in which the communications platoon was billeted and I borrowed a pistol. I led the prisoner along the road accompanied by

Lieutenant Colonel John P. Wemple commander 17th Tank Battalion, 7th Armored Division on the heights above Recht.
(Author's collection courtesy Colonel Wemple).

Sturmmann Einfalt. At the road fork, I took the right fork, which leads uphill. The American could only walk a few steps at a time; then we had to support him, as he could not continue. We came to a spot on the road and I turned right into the woods. Up to this point we had been leading the American. From there on I had him go to the wood in front of us. However, he did not reach the wood, only up to the edge of the wood approximately fifteen to twenty metres away from the road. I only went a few metres into the field and then I stopped and brought my weapon into position and I shot the American two or three shots. I am a good pistol shot. Normally, I had to test the repaired weapons, as I was the weapons sergeant. After the shooting I went into the chapel and returned the pistol. Then I returned to the stable and we all had lunch.'

Return to Petit Thier turning left at the main road in the direction of Vielsalm. Pause by the church in Petit Thier.

Early on the morning of 18 December, Headquarters CCR, 7th Armored Division, set out from Poteau in the direction of

Men of the SS-Leibstandarte pause to sample captured American cigarettes.

Vielsalm. Upon arrival here in Petit Thier, the men of CCR discovered that Lieutenant Joseph V. Whiteman of the 23rd Armored Infantry Battalion, separated from his column on the march south, had heard firing at Poteau. He had rounded up a collection of stray tanks, infantry, cavalry and engineers under the name of 'Task Force Navajo' to block the road to Vielsalm. The CCR Commander took over this roadblock and, as the force swelled through the day with incoming stragglers and lost detachments, extended the position west of the village. Thankfully, the German column at Poteau, however, made no attempt to drive on to Vielsalm. The main body of the 1st SS *Leibstandarte* Panzer Division needed reinforcements. The Panzergrenadier Regiment and the assault guns therefore left their assigned route and turned Northeast to follow the column passing through Stavelot.

Continue toward Vielsalm passing through Ville du Bois and upon entering Vielsalm, pause by the M4A1 Sherman tank on the left before the traffic lights.

This tank commemorates the role of the 7th Armored Division in the Battle of the Bulge.

Continue straight ahead past the traffic lights in the direction of Marche and stop at the junction with N68 (joining you from your right rear at the bottom of the hill).

This is General Bruce Clarke Square, named in honor of the wartime commander of CCB, 7th Armored Division. While not strictly speaking a 'square', it features a monument bearing the 7th Armored Division shoulder patch. Upon withdrawal to the far (west) Bank of the Salm River and establishment of the so-called 'Fortified Goose-Egg' American troops blew the road and rail bridges over the Salm effectively stopping any further enemy advance across the river in Vielsalm.

Suggested Reading:
MacDonald: Chapters 5,15,16 and 23.
Cole: Chapters 7,12 and 17.

CHAPTER 4

DASBURG-CLERVAUX-BASTOGNE-HOUFFALIZE

STARTING POINT: THE OUR RIVER BRIDGE AT DASBURG, 39 KILOMETRES EAST OF BASTOGNE.

German engineers demolished the Our River bridge here at Dasburg during their retreat to the German border in the autumn of 1944. Along with two other bridges at Ouren to the north and Gemünd to the south, this bridge was the only means of access for German armour to exit the Our River valley on their way to the villages sitting astride what came to be called the 'Skyline Drive'. Villages such as Marnach on the high ground west of the Our dominated roads leading west to Bastogne and beyond and would be defended tenaciously by elements of Major General Norman D. Cota's 28th Infantry Division and attached units.

German infantry assault troops began crossing the Our River prior to the opening artillery barrage in the pre-dawn darkness of 16 December. At this

It was at this point that the advance guard of the 2nd Panzer Division awaited the order to advance at dawn 16 December.

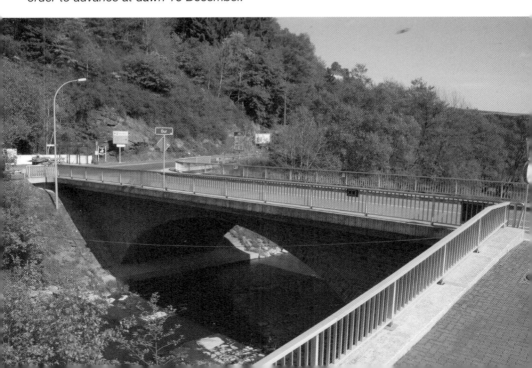

bridge site, unexpected complications meant that the men of Major Georg Loos' 600th Engineer Battalion couldn't begin construction of a replacement bridge until the attack began.

It took them until the early afternoon of the first day to complete the bridge at which point impatient tankers of *Oberst* Meinrad von Lauchert's 2nd Panzer Division began crossing the Our. Unfortunately, the eleventh tank doing so inflicted severe damage to the structure, which took another three hours to repair. To the south engineers completed the Gemund Bridge at about the same time.

Follow the Clervaux sign from the Dasburg Bridge west to Marnach and pass over the N7. In Marnach, on the bend before the church, on the right side of the street is a monument to the 28th Infantry Division and a plaque to the 707th Tank Battalion.

Men of Company B, 110th Infantry, under their battalion executive officer, Captain James H. Burns, ably supported by a platoon of towed guns of the 630th Tank Destroyer Battalion, fiercely defended Marnach until shortly after nightfall on 16 December. In nearby villages such as Hosingen, Heinerscheid and Munshausen, American infantry and artillerymen did their utmost to stop the German onslaught.

At the western end of Marnach, turn left on route 326 in the direction of Munshausen and pause in front of the village church.

Here, men of Company C, 110th Infantry, supported by six howitzers of the regimental Cannon Company and (on 16 December) by a platoon of medium tanks from the 707th Tank Battalion, inflicted heavy losses on the attacking soldiers of the 2nd Panzer Division's Reconnaissance Battalion. On 17 December, the gravity of the situation in Clervaux prompted the regimental commander, Colonel Hurley E. Fuller to withdraw the armored support from the defenders of Munshausen. On 18 December, when the Germans finally took the village, they discovered the body of one of their company commanders, on a path near this church with a bayonet stuck in his throat. According to MacDonald, the Germans were so impressed with the marksmanship shown by the defenders, that they nicknamed them 'The sharpshooters of Munshausen'.

Return to N18 turning left in the direction of Clerf (Clervaux). On the descent into town, pause at the overlook on the right for a spectacular view of the town and its castle.

From here you get a great view of the castle, strenuously defended by soldiers of the 110th Infantry's Headquarters' Company under Captains Claude B. Mackey

An American GI outside the Bertemes cafe/gas station in Marnach, examines abandoned German weaponry. (US Army Signal Corps).

and John Aiken Jr. Five Sherman tanks from a platoon of the 707th Tank Battalion under 1st Lieutenant Raymond E. Fleig, knocked out the lead German Mark IV on a hairpin bend below you effectively blocking this route into town.

Drive down into Clervaux and follow the signs for 'Bastogne' keeping the greater part of town off to your left. As you do so, note the GI statue commissioned by C.E.B.A. (a local group which studies the battle) to your left. Park in the next parking lot on the right and below the castle. Cross the street and walk back down

Clervaux after the battle. The castle was strongly defended by men of the 110th Infantry Regiment of the 28th Infantry Division. (US Army Signal Corps).

the main pedestrian access to the left which takes you back to the GI statue. As you face the statue, note the bronze plaque high on the wall of the bank to your left rear. It depicts the grateful citizens of Luxembourg welcoming their American liberators. Walk up to the castle and in the forecourt pause to look back toward the road that brought you into town. Inspect the Sherman tank and the German 8.8 cm Pak 43/41 then enter the inner courtyard to visit the Ardennes Battle Museum, open in June from 13:00 till 17.00 then in July till 15 September from 10.00 till 17.00. On Sundays and holidays (including Christmas) the museum opens from 13.00 till 17.00 and is closed throughout January and February.

Return to your car and continue in the direction of Bastogne crossing the railroad. Note the Claravallis hotel to your left and the rock face to its rear. Pause here.

This building served as regimental headquarters of Colonel Fuller's 110th Infantry Regiment. On the evening of 17 December, German tanks entered Clervaux from the north, crossed the railroad and opened direct fire upon the hotel. Colonel Fuller and some of his staff escaped up the rock face to the rear of an upstairs room only to be captured later on their way west of the town. At 18.39, the sergeant at the regimental switchboard called division to report that he was alone- only the switchboard was left.

Follow N18 in the direction of Bastogne until you reach the Antoniushof traffic island on N12.

By the evening of 17 December, the VIII Corps commander, Major General Troy H. Middleton, faced the problem of having insufficient numbers of men with whom to stop the German advance west of Clervaux. He ordered Colonel Joseph H. Gilbreth of Combat Command Reserve, 9th Armored Division, to place roadblocks here and at the next important junction at Fetsch. Here, at Antoniushof, Captain Lawrence K. Rose of Company A, 2nd Tank Battalion, positioned his task force comprising his own tank company, a company of armored infantry and an engineer platoon supported by a battery of guns from the 73rd Armored Field Artillery Battalion. Reconnaissance troops of von Lauchert's 2nd Panzer Division first approached Antoniushof on the morning of 18 December only to be followed that afternoon by tanks and armoured infantry. Under pressure after losing their artillery support, Task Force Rose withdrew from Antoniushof later that evening in the direction of Houffalize.

Turn left on N12 and drive on until you reach the junction with N874 sign posted 'Bastogne'. This is Fetsch.

Here, a second armored task force of Combat Command Reserve, 9th Armored Division, under Lieutenant Colonel Ralph S. Harper, established a roadblock comprising a company of tanks, a company of armored infantry and two batteries of the 73rd Armored Field Artillery Battalion. German tanks overran Task Force Harper, killing Colonel Harper whose infantry and few surviving tanks raced west to Longvilly. Colonel Theodore Seeley and men of the 110th Infantry tried in vain to stop the Germans who captured them.

Drive west on N874 to Longvilly stopping at the church.

Rather than proceeding into Longvilly, 2nd Panzer Division turned northwest in the direction of Bourcy. Von Lauchert's objective was not to capture Bastogne but rather to cross the Meuse River as quickly as possible. This gave Colonel Gilbreth and the remnants of Combat Command Reserve, 9th

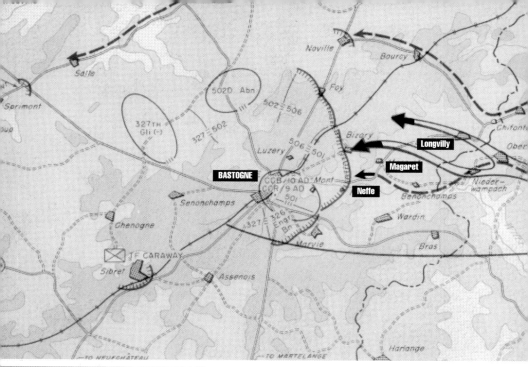

Armored Division, the time for a short-lived and much needed breathing space. Longvilly, five and a half miles from Bastogne, was the scene of considerable confusion. Stragglers rode or marched through the dingy village and no one seemed to know the precise location of the oncoming Germans, although rumour placed them on all sides. By 18 December, General Middleton was doing all he could to block the roads into Bastogne. Combat command B, 10th Armored Division under Colonel William Roberts, set up its command post at the hotel Lebrun just off the main square in Bastogne. From there he dispatched three combat teams to block three of the seven roads leading into the threatened city. Team Cherry, under Lieutenant Colonel Henry T. Cherry set up its headquarters in the

Oberst *Meinrad von Lauchert commander 2nd Panzer Division*
(Author's collection courtesy General von Lauchert).

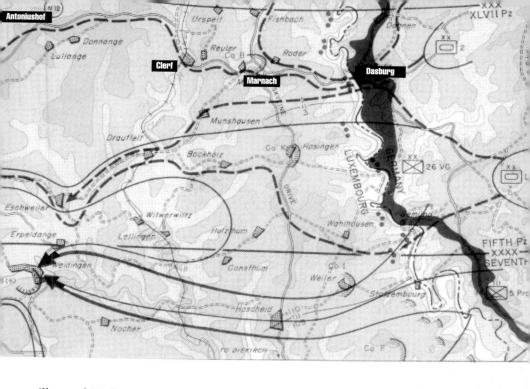

village of Neffe just east of Bastogne on the evening of 18 December. Its advance guard under 1st Lieutenant Edward P. Hyduke continued east to the western edge of Longvilly to assume defensive positions north, south and east of the village. By 19.00, the main body of Team Cherry under Captain William F. Ryerson was assembled on the road about a thousand yards west of Longvilly. *Generalleutnant* Fritz Bayerlein's Panzer Lehr, bypassed Longvilly to the south and captured Magaret, the next village to the west thus cutting the road to Bastogne. During the night, small groups of Germans made feeble attempts to pick off American vehicles crowding the streets of Longvilly. At Midnight in his command post in Neffe, Colonel Cherry learned that the Germans had captured Magaret thus separating his headquarters from the rest of the team here in Longvilly.

Continue west through the village until you reach the 'Grotto of Notre Dame' on the left side of the road. Stop here and note the bullet and shell fragment damage to the iron gates in front of the grotto.

Here, a force comprising Lieutenant Hyduke's remaining light tanks, armored cars and a platoon of tank destroyers from the 811th Tank Destroyer Battalion, managed to hold their ground for over an hour until Colonel Cherry ordered them to fall back and join the rest of the unit. Destroying their remaining vehicles,

Hyduke's men began walking cross-country to the west.

Drive towards Magaret, stopping on the slope leading down into the village.

This stretch of road is where the Germans destroyed the bulk of Team Cherry's vehicles with tank, artillery, antitank and rocket fire leaving a mass of twisted steel in its wake.

Drive into Magaret stopping where a sign points right in the direction of Bizory.

As Task Force Harper had struggled to defend Fetsch, Bayerlein's Panzer Lehr bypassed Fetsch through Oberwampach at which point, it was less than six miles from Bastogne. In Oberwampach, he sent a small force of tanks and panzergrenadiers to reconnoitre a minor road leading directly to Magaret only three miles from Bastogne. Despite the poor quality of this road, Bayerlein's advance guard captured Magaret shortly after the passage of Team Cherry on its way to Longvilly. Uncertainty as to the strength of the American unit now to his rear, caused Bayerlein to call a temporary halt to his advance upon Bastogne.

Drive into Neffe turning left at the stone chapel in the direction of Mont. Pass the first farm on your left and past the curve cross a small bridge. Up ahead, just before the road branches to the right, stands a farmhouse. Pause here.

This farm stands on the former site of Colonel Cherry's command post, the Château de Neffe. As the bulk of his team fought for its life at Longvilly and Magaret, Colonel Cherry and his staff were having a fight of their own here at the command post in Neffe, a mile and a quarter southwest of Magaret. Cut off from his main force, through the small hours of the 19 December, Cherry and his staff eagerly awaited reinforcements from the incoming 101st Airborne Division. At first light, a detachment of tanks and infantry of the Panzer Lehr hit the American tank platoon holding the crossroads in the centre of Neffe. The defenders stopped one tank with a bazooka round, but then broke under heavy fire and headed west along the road to Bastogne. One of the two American headquarters tanks in support of the roadblock got away, as did a handful of infantrymen who fell back to the château.

Just before noon, the Germans moved in to try and clear the stubborn defenders from the command post. Cherry's men held fast for over four hours using the automatic weapons lifted from their vehicles, and checking every enemy rush in a hail of bullets. Ultimately, a few determined Germans set the building alight when they threw incendiary grenades through the windows. A platoon of the 501st Parachute infantry arrived just in time to take part in the withdrawal. Their appearance and the covering fire of other troops behind them jarred the Germans enough to allow Colonel Cherry and his staff to break free. Before pulling out for Mont, the next village to the southwest,

Brigadier General Gerald J. Higgins acting Deputy Division Commander of the 101st Airborne Division at Bastogne.

(US Army Signal Corps photograph courtesy General Higgins).

Colonel Cherry radioed his commander Colonel Roberts the following message:

'We are pulling out. We're not driven out but burned out!'

Turn right, then keep left continuing straight ahead and eventually crossing N84 in the direction of Marvie and stopping by the village church. Note the turret by the community center on your right.

Here, yet another element of Colonel Roberts' Combat Command B, 10th Armored Division, Team O'Hara, commanded by Lieutenant Colonel James O'Hara, took up positions near Marvie aimed at blocking the road into Bastogne. On 20 December, Brigadier General Anthony McAuliffe, acting commander of the 101st Airborne Division, sent a battalion of his glider infantry to relieve the tired and hungry soldiers of Lieutenant Colonel Paul H. Symbol's under strength 35th Engineer Combat Battalion near Marvie. The changeover completed, one of O'Hara's outposts spotted a German column comprising four tanks and a rifle company approaching the village. Within one hour, O'Hara's medium tanks had accounted for the panzers and the glider infantrymen had beaten back the German infantry in disorder and occupied Marvie. In vicious close quarter fighting on 23 – 24 December at different times both sides claimed to have control of the village. This may well have led to an American air strike against Marvie by P-47's during the afternoon of 24 December. Much of the village burned as a result of these attacks but nonetheless the defenders kept hold of the western edge of the village.

Drive into Bastogne straight up N84 until you reach the tank on the central square today named 'Place McAuliffe'. Follow the sign for Liège (E25) and on E25 take exit 53 marked 'Hemroulle'. Drive into the village and stop by the church.

On 23 December, at a drop zone west of Bastogne between Hemroulle and Mande-Saint-Etienne, 241 C-47 aircraft dropped 144 tons of supplies, mainly artillery ammunition to the encircled defenders of Bastogne who, by then, were down to their last few rounds.

At one point in the fighting here, the defenders found themselves lacking suitable camouflage material. Major John D. Hanlon and a village councillor

American vehicles approach the market square in Bastogne from the rue d'Assenois. (US Army Signal Corps).

went from door to door asking the occupants for white sheets with which to camouflage the American vehicles. Hanlon returned post-war, bringing with him, a pair of white sheets for every home in the village, a gift from the people of his hometown in the United States.

> *Drive through Hemroulle in the direction of Champs, stopping with a narrow, blacktop road leading right in the direction of 'Rolley' and at the time of writing a few large trees on your left.*

On Christmas Day and 26 December 1944, elements of Generalmajor Heinz Kokott's 26th Volksgrenadier Division, supported by *Kampfgruppe* Maucke of the 15th Panzergrenadier Division, made a final desperate bid to break into Bastogne. A group of eighteen Mark IV tanks with Volksgrenadiers riding 'piggy-back' broke through the lines of Companies A and B of the 327th Glider Infantry Regiment. Just west of Hemroulle, about half the tanks wheeled left, defiling along a narrow cart path which led to the Champs to Bastogne road on which you are now parked. As they approached the road, the panzers formed in line abreast, now bearing straight toward Companies B and C of the 502nd Parachute Infantry, who were on their way to bolster the defenses at Champs. Lieutenant Colonel Steve Chappuis, commanding the 502nd, had but a few minutes to face his companies toward the oncoming tanks. Two tank destroyers of Company B, 705th Tank Destroyer Battalion, absorbed the initial shock before the Germans knocked them out as they fell back toward the Champs road. As the panzers rolled forward, Company C made an orderly withdrawal to the edge of a large wood on the east side of the road between Champs and Hemroulle. The paratroopers showered the tanks with lead, and the infantry clinging to the decks, fell to the snow covered ground. The tank detachment again wheeled into column, this time turning north toward Champs. Two of the other 705th Tank Destroyers that were supporting Company C caught the column in the process of turning and put away three of the panzers; the paratrooper's bazookas accounted for two more.

A burned out American M18 tank destroyer on the outskirts of Bastogne.
(US Army Signal Corps).

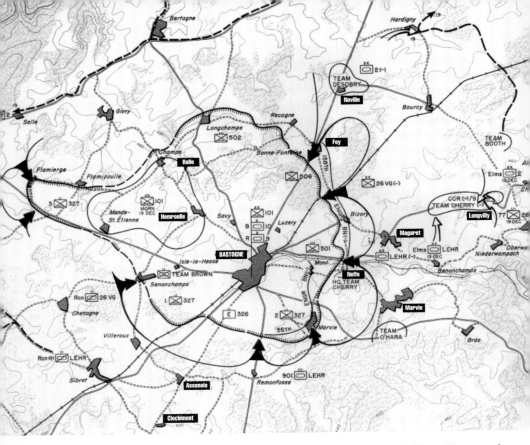

Fire from American tanks, tank-destroyers, parachute field artillery and bazookas decimated the half of the enemy tank-infantry formation which had kept on toward Hemroulle after knifing through the 327th foxhole line, effectively ending this German foray behind the American lines.

Turn right down the narrow road leading to Rolley and stop in front of the château.

This building served as the regimental command post of Lieutenant Colonel Steve Chappuis' 502nd Parachute Infantry.

Return to the main road and turn right in the direction of Champs. In the centre of the village, turn left in the direction of Mande-Saint-Etienne (not sign posted at the time of writing but spot marked by a cross commemorating military and civilian victims of both wars).

Drive uphill leaving the sign for Flamierge off to your right and return via Mande-Saint-Etienne to Bastogne.

In Bastogne, at the tank on Place McAuliffe, take N85 in the direction of Neufchâteau. Cross over E25 and in Sibret, turn left following a sign for Homprè.

150

Pass under E25 then take a left stopping immediately alongside the Belgian war memorial facing the hamlet of Clochimont.

On 18 December 1944, General Omar N. Bradley commander of 12th Army Group, called the Third Army Commander Lieutenant General George S. Patton Jr. to his Luxembourg City headquarters in the Hotel Alpha near the railway station. At this meeting, Patton first learned of the potentially catastrophic situation facing First Army to his north. When asked what help he could give, the Third Army commander immediately replied that he could intervene with three divisions 'very shortly'. He telephoned the Third Army chief of staff to stop the XII Corps attack forming for the following day and to prepare the 4th Armored and 80th Infantry Divisions for immediate transfer to Luxembourg.

By nightfall on the 18th December it became apparent that the First Army situation had deteriorated beyond expectation and at about 02.00 on 19 December Bradley called Patton to a meeting in Verdun later that morning for a meeting with the supreme commander General Dwight D. Eisenhower. At midnight the 4th Armored division began moving north to Longwy and at dawn the 80th Infantry Division started for Luxembourg City.

In anticipation of the tremendous difficulties this mission would entail, Patton ordered his Third Army Chaplain to compose the now legendary Weather Prayer:

THE WEATHER PRAYER

Almighty and most merciful Father, We humbly beseech Thee, of Thy great goodness, to restrain these immoderate rains with which we have to contend. Grant us fair weather for Battle. Graciously hearken to us soldiers who call upon Thee that, armed with Thy power, we may advance from victory to victory, and crush the opression and wickedness of enemies, and establish Thy justice among men and nations.

Amen.

General Creighton W. Abrams who, as a Lieutenant Colonel Commanded the 37th Tank Battalion, 4th Armored Division. Along with men of the 53rd Armored Infantry Battalion. This unit broke the siege of Bastogne. (Author's collection courtesy General Abrams).

It was from close to this spot, at 15.00 on the 26 December 1944, that Lieutenant Colonel Creighton W. Abrams 37th Tank Battalion and Lieutenant Colonel George L. Jaques' 53rd Armored Infantry Battalion intended to attack in the direction of Sibret. As both commanders pondered their next move, they spotted C-47 aircraft dropping supplies to the encircled defenders of Bastogne. Colonel Abrams then made a momentous decision and proposed they break through to Bastogne via Clochimont and Assemis, Jaques agreed.

At 15.20, Abrams radioed Captain William Dwight the battalion Operations Officer to bring forward the 'C-Team' comprising tanks of Company C of the 37th and halftrack-borne infantrymen of Company C of the 53rd. Another message, this time through an artillery liaison officer, gave the plan to the supporting 94th Armored Field Artillery Battalion and asked that someone tell the 101st Airborne that the armour was coming in. The 94th was already registered to fire on Assenois, but there was little time in which to transmit data to the division artillery or arrange a fire plan, Combat Command Reserve, alone among the 4th Armored Combat Commands, had no wire in. Continuous wave radio could not be counted on. Frequency modulation was working fairly well but they would have to relay all messages. Despite these handicaps, in fifteen minutes three artillery battalions borrowed from Combat Command B, (the 22nd, 253rd and 776th) were tied in to Shell Assenois when the call came.

Start driving through Clochimont towards Assenois stopping a few hundred yards short of the village.

Colonel Abrams had entrusted Captain Dwight with the breakthrough telling him 'It's the push!' By 16.20 all was ready and the 'C-Team' moved out, Shermans in the lead, and halftracks behind. Abrams stayed glued to his radio. At 16.34, he checked with the 94th Field Artillery Battalion to ask if he could get the concentration on Assenois at a minute's notice. Exactly one minute later, Lieutenant Charles P. Boggess called from the lead tank. Abrams passed the word to the supporting artillery. 'Concentration Number nine, play it soft and sweet.' A 'Time on Target' massed fire could hardly be expected given the state of communications, but the supporting thirteen batteries sent ten volleys crashing onto the drab village.

Eight German anti-tank guns ringed the village and fired a few wild shots before suffering direct hits from incoming artillery rounds or losing their crews to machine-gun fire from the tanks.

Drive to the dip on the road at the edge of Assenois. At this point, Lieutenant Boggess called for the artillery to lift, then plunged ahead without waiting to see if the 94th gunners had received his message.
Enter the village.

So close did the attack follow the artillery, that not a hostile shot was fired as the tanks raced into the streets. The centre of the village was almost as dark as night, the sun shut out by smoke and dust. Two tanks made a wrong turn. An incoming American shell knocked out one of the infantry halftracks since the

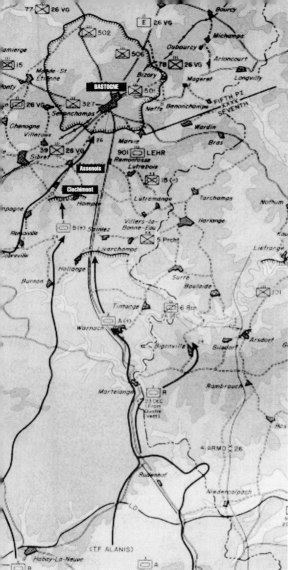

Sergeant John H. Parks of Mill Creek, Indiana as photographed on 10th December 1944 by a member of the 166th Photo Signal Company. Sergeant Parks served as a tank commander in the 2nd Platoon, Company B, of the 37th Tank Battalion. He died in action 23 December when the 37th engaged elements of the 5th Fallschirmjäger Division in Luxembourg during its drive to relieve the surrounded defenders of Bastogne. His remains were never recovered or positively identified and he was listed as 'Killed in Action/Body not recovered'. His name is inscribed on the Wall of the Missing at Luxembourg Military Cemetery.
(US Army Signal Corps).

initial fire plan had called for the supporting 155mm battery to plaster the centre of town and these shells were still coming in as the halftracks entered the streets. Far more vulnerable to the flying shell fragments than the tankers, the armored infantrymen leaped from their open vehicles and into the nearest doorway or behind a wall. In the smoke and confusion, the German garrison, a mixed group from the 5th Parachute and 26th Volksgrenadier Divisions, poured out of nearby cellars. The ensuing shooting, clubbing, stabbing melee was all that the armoured infantrymen could handle and the C-Team tanks rolled into the pages of U.S. Military History alone.

Drive straight on uphill to the Northeast until (at the time of writing) you reach woods on the left, pause here.

The relief column now consisted of three Shermans led by Lieutenant Boggess, followed by a halftrack that had blundered into the tank column and two more Shermans bringing up the rear. Boggess moved fast, his machine-gunner liberally spraying the woods on either side beside the road. A 300 metre gap developed between the lead three tanks and the last three vehicles giving the Germans time to lay a few Teller mines in front of the halftrack. The halftrack rolled over the first mine and exploded. Captain Dwight then rolled his two tanks onto the shoulder, the crews removed the mines, and the tanks raced on to catch up with Boggess.

Drive on a few hundred yards passing a minor road to the left (at the time of writing a recycling plant is on the right) and until you spot a group of decorative evergreens to your front right and a large open field on the left. Stop by the evergreens.

At exactly 16.50 on 26 December 1944, Lieutenant Boggess spotted some soldiers in friendly uniform preparing to assault the concrete pillbox now to your right. They were men of the 326th Airborne Engineer Battalion holding the defensive perimeter of Bastogne. His gunner fired three quick rounds at

The Belgian army pillbox on the outskirts of Bastogne, named in honour of Lieutenant Charles P. Boggess 37th Tank Battalion, 4th Armored Division. Evidence of battle damage can still be seen when his tank opened fire on this German held position.

the pillbox and its German occupants surrendered. The relieved engineers rushed forward to greet their liberators and very soon thereafter General McAuliffe came to meet Captain Dwight. Back near Clochimont, Colonel Abrams received a message from his commander, Colonel Wendell Blanchard asking what he thought of the possibility of breaking through to Bastogne.

By midnight on 26 December, 4th Armored had a secure hold on the road into the city.

Continue in the same direction turning left at the first sign for Bastogne. Upon reaching the main road, turn right in the direction of Arlon (N30) take the first exit at next traffic circle and at the sign for Lutremange, keep front left passing the tank turret and the 'Notre Dame de Bonne Conduite' chapel on your left. Continue downhill and over the next small ridge, stopping before the old farm on the left. Across the fields to your right rear, the building next to the metal barn was the Kessler farmhouse, to which German emissaries brought their now famous surrender demand.

Major General Joseph H. Harper who as a Colonel, commanded the 327th Glider Infantry Regiment of the 101st Airborne.
(US Army photo courtesy General Harper).

General McAuliffe.

On 22 December, four German emissaries, including two officers, came walking up the road from Remoifosse to Bastogne carrying a flag of truce. Soldiers of Company F, 327th Glider Infantry, took them to the farmhouse, then serving as command post of the company's Weapons Platoon. Eventually, a Major from Battalion took the terms to the division command post then in the Heintz Barracks in Bastogne. Colonel Joseph H. Harper, commanding the 327th Glider Infantry of the 101st Airborne, received a radio message ordering him to report to General McAuliffe. When Colonel Harper reached the Heintz Barracks, he reported to a basement room, at that time being used by the headquarters clerks for typing. General McAuliffe showed him a sheet of paper with the word 'N-U-T-S' typed in the centre. Colonel Harper thought the response amusing and asked the general if he could be the one to deliver the response

155

to the Germans.

In a letter to the author dated 3 August 1969, Major General Joseph H. Harper recalled his memories of events at the Kessler farmhouse:

'The Germans were waiting, still blindfolded, in the Company F command post, a Major and a Captain (actually a lieutenant). The Major, in a rather condescending manner asked "Is the reply in the negative or the affirmative? If in the affirmative, then we have the authority to negotiate further your surrender." The Germans' whole attitude and their assumption that we would consider surrendering made me angry. I replied "It is decidedly not in the affirmative" and added "If you continue this foolish attack, your losses will be tremendous."

'I then had them led to my jeep and took them back over a meadow road to the outpost where they had first entered our lines. Upon arrival, I told them to remove their blindfolds. I then said, "You will probably not understand what the word (Nuts) in the message means. It means the same as 'Go to Hell'" and stated further "'I want you to understand something else. If you continue to attack, we will kill every goddam German that tries to enter into this city." The Captain translated, they both turned red, saluted and said "This is war, we will kill many Americans." I returned their salute and said "on your way Bud", then, through a slip of the tongue added "Good luck to you". I of course, regretted this last remark.'

Return to Bastogne and park on the main square (Place McAuliffe). The square features a bust of General McAuliffe, a Sherman tank knocked out during the battle, and plaques honouring the 101st Airborne Division, 10th Armored Division and the 406th Fighter Group. Just off the square, on the right side of the Route Du Marche, stands the former Hotel Lebrun (at the time of writing a reclad non-descript building to the left of the current Hotel Giorgio), which served as the command post of 10th Armored Division's Combat Command B under Colonel William Roberts. To the south of the square on the Avenue de la Gare is the 101st Airborne Museum (www.airbornemuseumbastogne.com).

Exit the car park and drive east in the direction of the 'Mardasson', a star shaped monument dedicated on 4 July 1946 in honor of the United States and its role in the liberation of Belgium. Upon leaving the main road and turning left for the Mardasson, note the Belgian pillbox on the left, and the memorial named after Corporal Emile Cady, the first Belgian soldier killed in the defense of Bastogne in 1940. Continue around the bend then pause where the road splits in two, note the cone-shaped stone marker. This is the final stone of the 'Liberty Way', a series of such markers on the route between the Normandy Coast and Bastogne marking the advance of American troops inland after D-Day.

Contine up this road and park on the historical centre car park. (www.bastognehistoricalcenter.be/)

All around the town of Bastogne tank turrets symbolize and mark the defensive perimeter. (Author's collection).

The various tank turrets scattered around the city symbolise the tenacious defense of the encircled garrison by American troops during the battle.

Upon re-entering the city, at the first major intersection turn right in the direction of Houffalize, then take second exit at traffic circle down Route de la Roche in the direction of E25. The red brick buildings opposite the town cemetery, are the Heintz barracks (40 Route de la Roche), a Belgian army barracks, which served as the 101st Division command post during the siege.

Return to the N30 (main road towards Noville/Houffalize). In the village of Foy, turn right and Southeast in the direction of Bizory. Stop just before the road enters the trees of the Bois Jaques.

On the right side of the road (at the time of writing just inside the trees ahead of you, the traveller can still spot foxholes of the 2nd Battalion, 506th Parachute Infantry, immortalised in the book Band of Brothers by Stephen E. Ambrose.) Initially, the 506th attempted to attack the high ground to the North and overlooking Noville in support of Team Desobry, another of the Teams of Colonel Roberts' Combat Command B. However, they and the remnants of Team Desobry had to fall back to Foy under massive German pressure from the North. They then fell back to here to form the northern edge of the defensive perimeter around Bastogne. In his book Seven Roads to Hell *Donald Burgett graphically describes his experiences in Noville as a member of the 1st Battalion 506th and the subsequent withdrawal to Foy.*

Continue through the woods stopping at the far side just before reaching the old railroad line.

As a member of the 3rd Platoon, Company A of the 501st Parachute Infantry Regiment, Lieutenant Robert I. Kennedy served as assistant platoon leader. In a letter to the author, Bob Kennedy spoke of his experiences during the battle here in the Bois Jaques.

'On the evening of 19 December, the 2nd Battalion was unable to make contact with the 506th Regiment along the railroad track running from

In Noville, the house used as Major Desbory's command post still stands. (Author's collection).

Bastogne to Bourcy, which was the boundary between the 506th and 501st. The Germans evidently probed the area and found a large gap existed there. Company A of the 501st quickly pulled out (of its original position on the outskirts of Neffe) and went down the tracks to close that gap. As we approached the far edge of the woods located about 300 yards west of where the Bizory-Foy road crossed the railroad tracks, we hear the Germans coming straight at us. We deployed at the edge of the woods and waited until they were within yards of us. They wore white snow camouflage and we opened up with everything we had. When the fog lifted and daylight came, the open field in front of us was covered with German dead. We picked up several prisoners and had a few casualties of our own. The rest of the enemy withdrew to their own lines. No one told us that the Germans had surrounded us and captured the Division hospital. I made a trip to the chapel in the Bastogne seminary to visit the wounded from our company. Wounded and dying soldiers covered every square foot of floor space while only a few medics and sisters helping them, pretty much confirmed these rumours. Normally most of these men would have been evacuated to the rear. The piles of frozen bodies in the courtyard would also have been removed had the roads to the rear been open. On the return trip to the unit, I passed a huge circle of massed artillery facing outwards and firing in every direction of the circle. At night, you could see flashes of heavy gunfire in the distance to your left and right. You knew then, that you were surrounded. We didn't worry much about being surrounded because in airborne missions you are always surrounded. We did begin to worry about supplies since we weren't getting too much food or ammunition but we knew that eventually we would get an airdrop. On 23 December, the sky cleared, the sun came out, the first time we had seen blue sky. This alone raised the morale of the troops, and then in the middle of the morning came the planes. Hundreds of C-47's and fighters, it was one of the most spectacular sights I had ever seen. The sky was filled with coloured supply chutes and the fighters were buzzing the perimeter at treetop level. It must have been a terrible sight for the Germans.'

Return to the western edge of the woods making a brief pause overlooking the road into Foy.

First Lieutenant Harry E. Krig, a fighter pilot with the 513th Fighter Squadron returned to Foy on 21 September 2000. This was his 'trip of a lifetime' organised by his wife Pat and during which the author had the great privilege of tagging along. In an article entitled 'My Bastogne Story' Harry spoke of his first visit during which he got shot down in the vicinity of where you are now:

'In December, 1944 I was a pilot stationed in Mourmelon, France, a small town in close proximity to the Belgian, Luxembourg and German borders. Our headquarters was close to a 101st Airborne (paratrooper) base. Around December 16 news of the Battle of the Bulge reached us. Soon stories were told of Allied units being surrounded and Germans behind the lines in U.S. uniforms who were taking no prisoners as they advanced across Belgium. The 101st moved out to Bastogne to hold the town and its strategic roads.

First Lieutenant Harry E. Krig, Fighter Pilot with the 513th Fighter Squadron. German anti-aircraft gunners shot down Krig's plane on 30 December 1944 near Foy.
(Author's collection, courtesy Harry Krig).

'The weather was bad and extremely cold. I remember early morning briefings and then sitting around all day, grounded because of low ceilings, fog or snowstorms. I was flying a P-47 Thunderbolt and my flying log shows I flew missions on December 17, 23, 24, 25, 26, 27 and 30. This story is about the December 30 mission.

'We were scheduled to attack a tank column on the road to Bastogne. We were told to expect the tanks to be painted white as camouflage against the snow, and to be prepared for heavy anti-aircraft fire (flak). Our first flight went in, meeting heavy flak as expected. My flight, the second, was advised to avoid the flak by approaching from behind a wooded rise.

'As my turn came, I flew in so low that I remember my propeller ticking the treetops. To make my rocket firing run, I had to pull up to get a dive angle. I sighted on a white tank, fired, and then pulled up in a turn to avoid flying through the explosion. My exposed plane received hits in the engine and left wing and I knew I should bail out.

'We had been told US troops held a one-mile area surrounding Bastogne and we were instructed to bail out there, if possible. Bastogne was immediately to my left so I turned in that direction and pulled up. My engine quit and was on fire. Heavy black smoke was coming back over the cockpit. A large jagged hole was in my left wing and I could see ammunition belts hanging from the hole.

'The procedure for bailing out was to open the canopy at the lowest possible speed, trim the aircraft to level flight, and place your feet on the seat and dive toward the trailing edge of the right wing. I did all of this except for slowing the aeroplane. There wasn't time. As I stood up to make my dive the slipstream pinned me to the rear of the cockpit. I clawed my way out, slid down the side of the fuselage, and hit my left leg on the horizontal stabiliser of the tail section. I tumbled violently and had trouble getting hold of the 'D' ring to deploy my parachute. My altitude was no more than 500 to 600 feet and I remember the feeling of panic as I grasped the ring and pulled. Oh, how I pulled!

'I felt the shock of my parachute opening and just as I looked down, my feet touched the snow-covered ground. I realised my left leg was completely numb and useless as I extracted myself from the parachute harness. I rose to my hands and knees, looking around trying to figure out if I had landed in the safe area. I heard voices but could not distinguish the language. I ducked back down in the snow and covered myself with my white parachute.

'I eventually peeked out and saw a U.S. Army Medic standing at some distance, probably 250 yards away, waving at me from a grove of trees. Unable to walk, I started to crawl through the snow, trying to remain concealed under the parachute. It became too difficult to drag and I gave up on it. As I approached the tree, the Medic and another soldier ran out, grabbed me under the armpits and dragged me into the grove. They took me to a foxhole covered with logs and threw a blanket over me. Just then, we came under a mortar barrage. I remember the Medic saying, 'Oh, shit they saw us.' Suddenly, I had lots of company in the foxhole. After a time the shelling stopped but the noise continued as the Americans returned fire. My rescuers were from the 101st Airborne – friends from Mourmelon!

'I had bailed out in mid-morning and as the day wore on, pain replaced the numbness in my leg. I was wet from crawling through the snow and so cold I was shivering violently. The Medic returned and gave me a shot of morphine for the pain. He told me they would get me to a field hospital that evening. We talked some of the battle. He asked me if I would give him my .45 calibre pistol. Medics were not allowed to carry firearms, but, he said, in this battle no prisoners were being taken and Medics were unprotected. I did not say yes or no. He brought me a rifle in case of attack and pointed in the direction of the enemy. I noticed his finger pointing right down the furrow in the snow I made while crawling.

'Several times that afternoon we came under enemy mortar fire. Finally, darkness came and we travelled in a jeep into Bastogne. The hospital, a former church, had been hit and one side of it was covered with a tarp. My medic friend found a place for me among the patients lying in rows on stretchers. As he started to leave, I handed him my pistol.

'The hospital, treating both military and civilians, had a brightly-lit operating room at one end screened off with a tarp. There was continual activity there all night. My leg continued to swell and during the night I asked an attendant to slit my pant leg to relieve the pressure. Another shot of morphine enabled me to sleep.

'The next day I spent in a corner out of the way – a broken leg was, under the circumstances, a minor wound. I remember eating a cracker and cheese from a can as lunch. I learned I was to be evacuated by ambulance that night.'

Upon evacuation, Lieutenant Krig learned that he was to be flown to England, so rather than leave his buddies at the 513th, he bribed the pilot of a small observation plane to fly him back to the squadron at Mourmelon.

Return to Foy, crossing the main road (N-30) and following the sign for the German War Cemetery at Recogne. It can be found a few hundred yards past the local civilian cemetery on the left side of the road to Recogne.

On 4 February 1945 American Graves Registration began laying out a large

Recogne German war cemetery.
(Author's collection).

collecting cemetery on this site. They buried some 2,700 Americans and 3,000 Germans in two separate plots. In1946/47 they either repatriated the American dead or moved them to Henri-Chapelle and the Belgian authorities turned this into a permanent German cemetery holding 6,804 Germans soldiers. In 1984, the Belgian and German governments reached an agreement placing the care of German war graves in German hands.

Return to N-30 turning left in the direction of Noville. Upon reaching the village stop by the bus stop and the fourth house on the left.

Team Desobry of Colonel William Roberts' Combat Command B, 10th Armored Division, under Major William Desobry, supported by a tank destroyer platoon of the 705th Tank Destroyer Battalion rushed to defend Noville. Reinforced by the 1st and 3rd Battalions of the 506th Parachute Infantry, they tenaciously held the village until ordered to withdraw to Foy on 20 December. In his first-hand account of the bitter fighting here, entitled *Seven Roads to Hell* Donald R. Burgett graphically described their defence of the village in the face of attacks by German tanks and infantry. He placed particular emphasis upon the effects of artillery.

'Artillery is the most horrible, death-dealing, feared instrument of modern war. More men have been wounded, maimed, or killed by artillery than by any other means since the advent of gunpowder. When you are being pummelled by artillery there is nothing you can do to strike back. All you can do is lie there and listen to the shrieking, screaming shells coming in and the loud explosions they make when they hit. Your throat dries up and your lungs burn as you breathe in the burnt powder, dust and acrid smoke caused by the blasts. You instinctively hug the ground as hot, ragged fragments and splinters of shrapnel tear into trees, stone walls and human bodies. There is nothing you can do to fight back, while all around you flesh is being torn to red, bloody scraps.

Some men pray, some yell at the enemy and some just lie there quietly, in their holes, being bounced and jarred around while they await their fate. At times under heavy, prolonged shelling I found myself yelling, screaming at the enemy to stop. I would scream for the shelling to stop, for the enemy to come out face-to- face with us and get it over with. On the other hand, when it was our shells rumbling overhead toward the enemy, I would yell, "Give it to them! Don't stop until you've killed every goddamned one of them".*

* *By kind permission of Donald R. Burgett and Presidio Press*

This building, outside which you have stopped served as the joint command post of Team Desobry and Lieutenant Colonel James L. LaPrade's 506th Parachute Infantry.

During night fighting here in the centre of Noville a shell burst inside the building killing Colonel LaPrade and wounding Major Desobry. German troops captured the ambulance evacuating the unfortunate Major to Bastogne. He regained consciousness only to discover his newfound status as a Prisoner of War.

Drive north to Houffalize and upon descending into town note the Panther tank of Colonel Gerhard Tebbe's 16th Panzer Regiment of the 116th Panzer Division, a unit later decimated in the Verdenne Pocket.

Continue downhill into the centre of town turning left in the direction of Laroche and pause by the church, next to which is a monument commemorating civilian victims of the town's bombing by the RAF.

Continue out of town in the direction of Laroche and approximately 7 kilometres out of town turn left on the first road bridge crossing the Ourthe River, signposted Engreux. Upon crossing the bridge, park by the rock face on the far bank. Note the plaques commemorating the junction of First and Third Armies close to here on 16 January 1945, effectively cutting off the Bulge in the American lines.

Return to the main road turning left in the direction of Laroche. Park in the town centre.

Here in Laroche, there is evidence of the British role in the battle since elements of the British 51st Highland Division entered the town on 11 January 1945 to link up with their American counterparts, from Company C, 635th Tank Destroyer Battalion attached to the 4th Cavalry Group. A US Army Signal

The Achilles at Laroche. (Courtesy OPT).

Corps photographer immortalised this moment when he took a photograph of the link up. In recent times, Mr. Henri Rogister of CRIBA and Mr. Guy Blockmans of the Belgian Office for the Promotion of Tourism have helped identify the individual soldiers in the photograph. They have also managed to get eyewitness accounts from men in both units:

Carl Condon of Bismarck, Maryland served with Company C of the 635th and spoke of this picture:

'We were the 635th Tank Destroyer Battalion attached to the 4th Cavalry at that time. The 84th Infantry division was also in Laroche. I remember the town very well but was not aware that the picture existed. All of these Americans were our men from Company C. First Sergeant Ray Spangler of Topeka, Kansas, Corporal Harlen Mathis of Minneapolis, Minnesota and Staff Sergeant Max Beal of Coffeyville, Kansas.'

On the British side, Harris McAllister remembers the linkup:

'The picture of Corporal John Donald Sergeant F.D. 'Ricky' Richards and myself was taken after the capture of Laroche. We crossed over the wrecked/blown up bridge over the Ourthe River and met the American soldiers in an armoured car. We sat down and had coffee provided by them, round a fire of petrol and sand in a bucket in front of a garage. It was then that the photographer arrived with a reporter in a jeep and took a

Soldiers of US First and Third Armies join forces at Rensiwez, 16 January 1945.

The posed link-up at Laroche. (Courtesy OPT).

THIS MEMORIAL COMMEMORATES THE MEETING OF THE 1st BATTALION, BLACK WATCH
REGIMENT, 51st HIGHLAND DIVISION, AND THE 84th US INFANTRY DIVISION "RAILSPLITTER
WHO LIBERATED LA ROCHE-en-ARDENNE ON THE 11th JANUARY 1945

CETTE PLAQUE COMMEMORE LA RENCONTRE DE LA 51st SCOTTISH HIGHLANDS DIVISIO
"BLACK WATCH" ET DE LA 84th US INFANTRY DIVISION "RAILSPLITTERS"
QUI LIBERERENT LA ROCHE-en-ARDENNE LE 11 JANVIER 1945

The Link-up plaque. (Courtesy of OPT).

photograph of us. He realised we had different uniforms, and this was the Allied linkup. He then asked us to meet at the corner of Rue de la Gare and Route de Cielle and shake hands, which we did and he took a second, more appropriate photograph.'

Today, at the same spot, a marble plaque commemorates the incident while above town an 'Achilles' tank destroyer and other monuments recognise the role of British troops in the vicinity.

In a letter to the author dated 7 January 1979 the former XXX Corps Commander, Lieutenant General Sir Brian G. Horrocks spoke of the personality clashes between his boss Field Marshal Montgomery and his American counterparts:

'When the battle was over, he (Montgomery) stood up on the stage and told the audience how he had won the battle. This did not make for happy co-operation between the British and the Americans because **the Battle of the Ardennes was won by the extreme gallantry of young American soldiers.'**

In town there is also an interesting Bulge museum run by Mr. G. Bouillon the address for which is:

Musée Bataille Des Ardennes
Rue Chaumont 5
6980 Laroche en Ardenne
Telephone: International +32 (0)84 411.725
http:www.batarden.be
Suggested Reading:
MacDonald: Chapters 6,12,13,24 and 25.
Cole: Chapters 8, 13, 14,19 and 21.
Burgette: 'Seven Roads to Hell'.

General Der Panzertruppen,
Heinrich von Lüttwitz
Commanding General 47th
Panzerkorps whose Corps
surrounded Bastogne and
demanded the defenders'
surrender.
(Author's collection, courtesy General von Lüttwitz).

CHAPTER 5

'PARKER'S CROSSROADS' TO THE MEUSE RIVER

STARTING POINT: THE JUNCTION OF N30 WITH N89 30 KILOMETRES
NORTH OF BASTOGNE AND JUST OFF N25. LOOK OUT FOR THE CRIBA
PLAQUE AND 105MM HOWITZER ON THE NORTHWEST CORNER OF
THE CROSSROADS IN MEMORY OF THE DEFENDERS OF 'PARKER'S
CROSSROADS'.

Baraque de Fraiture was and still is a handful of buildings at the
crossroads south of the Belgian hamlet of Fraiture. The crossroads stands
on one of the highest summits of the Ardennes, a small shelf or tableland
at an elevation of 652 metres (2,139 feet). The roads, which intersect, are
important. N30 (then N15) the north-south road, was then the through paved
highway linking Liège and Bastogne. N28, (now N89) the east-west road, was
then classed as a secondary road but was nevertheless the most direct route for
movement along the northern side of the Ourthe River, connecting for
example, St. Vith with La Roche. In 1944, the crossroads and its few buildings
were on cleared ground, but heavy woods formed a crescent to the north and
west, and a fringe of timber pointed at the junction from the Southeast. In the
main, the area to the south and east was completely barren. Here the ground
descended, forming a glacis for the firing parapet around the crossroads.

Parker's Crossroads where a 105mm howitzer faces southeast.

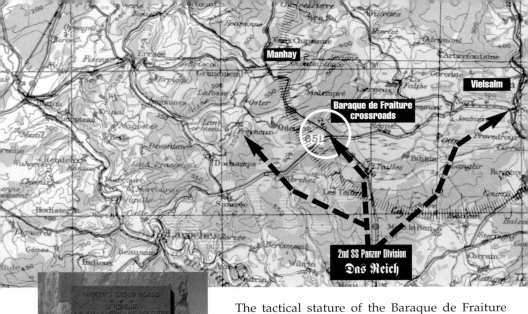

The tactical stature of the Baraque de Fraiture intersection was only partly derived from the configuration of the roads and terrain. The manner in which Major General Mathew B. Ridgway's XVIII Airborne Corps had deployed its units in the initial attempt to draw a cordon along the northwest flank of the German advance was equally important.

The mission assigned three task forces of the US 3rd Armored Division had been to close up to the Bastogne-Liège highway (with the crossroads as an objective), but it had not been carried out. East of the same highway the 82nd Airborne Division had deployed, but with its weight and axis of advance away from the crossroads. Circumstance, notably the direction of the German attacks from 20 December onwards, left Baraque de Fraiture, and with it the inner flanks of the two divisions, to be defended on a strictly catch-as-catch-can basis.

The CRIBA plaque upon which the Belgians commemorate their American liberators.
(Author's collection).

On the afternoon of 19 December, Major Arthur C. Parker III, successfully led three 105mm howitzers of the ill-starred 589th Field Artillery Battalion out of the melée on the Schnee Eifel east of St. Vith and here to Baraque de Fraiture. His mission was to establish one of the roadblocks that remnants of the 106th Infantry Division were preparing behind St. Vith.

The next day, four half-tracks mounting .50 calibre machine guns arrived from the 203rd Anti-aircraft Artillery Battalion, now moving in with the 7th Armored Division to establish the defensive lines around St. Vith. That night,

for the first time, the crossroads' defenders heard the sound of vehicles moving off to the southeast. (They probably belonged to *Oberst* Rudolf Langhaeuser's 560th Volksgrenadier Division, which that afternoon captured Samrée off to the southwest).

Before dawn, an eighty-man enemy patrol came up the road from Houffalize and the American Anti-aircraft gunners cut them apart whereupon they identified the dead and prisoners as belonging to the 560th. Among them was an officer of the 2nd SS *Das Reich* Panzer Division, scouting out the route of advance for his incoming division. In the afternoon, Troop D of the 87th Cavalry Squadron, earlier dispatched by the 7th Armored Division to aid Task Force Orr of 3rd Armored Division in a projected counterattack at Samrée, came in to join the crossroads garrison. The Troop leader had gone into Dochamps to meet Lieutenant Colonel William T. Orr of Task Force Orr, but finding Germans in town, disposed his men and vehicles under orders from General Hasbrouck of 7th Armored, that the crossroads must be held.

Fog settling over the tableland in late afternoon, gave the enemy a chance to probe the crossroads' defenses, but these jabs were no more than warning of things to come. Meanwhile, eleven tanks and a reconnaissance platoon from Task Force Kane of 3rd Armored Division arrived on the scene. The Americans spent the night of 21 December ringed around the crossroads; tanks alternating with armored cars in a stockade beyond which lay the rifle line. There was no sign of the enemy despite reports from all sorts of sources that German armour was gathering at Houffalize. Messengers coming in from the headquarters of the 3rd Armored and 82nd Airborne Divisions, all brought the same message: 'Hold as long as you can!'

Major General James M. Gavin, commanding the 82nd Airborne, was especially concerned by the threat to his division's flank developing at the crossroads and

Oberst *Rudolf Langhaeuser Commander 560th Volksgrenadier Division.*
(Author's collection courtesy General Langhaeuser).

went to talk the matter over with the 3rd Armored commander, Major General Maurice Rose at Rose's command post in Manhay. General Rose assured Gavin that his troops would continue to cover the western wing of the 82nd Airborne. Gavin nevertheless acted at once to send his 2nd Battalion, 325th Glider Infantry Regiment, from his division reserve to defend Fraiture, the village on a ridge +/- 1,300 metres northeast of the crossroads position. In addition, having made a personal reconnaissance of the area, Gavin ordered the regimental commander, Colonel Charles Billingslea, to dispatch a company of his glider infantry to reinforce the crossroads' defenders. The 2nd Battalion reached Fraiture before dawn on 22 December and Captain Junior R. Woodruff led Company F into the circle around the crossroads just before noon. This slight reinforcement was negated when Task Force Kane withdrew its tanks to stiffen the attack going on in front of Dochamps.

Both sides spent the day of 22 December in waiting. The 2nd SS *Das Reich* Panzer Division had more than its fair share of fuel supply problems and was moving in fits and starts. Mortar fire laid on by the German reconnaissance screen left in the area as the 560th Volksgrenadier Division advanced northwest, from time to time interrupted movement in and out of the crossroads position. That was all. During the day the 3rd Armored Division received some reinforcements; these were parcelled out across the front with a platoon from the 643rd Tank Destroyer Battalion going to the crossroads. Enroute south from Manhay on the night of the 22nd, the tank destroyer detachment lost its way and halted some distance north of the crossroads. German infantry surprised and captured the platoon in the early morning. Already *Das Reich* was moving to cut off and erase the crossroads garrison. Attack was near at hand, a fact made clear when the defenders captured an officer patrol from 2nd SS *Das Reich* at dawn near the American foxholes.

At daylight, shelling increased at the crossroads as German mortar and gun crews went into position; yet the long awaited assault failed to materialise due to lack of fuel. The 2nd SS *Das Reich* had only enough gasoline to move its reconnaissance battalion on 21 December for commitment near Vielsalm.

General der Waffen-SS Willi Bittrich, Commander 2nd SS Panzerkorps in the Ardennes.
(Courtesy General Bittrich).

Obersturmbannführer *Otto Weidinger, 4th Regiment* Der Führer *of 2nd SS Panzer Division* Das Reich *at Baraque de Fraiture.*
(Courtesy Otto Weidinger).

Late that evening, an exploding mortar round seriously wounded Major Parker. He initially refused evacuation but upon losing consciousness was sent to the rear. Major Elliott C. Goldstein, also of the 589th Field Artillery Battalion, then assumed command of the crossroad's defenders. Throughout daylight on 22 December, 2nd SS waited in its forward assembly areas till early evening when enough fuel arrived to set SS-*Obersturmbannführer* Otto Weidinger's 4th SS *Der Führer* Panzergrenadier Regiment, some tanks and an artillery battalion moving. In the course of the night the panzergrenadiers relieved the small reconnaissance detachments of the 560th, which had been watching at the crossroads and filed through the woods to set up a cordon west and north of the Baraque de Fraiture. SS-*Obersturmbannführer* Weidinger had placed a battalion to the right of the main north-south highway, and another battalion deployed around and to the rear of the crossroads.

In the pre-dawn darkness of 23 December the first move came, as the 2nd Battalion of the 4th SS *Der Führer* Panzergrenadier Regiment made a surprise

A German soldier on Reconnaissance armed with an MP44 assault rifle.
(Courtesy Roland Gaul)

attack on Fraiture only to be driven back after a bitter fight by the defending glider infantrymen.

Having lost the element of surprise, the Germans settled down to hem in and soften up the crossroads defense. They took radios from captured American vehicles and used them to jam the wave band on which the American forward observers were calling for fire. Whenever word flashed over the air that shells were on their way, enemy mortar crews dumped shells on American observation posts – easily discernible in the limited perimeter – making sensing virtually impossible. Late in the morning, Lieutenant Colonel Walter B. Richardson, who had a small force backing up Kane and Orr near Dochamps, sent more infantry and a platoon of tanks toward the crossroads. By this time, the German panzergrenadiers occupied the woods to the north in sufficient strength to halt the foot soldiers. The American tanks impervious to small arms fire reached the perimeter at about 13.00, whereupon the rifle line pushed out east and south to give the tankers a chance to manoeuvre.

At the crossroads time was running out. Shortly after 16.00, the German artillery really got to work, for twenty minutes pummelling the area around the crossroads. Then, preceded by two panzer companies (perhaps the final assault had awaited their appearance), the entire rifle strength of the 4th SS *Der Führer* closed upon the Americans. Outlined against the newly fallen snow, the line of defense was clearly visible to the panzers and the Shermans had no manoeuvre room in which to back up the line. The fight was brief, moving to a foregone conclusion. At 17.00 the Company F commander asked Billingslea for permission to withdraw; but Gavin's order was still 'Hold at all costs.' Within the next hour the Germans completed the reduction of the crossroads defense, sweeping up prisoners, armoured cars, half-tracks and the three howitzers. Three American tanks managed to escape under the veil of half-light. Earlier they had succeeded in spotting some panzers that were firing flares, and knocked them out. A number of men escaped north through the woods; some got a break when a herd of cattle stampeded near the crossroads, providing a momentary screen. Company F of the 325th Glider Infantry suffered the most but stood its ground until Billingslea gave permission to pull out. Ultimately, forty-four of the original one hundred and sixteen who had gone to the crossroads returned to their own lines. Drastically outnumbered and unable to compensate for weakness by manoeuvre, the valiant defenders of what today is known as 'Parker's Crossroads' had succumbed like so many other small forces at other crossroads in the Ardennes.

The dent made here at the boundary between the 3rd Armored and the 82nd Airborne Divisions could all too quickly turn into a ragged tear, parting the two and unravelling their inner flanks. The next intersection on the road to Liege, at Manhay was only four miles away to the north. From Manhay, the lateral road between Trois Ponts and Hotton would place the Germans on the deep flank and rear of both divisions. General Rose and General Gavin reacted to this threat at once; so did General Ridgway. Order followed order, but there remained a paucity of means to implement them. The deficit in reserves was somewhat remedied by the troops of the 106th Division and 7th Armored who, all day long, had been pouring through the lines of the 82nd Airborne after the hard-fought battle of St. Vith. General Hoge of CCB 9th Armored had been told at noon to send his 14th Tank Battalion to bolster the right flank of the 82nd. One tank company went to the Manhay crossroads; the rest moved to Malempré, two miles to the Southeast and off the Liege highway. Coincident with the German attack at Baraque de Fraiture, General Hoge received a torrent of reports and orders. By this time Hoge wasn't too sure as to either his attachment or mission. He finally gathered that the Baraque de Fraiture crossroads had been lost and CCB was to join the defense already forming to the north at Manhay.

Drive north of Baraque de Fraiture on N30 stopping at the first sign to the right for 'Malempré with open fields to both left and right.

On their way to Manhay, the attacking Germans initially bypassed Task Force Brewster of 3rd Armored Division here at Belle Haie. With the enemy now behind him Major Olin F. Brewster, the task force commander radioed for permission to pull out to the east in the direction of Malempré in the hope of finding it still to be in American hands. The advancing Germans knocked out two of Brewster's tanks whereupon he ordered his vehicles abandoned and released his men to find the American lines on their own – most of his command made it.

Continue north on N30 stopping in Manhay just before the road leading left (N807) toward Grandmenil (signposted at crossroads as 806 to Marche. N807 splits from N806 a few hundred yards down this road). The street running southwest of the crossroads leads to the 'Maison Communale' (Town Hall), in front of which stands a memorial to the 325th Glider Infantry Regiment of the 82nd Airborne Division.

The XVIII Airborne Corps mission as of 19 December 1944, was to block any further German advance along an irregular line extending from the Amblève River through Manhay and Houffalize to La Roche on the Ourthe River, placing the corps' right boundary twenty miles northwest of Bastogne. Three threatened areas were known to be in the newly assigned zone of operations. The Amblève River sector, where the 30th Infantry Division's 119th Infantry was deployed and the Salm River sector, especially at Trois Ponts where unknown to the 82nd Airborne, Company C of the 51st Engineer Combat Battalion still barred the crossings.

The third of these was the general area north of the Ourthe River where a vague and ill-defined German movement had been reported. The German capture of Houffalize had served to cut the main Bastogne-Liége highway N15 (Today N30) and their subsequent capture of 'Parker's Crossroads' gave them direct access north to Manhay – a distance of 6.4 kilometres. Manhay not only sat astride the main road to Liége but also the principal east-west road from Trois Ponts to Hotton. Major General James M. Gavin's 82nd Airborne Division therefore sent a company of its 325th Glider Infantry here to Manhay on the evening of 19 December 1944. On 20 December, Task Force Kane of 3rd Armored Division took up positions at Malempré, about 3,000 metres Southeast of Manhay. The village of Manhay represented a tactically untenable position. Hills to the east and west dominated the village, and to the Southeast extensive woods promised cover from which the enemy could bring fire on the crossroads. By reason of the ground, therefore, Malempré, on a hill to the south beyond the woods was the chosen objective. Task Force Kane reached Manhay then pushed advance elements as far as Malempré without meeting the enemy.

By dawn on 24 December *Gruppenführer* Heinz Lammerding's 2nd SS *Das Reich* stood poised to attack north of the Baraque de Fraiture toward Manhay. Lammerding planned to attack with his armoured infantry regiments to either side of the N15. The fuel problems he was having meant that although both groups possessed small panzer

SS-Gruppenführer
Heinz Lammerding.

174

Tanks of 2nd Armored Division and infantrymen of the 75th Infantry Division intermingle at an Ardennes road junction. (US Army Signal Corps).

detachments, the bulk of his tanks remained bivouacked in wood lots to the rear. The terrain ahead was only negotiable by small groups of armour and they had to husband their fuel for a short, direct thrust.

The initial attacks made by the 1130th Regiment of the 560th Volksgrenadier Division against Lamormenil and Freyneux proved disastrous with the attackers suffering severe losses.

During the night of 24 December, the Americans began rationalizing their over-extended lines by pulling the 82nd Airborne Division back to a much shorter front extending diagonally from Trois Ponts southwest to Vaux Chavanne, just short of Manhay. CCA of the 7th Armored Division was to withdraw to the low hills just north of the village and Grandmenil while retaining a combat outpost in Manhay itself. (Colonel Rosebaum, its commander protested to the effect that the high ground now occupied by his command south and Southeast of Manhay was tactically superior but without result).

The series of American manoeuvres begun on Christmas Eve proved both difficult and tricky to co-ordinate, particularly in the Manhay sector. Communications were not yet thoroughly established and tactical cohesion had not yet been secured. Communications between the 3rd and 7th Armored Divisions failed miserably. There had been so many revisions of plans, orders and counter-orders during 24 December, that Colonel Rosebaum didn't receive word of his new retrograde mission until 18:00. The withdrawal of CCA, 7th Armored and the elements of CCB, 9th Armored, south and southeast of Manhay was scheduled to begin at 22:30 – and most of these troops along with parts of 3rd Armored would have to pass through Manhay.

On the night of 24 December, the main body of *Das Reich* began moving

The village of Manhay showing signs of the heavy fighting which took place here on Christmas Day 1944.

toward Manhay. The seizure of Odeigne the previous night had opened a narrow sally port facing Grandmenil and Manhay, but there was no road capable of handling a large armoured column between Odeigne and the 2nd SS Panzer assembly areas south of the Baraque de Fraiture. On 24 December the commander of the 3rd SS *Deutschland* Panzergrenadier Regiment secured Lammerding's permission to postpone a further advance until German engineers could build a road through the woods to Odeigne. By nightfall on Christmas Eve engineers completed the road and Allied fighter-bombers had returned to their bases.

The 3rd SS *Deutschland* Panzergrenadier Regiment now gathered in attack formation in the woods around Odeigne, while tanks of the 2nd Panzer Regiment formed in column along the new road. To the east the 4th SS *Der Führer* Panzergrenadier Regiment sent a rifle battalion through the woods toward Malempré. By 21.00, the hour set for the German attack, the column at Odeigne was ready. Christmas Eve had brought a beautifully clear moonlit night; the glistening snow was hard-packed and tank going good.

About the time the German column started forward, the subordinate commanders of CCA, 7th Armored Division received word by radio to report here to be given new orders – the orders that is, for the general withdrawal north.

The commander of the 7th Armored position north of Odeigne (held by a company of the 40th Tank Battalion and a company of the 48th Armored Infantry Battalion) had just started for Manhay when he saw a tank column coming up the road toward his position. A call to battalion headquarters failed to identify these tanks, but since the lead tank showed the typical blue exhaust fumes of a Sherman, it was decided that this must be a detachment from the 3rd Armored Division. Suddenly, a German Panzerschreck rocket blasted from the woods where the Americans were deployed; German infantry had crept in close to the American tanks and their covering infantry. Four of the Shermans fell victim to enemy panzerschrecks in short order and two more were crippled, but the crippled tanks and one still intact managed to wheel about and head for Manhay. The armored infantry did likewise.

A thousand metres or so further north stood another 7th Armored roadblock, defended by an under strength rifle company and ten medium tanks which had been dug in to give hull protection. Again the enemy-crewed Sherman leading the German column deceived the Americans. When almost upon the immobile American armour the Germans cut loose with flares. Blinded and unable to move, the ten Shermans were so many sitting ducks. German tank fire hit most of them as their crews hastily evacuated their vehicles. The American infantry in turn fell prey to the attacking panzergrenadiers moving through the woods bordering the road and fell back in small groups toward Manhay.

It was now a little after 22.30, the hour set for the 7th Armored move to the new position north of Manhay. The covering elements of 3rd Armored had already withdrawn without notifying CCA of the 7th. The light tank detachment from Malempré had left the village (the grenadier battalion from *Der Führer* moving in on the tankers' heels) and the support echelon of CCB 9th Armored had already passed through Manhay. The headquarters column of CCA 7th Armored was just on its way out of the village when the American tanks that had escaped from the first roadblock position burst into the village. Thus far the headquarters in Manhay knew nothing of the German advance – although a quarter of an hour earlier the enemy gunners had shelled the village. A platoon commander attempted to get two of his medium tanks into positions at the crossroads itself, but the situation quickly degenerated into a *sauve qui peut* when the leading panzers stuck their snouts into Manhay. Confusion reigned supreme as panzer ace SS-*Oberscharführer* Ernst Barkmann's Panther number 401 raced at top speed into the village, he and his crew thinking they'd been left behind by the rest of their

SS-Oberscharführer
Ernst Barkmann.

platoon. They arrived in Manhay to find the place full of American vehicles and the road to the west occupied by three Shermans. Barkmann decided to head north of Manhay passing several enemy tanks as his Panther roared up the main street. Crushing an American jeep and colliding with a parked Sherman, Panther 401 knocked out a pursuing Sherman then sought shelter in the woods north of the village.

Meanwhile the fighting raged in Manhay and in a last exchange of fire, the Americans accounted for two of the panzers but lost five of their own tanks at the rear of the CCA column. Thus Manhay passed into German hands. As the sounds of the battle died down, Barkmann and his crew drove slowly back down the road into Manhay passing numerous burning vehicles to rejoin their comrades.

Turn west (left on the N806) in the direction of Grandmenil and, driving up the main road (N807), keep an eye out for a bus stop on the right beside which stands a Panther tank of the 2nd SS. Diagonally across the main road from the tank is a monument to the 289th Infantry Regiment of the 75th Infantry Division, the 3rd Armored Division and a plaque to the 951st Field Artillery Battalion, VII Corps, 1st Army.

On the main street in Beffe, two curious GI's from the 75th Infantry Division inspect an abandoned Waffen-SS Kubelwagen. (US Army Signal Corps).

American GI examines a captured German 7.5 cm anti-tank gun.

In the early morning hours of Christmas Day at about 03.00, a column of eight tanks from the 2nd SS preceded by an enemy crewed Sherman passed west through Grandmenil in the direction of Erezée.

> *Continue west of Grandmenil (following signs to Erezee N807) and pause on a series of uphill bends about 3.3 kilometres west of the village. This spot is locally known as Troup du Loup.*

By this stage in the battle, the Americans were moving in more reinforcements in the shape of the 75th Infantry Division. Upon reaching Troup du Loup, troops of the 3rd Battalion, 289th Infantry attempted to set up positions blocking the road to Erezée and came under attack by this German column. The attacking armour wrought havoc among the infantrymen to either side of the road as the lead Panther ran over and destroyed several American vehicles and trailers. Several GIs fired bazooka rockets at the enemy tanks but none detonated since in their haste, the inexperienced soldiers had forgotten to remove the safety pins permitting them to arm the projectiles. Corporal Richard F. Wiegand seized the initiative, getting behind the lead tank and succeeding in destroying its engine before being killed by an enemy shell. The second Panther in line then tried to push the wrecked vehicle off the road but proved unable to do so. The wrecked tank remained in position effectively blocking the road whereupon the others pulled back in the direction of Grandmenil.

Following the engagement at Trop du Loup. It took some time for the US 3rd Battalion, 289th Infantry to reorganise, but by 08.00 the battalion set off on its assigned task of clearing the woods southwest of Grandmenil. At the same time the rest of the regiment, on the right, moved into an attack to push the outposts of the 560th Volksgrenadier Division back from the Aisne River. Brigadier General Doyle A. Hickey, the CCA, 3rd Armored commander, however, needed more help than a green infantry regiment could give if the 3rd Armored was to halt 2nd SS *Das Reich* and restore the position at Grandmenil. General Rose carried his plea for assistance up the echelons of command, and finally CCB of 3rd Armored was released from attachment to the 30th Infantry Division in the La Gleize sector to give the needed armoured punch.

Early that afternoon, Task Force McGeorge (a company each of armoured infantry and Sherman tanks) arrived west of Grandmenil. The task force was moving into the attack when disaster struck. Eleven P-38s of the 430th Fighter Squadron, which were being vectored onto their target by 7th Armored Division, mistook McGeorge's troops for Germans and made a bombing run over the wooded assembly area killing three officers and thirty-six men in the process. The communications failure between the 3rd and 7th Armored Divisions had cost dear. Task Force McGeorge mounted a fresh attack at 20.00; McGeorge's armoured infantry and a company from the 289th preceding the American tanks in the dark. Within an hour, five tanks and a small detachment of infantry in halftracks were in Grandmenil, but the enemy promptly counterattacked and restored his hold on the village.

The 2nd SS *Das Reich* Panzer Division had nevertheless failed on 25 December to enlarge the turning radius it so badly needed around the Grandmenil pivot. The German records show clearly what had stopped the advance. Every time that the 3rd SS *Deutschland* Panzergrenadier Regiment formed an assault detachment to break out of the woods south and west of Grandmenil, American artillery observers located on the high ground to the north, brought salvo after salvo crashing down. All movement along the roads seemed to be the signal for the much-feared Allied fighter-bombers to swoop down for the kill. To make matters worse, the 9th SS *Hohenstaufen* Panzer Division had failed to close up on the 2nd SS *Das Reich* Panzer's right. *Gruppenführer* Lammerding dared not swing his entire division into the drive westward and thus leave an open flank facing the American armour known to be in the woods north of Manhay.

On the morning of 26 December the 4th SS *Der Führer* Panzergrenadier Regiment attacked northward using Manhay and the forest to the east as a line of departure. The 3rd SS *Deutschland* Panzergrenadier Regiment would have to make the main effort, forcing its way out of Grandmenil to the west in the direction of Erezée.

The German attempt to shake loose and break into the clear proved abortive. On the right, the 4th SS *Der Führer* Panzergrenadier Regiment sent a battalion from the woods east of Manhay into an early morning attack that collided with the 325th Glider Infantry Regiment of the 82nd Airborne Division and the Americans drove them off. By daylight, the enemy assault force was in full retreat, back to the woods. Plans for a second attack north of Manhay came to nothing since by then, the Americans held the initiative.

At the same time, the Germans tried to move west of Grandmenil, they also tried attacking to the northwest in the direction of Mormont, hoping to flank Erezée. The westward move began at false dawn, by chance coinciding with Task Force McGeorge renewal of its attack to enter Grandmenil. The road limited the action to a head-on tank duel. McGeorge's Shermans proved no match for the Panthers which out-gunned them. When the shooting died down, the American detachment had only two medium tanks left in operational condition.

Sometime after this skirmish, one of the American tanks, that had reached Grandmenil during an attack the previous evening, suddenly came alive and roared out to join the task force. Captain John W. Jordan of the 1st Battalion, 33rd Armored Regiment, had led five tanks into the village, but during the earlier fight four had been hit or abandoned by their crews. Jordan and his crew sat through the night in the midst of the dead tanks, unmolested by the enemy. When Captain Jordan reported to his headquarters, he told of seeing a column of at least twelve Panthers, rumbling out of Grandmenil in a northerly direction. The 3rd Armored put up a liaison plane to locate the enemy armour but to no avail. Company L of the 289th Infantry knocked out the lead Panther in this group as the column passed through a narrow gorge on the road to

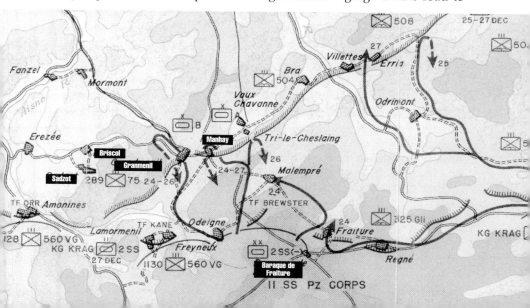

Mormont and suffered numerous casualties as bazooka teams and tanks fought it out. German reports stated that this road was blocked by fallen timber and that intense American artillery fire blocked all movement north of Grandmenil. Whatever the reason, this group of tanks made no further effort to force the Mormont road.

Task Force McGeorge received sixteen additional Shermans at noon and a couple of hours later on the heels of three-battalion artillery shoot, burst through to retake Grandmenil. The pounding meted out by the 3rd Armored gunners apparently drove most of the panzergrenadiers in flight from the village and by dark, the 3rd Battalion, 289th Infantry had occupied half the village and held the road to Manhay.

Continue west on N807 and as you enter Briscol pause by the small church on the left in order to see the Belgian Touring Club stone marker indicating this high point in the German offensive. Continue west and turn left following the sign for Sadzot. Drive up into Sadzot swinging right at the top of the village. Here stands a monument to the 3rd Armored Division; 75th Infantry Division; 509th Parachute Infantry Battalion; the 289th Infantry Regiment and Company B of the 87th Chemical Mortar Battalion.

As 1944 came to a close, the Sixth Panzer Army made one last effort to breach the American defenses between the Salm and Ourthe Rivers. This small village was the epicentre of that stage in the battle. It was an action fought at squad and platoon level and later nicknamed 'The Sad Sack Affair' by the Americans who fought there.

Having failed in its attempts to break through at Manhay and Grandmenil, the 2nd SS *Das Reich* Panzer Division began to parcel out its troops. Some were left to cover the deployment of the 9th SS *Hohenstaufen* Panzer Division as it extended its position in front of the 82nd Airborne Division to take over the one time 2nd SS *Das Reich* Panzer Division sector. Other units shifted west to join the incoming remnants of the 12th SS *Hitlerjugend* Panzer Division, by then a shadow of its former self after suffering tremendous losses in the battle for the 'Twin Villages' of Krinkelt-Rocherath. The plan was to cross the Trois Ponts – Hotton road in the vicinity of Erezée and regain momentum for the drive to the northwest. The forces actually available were considerably less than planned. Traffic jams, a series of fuel failures and Allied air attacks had combined to slow down the movement of the 12th SS *Hitlerjugend* Panzer Division and just as the division was nearing the Aisne River, German Command OB West had seized the rearward columns for use around Bastogne. By the 27 December, the date set by 6th Panzer Army for the new attack, all 12th SS *Hitlerjugend* Panzer Division could muster was its 25th SS Panzergrenadier Regiment, most of which was already in the line facing 3rd Armored Division. The 2nd SS *Das Reich* Panzer contribution to the attack force was limited to *Sturmbannführer* Ernst Krag's *Kampfgruppe* Krag consisting of the reinforced divisional reconnaissance battalion, a battalion of self-propelled guns and two rifle companies. The attack was scheduled to begin at midnight. During 27 December the lines of General Hickey's CCA 3rd Armored Division had been redressed. In the process, the 1st Battalion of the 289th Infantry had tied in with Task Force Orr of the 3rd Armored on the Aisne River while the 2nd Battalion continued the 3rd Armored line through the woods southwest of Grandmenil. Unknown at the time, a one thousand-yard gap had developed south of Sadzot and Briscol between these two battalions. At zero hour, the German assault started forward through the deep woods; the night was dark, the ground pathless, steep and broken. The grenadiers made good progress, but the radio failed in the thick woods and it would appear that some of the attackers became disorientated. At least two companies of the 25th SS Panzergrenadier Regiment did manage to find their way through the gap between the battalions of the 289th and followed the creek into Sadzot, where they struck about two hours after the jump-off.

SS-Sturmbannführer *Ernst Krag.*

The course of the battle as it developed in the early morning hours of 28 December is extremely confused. The first report of the German presence in Sadzot was relayed to higher headquarters at 02.00 by artillery observers belonging to the 54th Armored Field Artillery Battalion, whose howitzers were positioned north of the village. The two American rifle battalions, when queried, reported no sign of the enemy. Inside Sadzot were bivouacked Company C of the 87th Chemical Mortar Battalion and a tank destroyer platoon; these troops rapidly recovered from their surprise and during the melée established a firm hold on the north side of the village. General Hickey immediately alerted the US 509th Parachute Infantry Battalion near Erezée to make an envelopment of Sadzot from west and east, but no sooner had the paratroopers deployed than they ran into *Kampfgruppe* Krag.

This engagement in the darkness seems to have been a catch-as-catch-can affair. The American radios, like the German radios, failed to function in this terrain (the 3rd Armored communications throughout the battle were mostly by wire and runner). Confusion caused the Germans to put mortar fire on their own neighbouring platoons. Squads and platoons on both sides carried on the fight firing at whatever moved. At daylight, the paratroopers got artillery support, which far outweighed the single battalion behind the enemy assault force, and moved forward. By 11.00, the 509th had clicked the trap shut on the Germans inside Sadzot.

There remained the task of closing the gap between the two battalions of the US 289th. At dark on 28 December, General Hickey put in the 2nd Battalion of the 112th Infantry, but this outfit, hastily summoned out for the fight, lost its direction and failed to seal the gap. Early on the morning of the following day, Hickey, believing that the 112th had made the line of departure secure, sent the 509th and six light tanks to attack toward the southeast. In the meantime, the Germans had reorganised, put in what was probably a fresh battalion and begun a new march on Sadzot. In the collision that followed, a section of German 75mm anti-tank guns destroyed three of the light tanks and the

Germans who died when the 505th Parachute Infantry Regiment fought the 1st and 2nd Battalions of SS Panzergrenadier Regiment 25 of the 12th SS Panzer Division at Sadzot. (US Army Signal Corps).

paratroopers fell back, but so did the enemy.

During the morning, the 2nd Battalion, US 112th Infantry, got its bearings – or so it was believed – and set out to push a bar across the corridor from the west. Across the deep ravines and rugged hills American troops were sighted, and believing them to be the 2nd Battalion, the troops of the 112th veered toward them. What had been seen, however, proved to be the paratroopers of the 509th. After this misadventure, and the jolt suffered by the paratroopers, Hickey and the battalion commanders concerned, worked out a co-ordinated attack. First, the paratroopers put in a twilight assault, which forced the Germans back. Then, the 2nd Battalion 112th made a night attack with guiding this time on 60mm illuminating mortar rounds fired by the 2nd Battalion of the 289th. Crossing through deep ravines, the infantrymen of the 112th drove the enemy from their path. At dawn on the 29th, the gap was finally closed.

The German failure to penetrate through the Erezée sector on 28-29 December, was the last serious bid by the Sixth Panzer Army in an offensive role. On that day, *Generalfeldmarschall* Model ordered 6th Panzer Army to go over to the defensive and began stripping it of its armour. The German commanders left facing the VII and XVIII Airborne Corps east of the Ourthe River, record a number of attacks being made between 29 December and 2 January. The units involved included infantry detachments from the 9th SS as well as the 18th and 62nd Volksgrenadier Divisions. Ordering these weak and tired units into the attack when the German foot soldier knew that the great offensive was ended, was one thing. To press the assault itself, was quite another. The American divisions in this sector note only at the turn of the year 'Front quiet', or 'Routine patrolling'. The initiative had clearly passed to the Americans.

Return to the main road (N807) turning left (west) in the direction of Erezée. Drive through Erezée and continue west on N807 passing through Fisenne and Soy. West of Soy on N807, watch out for the crossroads named in honor of the 517th Parachute Infantry Regiment to the northwest corner of which is a monument to the 517th. Pause here.

In May 1992, a group of veterans of the 1st Battalion, 517th Parachute Infantry Regiment returned to Belgium for the dedication of this monument. The 1st Battalion incurred 139 casualties with fourteen men killed in action during its fighting in the Soy-Hotton-Lamormenil area from 23-26 December 1944. Artillery and tank fire reduced this crossroads (locally known as 'Quatre Bras') to a scene of utter desolation. The stench of cordite, charred flesh and white phosphorous hung in the air for days after the capture of the crossroads area. A lone pine tree survived the rigors of battle only to be cut down some forty-seven years later by foresters unaware of its place in history.

After pausing at the 517th monument turn left at this same junction off N807 and at the downhill bends pause by the stone monument on the left.

As a young boy, Florent Lambert lived through the battles in this area and never forgot the debt he and his countrymen owed their allied liberators. On 3 January 1945, Captain James M. Burt of Company H, 3rd Battalion, 66th Armored Regiment of the 2nd Armored Division, was leading a column of medium tanks down this hill in the direction of Melines. Driving these vehicles on this icy slope proved tricky and as Captain Burt neared the bottom of the hill he heard a violent explosion to his rear. Just across the valley, a group of civilians preparing to leave the area also heard the explosion and turned to see thick smoke rising above the trees. As the tank column jarred to a halt, men ran in both directions to find out what had happened. Some infantrymen of the 84th Infantry Division had been riding 'piggy-back' aboard one or more of the long-barrelled Shermans. The tank, commanded by Lieutenant George C. Connealy, had been inching its way down the road when it skidded on the hard-packed ice and snow off the edge of the winding road. Upon doing so, it struck a daisy chain of mines that detonated simultaneously blowing the tank turret clear across the road, killing Lieutenant Connealy, his crew and the hitch-hiking GIs. Florent Lambert never forgot those young men who gave their lives that cold winter's day, and in their honor he built this monument.

Continue downhill keeping to the right at the bottom and past the road to Beffe (signposted Werpin). As you then drive uphill, on the right is another monument

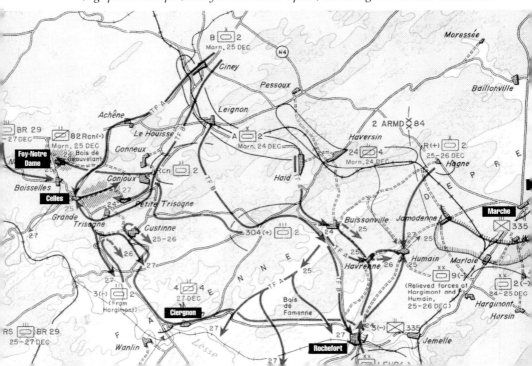

erected on the initiative of Florent Lambert.

This monument commemorates several American units, which served in this area at various points throughout the battle. The units include 3rd Armored Division, 75th Infantry Division, 2nd Armored Division and the 84th Infantry Division. It also features a portrait of Corporal John Shields of Company C, 23rd Armored Infantry Battalion, 7th Armored Division whose remains were discovered about fifty yards further up the road in the ditch on the right hand side by Florent Lambert's father in 1947.

Continue up the road keeping an eye out for a small stone cross on the right, which shows where Mr. Lambert Sr. discovered Corporal Shields remains. Continue straight ahead in the direction of Werpin. As the road begins to level off, the wooded hill to the left is known as 'La Roumière'. Pause with the high wooded ground off to your left.

The arrival of the US 75th Infantry Division in the European Theatre, more specifically, in the 3rd Armored Division sector, promised the needed rifle strength to establish a solid defense in the rugged country east of Hotton and along the bluffs of the Aisne River. To establish a homogenous line the Americans would have to seize the high, wooded and difficult ground south of the Soy-Hotton road (N807), and at the same time, push forward to close up to the banks of the Aisne River over the tortuous terrain south of the Erezée-Grandmenil road. With two regiments of the 75th attached to the 3rd Armored (the 289th and 290th Infantry Regiments), General Rose ordered a drive to

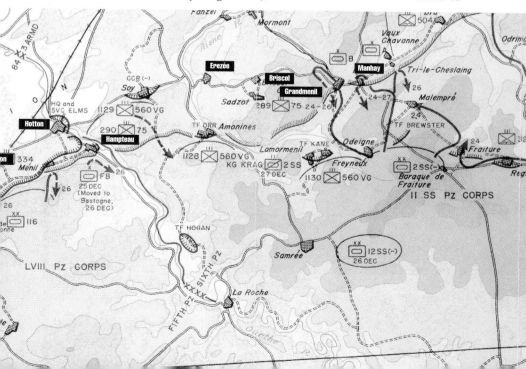

cement the CCA wing in the west.

The units of the 75th had been scattered in widely separated areas after their arrival in Belgium. A smooth-running supply system had not yet been set up, and to concentrate and supply the rifle battalions would prove difficult. Colonel Carl F. Duffner's 290th Infantry received orders at 16.00 on the 24 December to assemble at Ny for an attack to begin two hours later. There ensued much confusion, with orders and counter-orders, and finally the attack was re-scheduled for 23.30. The regiment had no idea of the ground over which it was to fight but did know that the line of departure was then held by a battalion or less of the 517th Parachute Infantry Regiment deployed along the N807 between Soy and Hotton. The 2nd and 3rd Battalions were chosen for this first battle, their objective La Roumière.

About midnight on the 24 December the battalions started their assault companies forward, little did they know it but the men of the 3rd Battalion were embarking upon a nightmare mission. Second Lieutenant Paul B. Ellis Jr. commanded the 2nd Platoon of Company K that fateful Christmas Eve as they reached the crest of La Roumière. In a letter to the author dated 8 October 1991, he recalled the attack on the hill:

'As my platoon moved from right to left along the crest of the hill, we spotted a machine-gun nest with four Germans in it. They were firing down the hill and I don't think they saw us. Cyril Gerwitz and I tossed two grenades in the emplacement and either killed or knocked out all four

Germans. A man from my platoon went in and made sure the war was over for all four Germans. Private First Class Gerwitz was my runner. Each officer had a runner who was known by the company commander, to relay messages. When my platoon ran out of ammunition on top of the hill, I ordered Cyril to leave. I still had a few rounds in my carbine to cover him and the others. He would not go. When I ran out of "ammo", we took off down the hill and a little German in a greatcoat that reached his ankles came after us firing a "burp-gun" (machine pistol) as he ran 75 to 100 yards behind us. We had almost reached the ditch beside the road when he fired a long burst that killed Gerwitz and wounded me.'

Lieutenant Ellis' platoon sergeant, 'Woody' Woodrome killed the pursuing German who'd followed Ellis to the edge of the road. Losses in this débacle were severe with most of the officers either killed or wounded. On the

PFC Cyril J. Gerwitz the runner for 2nd Platoon, Company K, saved the life of Lieutenant Ellis when he gave his own. (Author's collection, courtesy Paul and Rosemary Ellis).

afternoon of Christmas Day, more infantry arrived (probably from the 517th Parachute Infantry), plus a platoon of tank destroyers, and a fresh assault was organised. This carried through the woods and onto the crest of the slope. The 290th Infantry Regiment had undergone their 'Baptism of Fire'.

Continue through Werpin bearing right at the church and proceed to Hampteau. Here, turn right on N833 towards Hotton and in the centre of town pause in the vicinity of the Ourthe River Bridge, which is off to your right side.

Just north of the bridge note the Hotel de L'Ourthe that from 20 December served as the forward command post of General Maurice Rose's 3rd Armored Division.

On the southeast end of the bridge note the plaque to Lieutenant Colonel Harvey Fraser's 51st Engineer Combat Battalion.

The town of Hotton is built astride the main channel of the Ourthe River at a point where the valley widens. Here, a series of roads converge to cross the river and proceed on the West Bank to the more important junction centre at Marche from which roads radiate in all directions. Here in 1944, a Class 70 two-way wooden bridge spanned the river. In the buildings on the East Side about two hundred men from the service detachments of the 'Spearhead' 3rd Armored Division and its Combat Command Reserve prepared to defend the town. In addition, one light and one medium tank were positioned on the east bank. Across the river the following units defended the western end of the bridge. The 1st Platoon of Company A, 51st Engineer Combat Battalion; a squad from Company B of the 51st; a squad of engineers from 3rd Armored Division with a 37mm anti-tank gun; two 40mm Bofors Anti-aircraft guns; several bazooka teams; and some 50 calibre machine guns. An additional engineer squad from the 51st guarded a footbridge at Hampteau, two thousand yards south of Hotton.

At about 07.00 on 21 December 1944, twenty-five German infantrymen crossed the Ourthe River at Hampteau in an initial probe of the Hotton defenses by the 116th *Windhund* (Greyhound) Panzer Division. About half an hour later, mortar and small arms fire heralded the opening attack against the bridge defenders. Despite casualties and confusion Major Jack W. Fickessen, executive officer of the 23rd Armored Engineer Battalion hastily set up the defense of the bridge. His men drove engineer trucks out to block the roads then distributed bazookas and machine guns for a close-in defense of the

Second Lieutenant Paul B. Ellis commander of The 2nd Platoon, Company K of the 290th Infantry Regiment in the action at La Roumière.
(Author's collection, courtesy Paul and Rosemary Ellis).

Anti-tank gunners of the 84th Infantry Division see to the maintenance of their 57mm anti-tank gun. (US Army Signal Corps).

town. Taking advantage of the woods that came right up to the eastern edge of Hotton, four or five enemy tanks rumbled forward to lead the assault. The Germans immediately knocked out both American tanks on the east side of the river but on the opposite bank, an American tank destroyer suddenly appeared and knocked out one of the attacking Panther tanks. Although the German infantry managed to gain control of about half the buildings on the east bank, the Americans defending the remainder and those on the other bank prevented the enemy from reaching the bridge.

At his command post in Marche, Lieutenant Colonel Harvey 'Scrappy' Fraser, commander of the 51st Engineers remained in constant telephone contact with his men on the spot who gave him a running commentary on the fighting in progress. As the situation began to deteriorate, Fraser called General Bolling of the 84th Infantry Division to request support. General Bolling refused this request indicating that he couldn't accept as factual, reports from 'on the spot' eye-witnesses.

At 08.53 the telephone line between Fraser and his men in Hotton went out so he and his driver drove to Hotton to join the defenders at the bridge. In the course of the morning, the defenders knocked out some four enemy tanks. Private Lee J. Ishmael, Fraser's driver knocked out one such tank while manning a 37mm anti-tank gun when its crew proved reluctant to do so.

Later that afternoon, the Germans managed to damage the wiring leading to the demolition charges on the bridge. Under enemy small arms fire, Lieutenants Floyd D. Wright and Bruce W. Jamison of the 51st Engineers waded through chest deep, ice cold water and succeeded in repairing the wiring. The engineers had the situation well in hand by the time reinforcements from the 334th Infantry of the 84th Division arrived.

Turn west (left) on N86. As you climb up out of town take the left turning marked Menil where you see a sign for the British and Commonwealth War Cemetery (Hotton War Cemetery). Continue on this road until you reach the cemetery on your right.

Here lie buried 667 British and Commonwealth war dead including casualties from the 'Battle of the Bulge'. Although in Allied terms essentially an American battle, elements of the British XXX Corps and 6th Airborne Division deployed and fought in the area. At La Roche, a fine marble plaque and other monuments commemorate the role of British units in the battle. About fifteen miles southwest of Hotton, in an attack against the Germans defending the village of Bure, the 13th Battalion of the Parachute Regiment suffered some 189 casualties. Sixty-eight lie buried in this cemetery. Theirs was indeed a valiant story. For those wishing to make a side trip to Bure, a memorial to the 13th Battalion stands outside the village church while inside a Roll of Honor lists the men of the battalion and the Belgian Special Air Service killed in the vicinity of the village.

Return to N86 turning west (left) in the direction of Marche. In Bourdon, turn left in the direction of Verdenne/Marenne. Cross the railroad and climb the hill to your front, keeping to the same road, Pass the local soccer pitch to your right and keep right, passing the monument to the Verdenne Pocket. Continue towards the outskirts of Verdenne passing the grounds of the Château de Verdenne (private property) to your left and stop at the entrance to the village.

On the night of 23 December, two companies (dismounted troops of the 116th Panzer Division's reconnaissance battalion) infiltrated the American lines at the junction point between the 334th and 335th Infantry Regiments. They stealthily worked their way forward and by dawn were to the rear of the 334th. There they sought cover on the wooded ridge north of Verdenne. This village, outposted by the Americans, was the immediate goal of the German attack planned for 24 December. Commanding the Marche-Hampteau road – roughly the line held by the left wing of the 84th Division – it afforded immediate access via the good secondary route to Bourdon on the main Hotton-Marche highway (N86), and its possession would offer a springboard for the German armoured thrust.

A delay in fuel supply meant that the 116th Panzer did not attack at daylight on 24 December. Instead, the division commander, Generalmajor Siegfried von Waldenburg, sent detachments of his 60th Regiment into the Bois de Chardogne, the western extrusion of a large forested area partially held by the Germans southwest of Verdenne. Unusual movement in the woods alerted the

Americans to the enemy presence during the morning so General Bolling sent the 1st Battalion, 334th Infantry supported by three tank platoons of the 771st Tank Battalion to trap the infiltrators. The American tanks suddenly appeared on the wooded ridge north of Verdenne and ran head on into the enemy just assembling at the wood's edge in assault formation. The Germans broke and fled, some fifty surrendered and the Americans cleared the woods.

About an hour after the above incident, five enemy tanks and two halftracks accompanied by a hundred or so grenadiers, struck Verdenne from the south and in the process, captured the village. They then pushed on to the château and that evening drove the wedge even deeper.

Companies I and K of the 334th Infantry fell back to a new line barely in front of the crucial Marche-Hotton road, and German light artillery moved up to bring the road under fire.

Return to the 'Verdenne Pocket' monument and stop.

General Bolling then ordered his reserve, the 333rd Infantry, to send its 3rd Battalion to re-take Verdenne. As they entered the woods in the pitch-black dark, the men of Company K ran into a column of seven or eight tanks. Sergeant Donald Phelps manning the point went forward to check the lead tank. As he pounded his fist on the side of the vehicle, the hatch opened slowly and a somewhat curious voice asked 'Was ist los?' Immediately a firefight broke out and under machine gun fire from the tanks the men of Company K sought cover in the roadside ditches. Sergeant Phelps and his buddies had run smack into a battalion-size force of forty tanks, armored infantry and supporting engineers and artillery of the 116th Panzer Division. Severely lacerated before they could break away, the remaining forty men of Company K joined the main assault against Verdenne an hour later.

Intense American artillery fire softened up the Germans in Verdenne and the attacking GIs succeded in getting clear through the village – although fighting resumed at daylight with the dangerous task of house-clearing. Some 289 German soldiers surrendered by the end of Christmas Day.

The seizure of Verdenne cast a loop around the German tanks and infantry in the woods north of the village. At noon on Christmas Day a tank company of the 16th Panzer Regiment tried an assault in staggered formation against Verdenne but found Company B of the 771st Tank Battalion waiting for them and lost nine tanks – its entire complement.

Von Waldenburg still hoped that the detachment in the woods could be saved, for during the day *Oberst* Otto Remer's Führer Escort Brigade came in on his right, freeing the troops he had deployed to watch Hampteau and the Hotton approaches. More than this, he apparently expected to use the wedge which would be created in reaching the pocket as a means of splitting the Marche-Hotton line and starting a major advance westward.

Tankers attached to 84th Infantry Division on the look out for enemy activity. An abandoned German "Kubelwagen" stands snow covered behind them.
(US Army Signal Corps).

The area in which the Germans were hemmed posed a very neat problem in minor tactics. It was about 800 yards by 300, densely wooded and shaped with an inner declivity somewhat like a serving platter. Guns beyond the rim could not bring fire to bear on the tanks inside, and tanks rolling down into the pocket would be in the same position if they moved up and over the edge. Assault by infantry could be met by tank fire whether the assault went into or came out of the pocket.

Companies A and B of the 333rd Infantry tried such an assault in a pre-dawn attack on 26 December. The American skirmish line, its movements given away by the snow crackling underfoot, took a number of casualties and was beaten back, but it gave some test of the enemy strength, now estimated to be two rifle companies and five tanks. Actually, most of the Germans in the 1st Battalion, 60th Panzergrenadier Regiment, took part in the fighting at the pocket or in attempted infiltration through the woods to join their comrades there. One such relief party, led by a tank platoon, did cut its way in on the morning of the 26 December. Now that the enemy had been reinforced, the 333rd infantry decided to try the artillery, although not before the regimental commander had been assured that the gunners would fire with such minute accuracy as to miss the friendly infantry edging the pocket. Throughout the rest of the day, an 8-inch howitzer battalion and a battalion of 155mm guns hammered the target area intent on jarring the panzers loose, while a chemical mortar company tried to burn them out.

On 27 December, patrols edged their way into the pocket to find nothing but abandoned tanks. The previous evening, von Waldenburg learned that the

Some fifty years after the battle Mr and Mrs Fautré-Blétry show their continued appreciation for the 'Railsplitters' by painting the 84th Division patch on their gable end. (Author's collection).

Führer Escort Brigade was being taken away from his right flank and that he must go over to the defensive at once. Still in radio contact with his troops in the pocket, he ordered them to come out, synchronising their move with an attack toward Menil at dusk. Perhaps the feint at Menil served its purpose – in any event, most of the grenadiers made good their escape, riding out on the tanks still capable of movement.

Return to N86 turning left in the direction of Marche. Just before reaching the town cemetery in Marche, note the red brick house on the left side of the road. For the fiftieth anniversary of the battle, the owner painted a large 'Rail-splitter' patch on the eastern gable end in honor of the 84th Infantry Division. From here head to the 'Musee de la Farenne' at 22 Rue du Commerce. On the wall in the courtyard of this building are plaques commemorating the 84th Division and its commander, Brigadier General Alexander R. Bolling.

On 19 December, US General Bolling received orders to make ready for relief by the 102nd Infantry Division, and by noon the next day, his leading regimental combat team, the 334th, was on the road from the Roer River front to Belgium. First Army ordered General Bolling to assemble the 84th in the sector of Marche.

He set up his command post in Marche late on the afternoon of 21 December. The only friendly troops he found in the neighbourhood were those of Lieutenant Colonel Harvey 'Scrappy' Fraser's 51st Engineer Combat Battalion, whose command post was also in Marche. This battalion was part of a small engineer force, which VII Corps had gathered to construct the barrier line along the Ourthe River. Colonel Fraser spread out his two companies at roadblocks and demolition sites all the way from Hotton, on the river, to a point just south of the Champlon crossroads on the Bastogne-Marche highway (N4).

The first word of an attacking enemy reached the 84th Division command post in Marche at 09.00 on 21 December, but the attack was being made at Hotton, to the Northeast, where the 116th Panzer division had earlier started

Anglo-American traffic on a street in Marche. (US Army Signal Corps).

its assault against the Ourthe River Bridge. General Bolling ordered his single regimental combat team, the 334th under Lieutenant Colonel Charles E. Foy, to establish a perimeter defense around Marche. Meanwhile Colonel Fraser had asked for help in the fight at Hotton, but by the time troops of the 334th reached the scene in mid-afternoon, the embattled engineers and soldiers of 3rd Armored Division had halted the enemy in their tracks and saved the bridge. General Bolling received word from army headquarters that his division was to hold the Marche-Hotton line. By midnight on the 21 December, he had his whole division and the 771st Tank Battalion assembled and in process of deploying on a line of defense. About dark, as the second team de-trucked, Bolling relieved the 334th of its close-in defense of Marche and moved the 2nd and 3rd Battalions out to form the left flank of the division, this anchored at Hotton where troops of the 3rd Armored Division had finally been met. The 335th Infantry, under Colonel Hugh C. Parker, deployed to the right of the 334th with its right flank on N4 and its line circling south and east through Jamodenne and Waha. Colonel Timothy Pedley's 333rd Infantry, the last to arrive, assembled north of Marche in the villages of Baillonville and Moressée ready to act as cover for the open right flank of the division – and army, or as division reserve. During the night, the regiments pushed out a combat post line, digging in on the frozen ground some thousand metres forward of the main position, which extended from Hogne on highway N4 through Marloie and along the pine-crested ridges southwest of Hampteau. The division was now in position forward of the Marche-Hotton road (N86) and that vital link appeared secure. Earlier in the day, the 51st Engineer roadblocks on the Marche-Bastogne highway had held long enough to allow the 7th Armored Division trains to escape from Laroche and reach Marche. At

19.30 the tiny engineer detachments received orders to blow their demolition charges and fall back to Marche, leaving the road to Bastogne in German hands.

Continue on N836 in the direction of Rochefort via Jemelle. Stop in Rochefort town centre.

On 24 December 1944, the hottest points of combat in this sector were Rochefort, Buissonville and the Bourdon sector east of the Marche-Hotton road (N86). A couple of hours after midnight, *Generalleutnant* Fritz Bayerlein's Panzer Lehr began their main attack against the defenders of Rochefort. The Americans held fast and made a battle of it in houses and behind garden walls. Companies I and K of the 333rd Infantry, 84th Division, concentrated in and around the Hotel du Centre, dug in a brace of 57mm anti-tank guns and a selection of heavy machine guns in front of the hotel, and so interdicted the town square. About 09.00 on Christmas Eve, the 3rd Battalion lost radio contact with division, but four hours later, one message did reach Rochefort: an order from General Bolling to withdraw. By this time, a tree burst had put the anti-tank guns out of action. To disengage from this house-to-house combat wouldn't be easy. Fortunately, the attackers had their eyes firmly fixed on the town centre market place, apparently with the objective of seizing the crossroads there so that armoured vehicles could move through from one side of town to the other.

The Germans were so preoccupied that they neglected to bar all exits from Rochefort. Driven back into a small area around the battalion command post, where bullet and mortar fire made the streets an inferno, the surrounded garrison made ready for a break. Enough vehicles had escaped damage to mount the battalion headquarters and Company M. The rest of the force formed up for a march out on foot. At 18.00, the two groups made a concentrated dash from the town, firing wildly as they went and hurling smoke grenades, which masked them, momentarily, from a German tank lurking nearby. The vehicular column headed west for Givet without being ambushed. The foot elements headed north with the intention of reaching the outposts of a 3rd Armored Division task force known to be thereabouts, but the seemingly ubiquitous presence of enemy troops severely hampered movement. During the night, battalion sent some trucks east of Givet and located parts of Companies I and K. Patrols from the 2nd Armored Division picked up two officers and thirty-three men of Company I in an exhausted state and returned to the American lines. The defense of Rochefort had not been too costly: the defenders left behind fifteen wounded men in the care of a volunteer medic while the attackers captured or killed a further twenty-five. *Generalleutnant* Bayerlein, commander of the Panzer Lehr, who himself fought in both engagements, would later rate the American defense of Rochefort as comparable in courage and significance as that of Bastogne.

Take N911 in the direction of Ciergnon. West of Ciergnon turn right on N94 in the direction of Celles/Dinant. Once through Celles, pause at the junction with N910 and note the wrecked Panther in front of the café to your right.

In its attempt to cross the Meuse River, the 47th Panzer Korps' 2nd Panzer Division's reconnaissance element reached the village of Foy Notre Dame, between here and Dinant, at midnight on 23 December. In support of this spearhead, the 2nd Panzer Division commander, Oberst Meinrad von Lauchert sent Major Ernst von Cochenhausen's Kampfgruppe *forward. This battered hulk is what is left of* Kampfgruppe *von Cochenhausen's lead tank after it struck a mine early on the morning of 24 December. Later, the village council moved it to its present location.*

Private Patrick E. Shea a BAR gunner with Company B, 329th Infantry Regiment of the 83rd Infantry Division. He and his company repulsed enemy attacks at Rochefort for two days 6/1/45. (US Army Signal Corps).

Continue north on N94 to Celles (signposted Dinant) crossing N910 and in Boisselles take a minor right under N97 following the sign for Foy Notre Dame. Upon entering the village after passing under the arch, turn left then at the church turn right. Just past the church, watch out for a Belgian Touring Club stone marker and a cross on your right.

It was in and around this village that the 2nd Panzer Division spearhead was annihilated. Thanks to intelligence gathered by two local former Belgian army officers, Captain Jaques de Villenfagne de Sorrines and Lieutenant Philippe le Hardy de Beaulieu, British troops in nearby Sorrines learned of the proximity and precise location of German troops, vehicles and guns. On 24 December, American and British units supported by ground-strafing P-51s put pressure on the Germans in and around Foy Notre Dame, effectively wiping them out over the next couple of days. Major General Ernest N. Harmon's US 2nd Armored Division was instrumental in this destruction of the 2nd Panzer Division. Von Lauchert's men had achieved the deepest penetration in Hitler's last desperate attempt to snatch victory in the West.

Return south and pass under the N97 turning right, then a little further, turn right again back under the N97 onto N94. Follow N94 west and downhill turning right toward Dinant at the Meuse River. Stop by the large triangular rock formation on the east bank known as the 'Rocher Bayard'.

During the night of 23 December, three men of *Obersturmbannführer* Otto Skorzeny's 150th Panzer Brigade, driving a captured American jeep, reached the Rocher Bayard only to be stopped dead in their tracks by men of the British 29th Armoured Brigade. A stone positioned close to the north side of the rock marks this as the furthest point west reached by any German soldier in WACHT AM RHEIN.

Continue on into Dinant for a couple of well earned Belgian Trappist beers!

Suggested Reading:
MacDonald: Chapters 26,27 and 29.
Cole: Chapters 16,22 and 23.
Breuer: *Bloody clash at Sadzot.*
Fowle and Wright: *The 51st Again.* Chapters 5, 6 and 7.
Pallud: *The Battle of the Bulge: Then and Now* Parts 3 and 4.

Brigadier General W.B. Palmer VII Corps Artillery Commander. (US Army Photo, courtesy General Palmer).

CHAPTER 6

WALLENDORF-HOESDORF

In editing this itinerary which looks at the Westwall, or Siegfried Line, I turned to my friend Roland Gaul, without doubt the leading authority on this area. In 1982, a small group of enthusiasts and militaria collectors founded the Diekirch Historical Society, a non-profit organisation, entirely composed of volunteers, that was to become the platform for the future Diekirch Military Museum. As one of the founding members, Roland Gaul, himself a prolific author and true expert on the battles in this area, has kindly permitted me to make use of the museum's brochure entitled *Promenade du Souvenir*. This is a seventeen kilometre walking tour which starts in Hoesdorf and is marked by blue signs bearing white stars.

<u>START POINT: THE PATTON MONUMENT ON THE LEFT SIDE OF N7 AT THE EASTERN EDGE OF ETTELBRÜCK.</u>

In Ettelbrück this fine monument and a small museum (www.patton.lu) in town pay tribute to the commander of Third Army, Lieutenant General George S. Patton Jr. The General is buried in the Luxembourg U.S. military cemetery close to the national airport.

Drive east to Diekirch passing the old railway station on the left (still sporting traces of small arms fire) and stop just past the Hotel de Ville on the right.

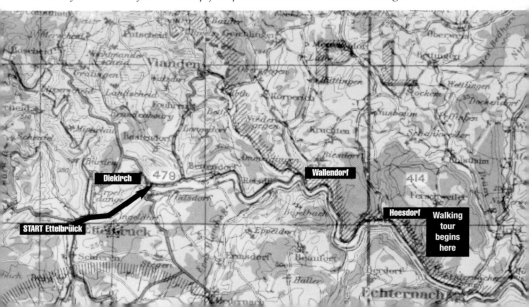

In the municipal park off to your right is a memorial commemorating American units that passed through town at various stages in 1944-45. There is also a walkway in memory of the Luxembourg citizens who were either deported by the Nazis or conscripted and sent off to the eastern front. At the turn of the millennium as part of a project called 'M-2000' the authorities here in Diekirch erected a memorial commemorating in a condensed fashion, the country's military history. A pamphlet produced by the Diekirch Historical Society entitled Diekirch and surrounding areas during the Bulge 16 December,1944 - 21 January, 1945, *recalls events in the town:*

'During the Nazi occupation, the city of Diekirch became an administrative centre for the NSDAP (Nazi party), responsible for the smaller communities in northern Luxembourg. At the same time, Diekirch was also a secret site of Luxembourg resistance against the German occupants.'

On 11 September 1944, armoured and mechanised infantry elements of the US 5th Armored Division, liberated Diekirch, after patrols of the 85th Cavalry Reconnaissance Squadron had touched base with several local civilians to find the Germans no longer held the town. Prior to abandoning Diekirch, on 9 September, the retreating Germans blew the Sauer River Bridge. News of the subsequent arrival of American troops spread like wildfire and within minutes, thousands of townspeople poured onto the streets to welcome their liberators with flowers, drinks and above all, tears of joy in their eyes. Church bells rang; children rode Sherman tanks while townspeople and soldiers danced in the street in an indescribable atmosphere of exhilaration at their liberation.

An acute shortage of jerrycans prompted the US army to put up signs urging the populace to hand in any cans they found. (US Army Signal Corps).

Whereas military operations in Belgium and the nearby German border town of Wallendorf continued, normal life gradually returned to Diekirch. A US Civil Affairs detachment commanded by Lieutenant Colonel Charles Mathews established its headquarters in town to assume responsibility for Northern Luxembourg. In early October 1944, troops of the 8th Infantry Division replaced remaining elements of 5th Armored Division. Operating from Diekirch they undertook extensive patrol and intelligence activity along the German border. No significant combat activity took place during that time.

In turn, Major General Norman D. Cota's 28th Infantry Division replaced the 8th after suffering heavy losses in the battle of the Hürtgen Forest and moved into this 'quiet' sector of Luxembourg to rest and refit. Lieutenant Colonel James Rudder's 109th Infantry Regiment assumed positions in the greater Diekirch area with two battalions on the defensive 'front' line overlooking the Our River. Colonel Rudder's 3rd battalion, in reserve here in Diekirch, took hot showers, received new clothes and above all, the spontaneous hospitality of the town's grateful citizens. U.S.O. shows entertained the troops featuring such notable stars as Mickey Rooney and Marlene Dietrich. Other than sporadic artillery and counter-battery fire, neither side took offensive action of any significance. (At that time German troops were already moving into assembly areas in the Siegfried Line for their forthcoming counterattack). Combat intelligence and reconnaissance missions continued in attempts to find any weaknesses in the German defensive line. Occasional German patrols entered Luxembourg but on the whole, a sort of 'gentleman's agreement' deadened the effects of war.

The citizens of Diekirch enjoyed a traditional turkey dinner on Thanksgiving Day in a unique atmosphere of Luxembourg-American friendship. Needless to say, children enjoyed Hershey bars, chewing gum and candy, while their parents invited American GIs to sample local specialities. By early December the reorganisation of the 109th was completed when new replacements arrived and the regimental sector of responsibility redefined. As a consequence, the 2nd and 3rd Battalions were assigned to the front line (two companies of each), whereas the entire 3rd Battalion remained in reserve at Diekirch.

The Regimental headquarters moved to Ettelbrück. Gun batteries of the 107th and 108th Field Artillery Battalions provided fire support along with Sherman tanks of the attached 707th Tank Battalion. In case of emergency, nearby batteries of Combat Command A, 9th Armored Division (3rd Field Artillery Battalion) as well as other elements of the 28th Infantry Division could be called upon for support if needed.

During the second week of December, the weather turned very cold: there was light snow on the ground that often turned into mud, there was also rain, snow, sleet and above all, fog. GIs in their foxholes did their best to keep warm and dry as they dreamt of Christmas and a not too distant end to the war.

On 16 December 1944, at 05.30 am, all hell broke loose when, quite unexpectedly, German artillery opened up with a deadly and intense rain of shells and rockets. The thirty minute barrage pinned down the men of the 109th who initially didn't realise what was going on. Shells ploughed into the US front line positions while others set alight various buildings in Diekirch. Massive German infantry attacks across the Our River followed the artillery barrage that signalled the start of the Battle of the Bulge. At first light, all front line companies of the 109th Infantry between Vianden and Wallendorf reported communications problems and attacks by German infantry. Enemy soldiers of the 915th and 916th Regiments of the 352nd Volksgrenadier Division crossed the swollen Our River to attack the 3rd Battalion of the 109th while the 914th Regiment and elements of 5th Parachute Division attacked Rudder's 2nd Battalion. Backed up by their own 81mm mortars, the 105mm howitzers of Lieutenant Colonel James Rosborough's 107th Field Artillery Battalion and the 155mm batteries of the 108th Field Artillery Battalion both positioned on the high ground north of Diekirch – Rudder's men defended themselves well. The attacking Germans made some progress against the 2nd Battalion when they surrounded and captured men of Company E holding the village of Fouhren. On 18 December, German pressure increased considerably and harsh fighting on the morning of 19 December prompted Colonel Rudder to order his men to pull back behind Ettelbrück to a new defensive line. The 3rd Battalion moved through Bettendorf and Gilsdorf after destroying the Sauer river bridges to deny the enemy usage thereof and reached Diekirch late afternoon on 19 December having suffered considerable losses. Together with the local authorities, resistance fighters and police, the 3rd Battalion executive officer, Captain Harry Kemp, worked out an emergency evacuation order for the population of Diekirch in such a way as not to interfere with the battalion retrograde movement. The civilians left Diekirch around midnight via the still intact Railway Bridge then off to the south while the remaining troops of the 109th established new positions on the high ground overlooking Ettelbrück. According to civilian eyewitnesses (some had missed the evacuation), the first Germans entered Diekirch in the early morning hours of 20 December.

The German advance continued through Ettelbrück in the direction of Feulen, Mertzig, Michelbuch, Pratz and Bettborn, where on Christmas Day 1944, attacking elements of the 80th Infantry Division of Patton's Third Army pushing up from the South stopped them.

On 23 December, American troops recaptured Ettelbrück while elements of the 80th Division and the 109th Infantry Regiment attacked the more advanced enemy forces around Mertzig who were suffering from a lack of armoured and inadequate artillery support. After a desperate struggle, the Germans abandoned all their heavy equipment and those who had not been killed or captured, tried to pull back to a new defensive line behind the north bank of the Sauer River in the Diekirch-Bettendorf sector. In the meantime, units of the 5th Infantry Division (again of Patton's Third Army) took up position on the high ground overlooking the South bank of the Sauer, thus preventing any German attempt at crossing the river. Early January found American troops well entrenched on this new line and awaiting orders to counterattack, while the Germans tried to hold the same sector on the opposite bank. After a very heavy late December snowfall, temperatures plummeted and the weather took a severe turn for the worse. On the US side, the 2nd and 10th Infantry Regiments of the 5th Division carried out extensive patrol activity aimed at probing weaknesses in the German line. On 10 January 1945, a six-man patrol, of the 10th Infantry Regiment penetrated Bettendorf at night and captured several German prisoners, one of whom, an NCO had valuable papers on him. These documents were of great help to the Regimental Executive Officer of the 10th Infantry, Lieutenant Colonel William K. Breckinridge and his staff in finalising plans for the division's attack in this sector. On the left flank, the 2nd Infantry Regiment found out that Diekirch was only heavily defended in two places.

The American counterattack in the Sauer River sector (Diekirch-Bettendorf) by the 5th Infantry Division jumped off at 03.00am on 18 January while its right flank neighbour, the 4th Infantry Division joined in from Moestroff-Wallendorf. The objective was to cross the river and push twenty kilometres north as far as Hoscheid and clear the remaining German pockets of resistance. Wishing to retain the element of surprise, the two American divisions did not call upon their artillery to support the attack, unless the attacking infantry encountered stiff resistance.

Soldiers of the 7th Engineer Combat Battalion ferried the GIs of the 2nd Infantry Regiment across the icebound Sauer River near Diekirch and the companies of the 10th Infantry near Bettendorf. Unfortunately, the Germans, having insufficient troops to defend the sector, had heavily mined the banks of the Sauer River. The mines, mostly of a non-metallic type, proved difficult to detect and caused heavy casualties as did fire from numerous automatic weapons. Sporadically, German *Nebelwerfer* rocket batteries also fired at the crossing points. On 19 January, a two-pronged attack by the 2nd Infantry Regiment succeeded in re-taking most of Diekirch while the 110th Infantry

German prisoners of Grenadier Regiment 914 from the 352nd Volksgrenadier Division captured near Merzig, December 1944. (US Army Signal Corps).

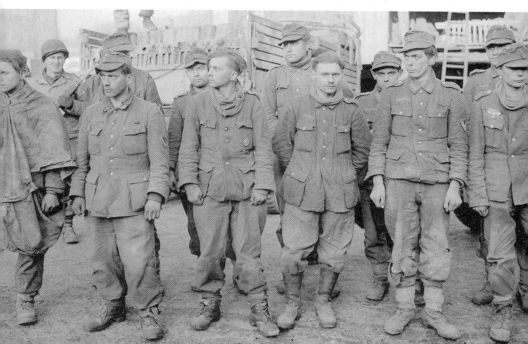

Regiment took Gilsdorf and Bettendorf. After consolidation of the US bridgehead near Diekirch, Sherman tanks broke up the last German resistance in the northern part of town. Around noon on 21 January 1945, the last German troops surrendered on the high ground north of Diekirch and the city was thus definitely liberated. About 60 percent of the buildings in town had been badly damaged by shellfire and its citizens returned to their shell-torn city in March 1945, after US engineers cleared all mines from the area.

Continue into Diekirch following the signs for Echternach until you reach the centre of Bettendorf where you turn right on route 357 to cross the Sauer River Bridge.

This bridge bears a plaque honouring Lieutenant Colonel William M. Breckinridge, regimental executive officer of the 10th Infantry Regiment of the 5th Infantry Division who planned the attack on Bettendorf. There is also a monument to the 5th Infantry Division's 10th Infantry Regiment in a corner of 'Major-General William Breckinridge Square' (on the left after crossing the bridge). On 20 January 2001, an additional bronze plaque portraying the crossing of the Sauer on 20 January 1945, was fixed to a triangular stone about 200 metres from the afore-mentioned memorial. This plaque is a masterpiece, copying the original picture taken in 1945 at this exact location.

Return to the main road (N-19) turning right in the direction of Echternach. Upon arrival in Reisdorf take the left turn just prior to reaching the bridge and continue straight on to the Our River Bridge at Wallendorf-Pont. Across the Our note the bunker in front of you at the 'T' junction.

This bunker is in fact a reinforced concrete 'pillbox' established as an observation and listening post with a clear view of the bridge spanning the Our and overlooking 'enemy' territory (Luxembourg was neutral at that time). In September 1944 it looked out over American held ground on the West Bank of the Our. This bunker had a two or four-man crew with an armoured gun post to accommodate an automatic weapon.

As the smallest of its type, it was commonly known as 'Panzerwerk C' or simply 'C-Werk' in the classification system of German defensive structures. It was one of the very first of this type constructed in this section of the Westwall parallel to the Our River, marking the border between Luxembourg and Germany. Early planning and excavation work for the construction of the Westwall (a static and heavily-armed defensive structure that almost stretched from the North Sea to the Swiss border, following the political and natural borders of pre-war Nazi Germany,) had already begun in 1936. The Westwall represented in fact the counterpart to the French Maginot Line and can be seen as still in line with military doctrine based upon the World War 1 (static front)

A section through a bunker in the Siegfried Line – constructed in the 1930s – it was given wide publicity. This defensive system was to remain untried until late 1944.

experience. For camouflage and deception purposes, the entire operation was then called 'Bauvorhaben in Westen' (construction enterprise in the West). It was only in 1938 (after a major public speech by Hitler), that the enterprise became known to the world as the 'Westwall'.

The bunkers and pillboxes along the Our River, which were all located and constructed to support each other with interlocking fire in case of enemy attack, were normally of this type (C-Werk), serving primarily as a solid medium artillery shell-proof shelter for front-line observation teams. A field wire and telephone network connected the various bunkers amongst themselves and with larger structures further back. There were no anti-tank 'Dragon Teeth' obstacles in this sector unlike further north however, barbed wire obstacles and mine fields usually located in front of the bunker's field of fire and toward the river, supplemented the bunker's protection.

The stone wall constructed in front of this actual pillbox was in fact a deceptive camouflage measure aimed at giving the impression of a garden wall. Other bunkers of this type could be camouflaged as a shed, stable or heavily covered and overgrown with natural vegetation. Furnishings included 2 or 3 cots, a table, benches, a drinking water, storage, ration and ammunition cache, lighting and communications equipment, a ventilating system and sometimes, a stove. Larger bunkers also had special mounts for periscopes, or other sighting equipment. The gun port was normally reinforced with thick armour plate, leaving only a narrow slit for observation or a weapon. A heavy gas tight access door was usually built into the rear side of the bunker.

Prior to 10 May 1940 (beginning of the German campaign in the West), the present pillbox served in its intended capacity and, with the fall of Luxembourg and Belgium, along with the rest of the Westwall, became redundant. Many such bunkers were cleared of their weapons and leased to farmers for agricultural storage. In late summer, 1944, with the German retreat to the borders of the Reich, the Nazi leadership made a major effort to re-arm the Westwall to defend its borders. With the wartime advances in arms technology since the building of the Westwall, most of the larger bunkers (especially those intended to house anti-tank or artillery pieces) could no longer accommodate the larger calibre weapons and hence became almost useless, as time didn't permit sufficient upgrading.

The first Americans hit the German border in this area on 11 September 1944 to find most of the small bunkers on the immediate front line unoccupied, however the Westwall remained a powerful psychological weapon in the eyes of allied troops who over-estimated its potential. Following the American retreat from the Wallendorf sector after limited initial success by elements of the 5th Armored Division supported by the 112th Infantry regiment of the 28th Infantry Division. In late September 1944, and the following 3-month 'quiet' period prior to the German attack on 16 December, this bunker was only occupied under cover of darkness. It acted as a listening and observation post toward the opposing high ground, then occupied by soldiers of the 109th Infantry and only put up limited resistance to U.S. forces in February 1945 during the opening phase of the invasion of Germany. American and French engineers destroyed most of the nearby bunkers and pillboxes during the post-war occupation years.

Facing the bunker, turn right and drive toward the town centre church. Upon reaching the church turn left following the sign bearing five crosses (symbol of the German War Graves Organisation) and marked 'Kriegsgräbstätte'. The Cemetery entrance is on the right hand side opposite the parking lot of the Hotel Wallstein.

A flat tire in Bettendorf. (US Army Signal Corps).

The 'Volksbund Deutsche Kriegsgräberfürsorge' maintains the small Wallendorf German war cemetery containing the remains of 326 German soldiers who died during fighting in the larger Wallendorf area on both riverbanks between September 1944 and February 1945.

The river crossing at Bettendorf 18 January 1945. (Courtesy, Roland Gaul).

As can be seen from the grave markers, most of those buried here were quite young. Units represented include the 2nd Panzer Division, 108th Panzerbrigade, 212th, 276th and 352nd Volksgrenadier Divisions, 5th Fallschirmjäger Division, Volkswerferbrigade 18, Volksartilleriekorps 406 and other smaller Corps support and engineer units.

Occasionally, the remains of soldiers are found and buried, the last one being in 1993 near Bettendorf.

At 05.30am on 16 December 1944, after a thirty minute intense artillery and *Nebelwerfer* rocket barrage, German troops of the 352nd Volksgrenadier Division, crossed the Our River in the Wallendorf-Gentingen sector to assault the American positions atop the Hoesdorf-Bettendorf Plateau. Their objective was to capture the vital road to Diekirch/Ettelbrück as well as the Sauer (Süre) River bridges in this sector. There followed three days of intense fighting in the woods, during which both sides suffered numerous casualties. The remaining troops of the 109th Infantry Regiment withdrew in the direction of Diekirch and further south destroying the Sauer bridges as they went. The 352nd Volksgrenadier Division made further progress till shortly after Christmas when elements of Patton's Third Army counterattacked.

From late December 1944 through till the end of January 1945, the bunkers in the greater Wallendorf sector were primarily occupied by German rear echelon and guard units as a weak defensive force to channel logistics.

On 7 February 1945, the bunkers became key targets when attacked in combined action by artillery, infantry and engineer elements of the 4th, 5th and 80th U.S. Infantry Divisions during the initial phase of the Our and Sauer River crossing operations preceding operations in Germany. Flame-throwers, shaped charges and explosives, as well as artillery destroyed numerous bunkers and pillboxes. Poorly armed and equipped, the Westwall bunkers were no longer a match for overwhelmingly superior US forces.

Upon leaving the cemetery, carry on uphill for about another four hundred yards and at the intersection of two small country roads stands another bunker, park here.

Construction workers of the 'Organisation Todt' probably completed construction of this 'B-Werk' type bunker in 1938. The larger structure with reinforced concrete walls up to a maximum thickness of 1.5 metres, was designed to serve as an observation bunker located on the heights overlooking the confluence point of the Our and Sauer Rivers, as well as the high ground on the Luxembourg side. This type of bunker was well furnished and could provide room for a squad (ten to twelve men). In addition to optical observation and communications equipment, a power unit, ration and ammunition storage, its main armament normally consisted of machine guns, an automatic grenade launcher, and sometimes, a static directional flame-

The Führer on a pre-war inspection of the Westwall visits a newly constructed bunker. Many such fortifications still exist on the east bank of the Sauer River. Right: *Hitler is reputed to have visited this same bunker prior to the Second World War.*

thrower for close defense. Again, this bunker was probably disguised as a garden house by means of a mock wooden front structure camouflaged with natural overgrowth and had overlapping fields of fire with smaller neighboring *C-Werk* type pillboxes.

According to a local eyewitness, Hitler, visited here while on an inspection tour of the Westwall in the Eifel around 22-28 August 1938. He is said to have stopped briefly to visit this very bunker and from its top, took a look into Luxembourg.

After the German invasion of Luxembourg on 10 May 1940 and throughout the Wehrmacht's ensuing campaign in the West, (*'Fall Gelb'* – 'Plan Yellow'), this structure lost its military importance. In August 1944 the Germans hastily re-occupied and armed it, when alarming news of the American advance made it obvious that Wallendorf was once again to become the front line. During the year of occupation, the Westwall had lost its significance and the bunkers stripped of their weapons systems. Lack of proper maintenance meant that communications lines, power units and ventilation equipment were in poor condition when the Americans hit the Westwall in the fall of 1944.

On 14 September 1944, after a four to five hour artillery preparation, mechanised elements of Combat Command Reserve, 5th Armored Division supported by troops of the 112th Infantry Regiment attacked to seize a bridgehead across the Sauer in order to probe the Westwall defenses in the direction of Bitburg. Luxembourgers escorting the Americans informed them of this bunker's existence so they shelled it with 155mm projectiles. The shelling ripped off the bunker's natural camouflage leaving it exposed to observation by the attackers. Heavy fighting in and around Wallendorf and subsequently the neighboring villages continued until 23 September, when, lacking adequate logistics and flank protection, the US task force had to withdraw. It had suffered sizeable casualties as a result of constant counterattacks by various German armoured and infantry elements, which were, then globally under the command of either 1st SS Panzerkorps or LXXX Armeekorps. Needless to say, the town of Wallendorf was almost completely wiped out by artillery fire and strafing by fighters of the 9th US Air Force.

Still today there are myths (primarily) on the American side concerning the unconfirmed story of Wallendorf civilians waving white flags from their houses to lure the Americans into a trap. Another story mentions the 'Ghost of Wallendorf' – a woman in white clothes directing artillery fire by moving from target to target. On the other hand, Nazi propaganda then alleged that the 'American Murderers' deliberately wiped out Wallendorf and its inhabitants as a powerful message that the German soldier must never yield to protect the homeland.

The Panzerwerk C *pillbox at Wallendorf. It served as a medium artillery shell-proof shelter for front-line observation teams.*

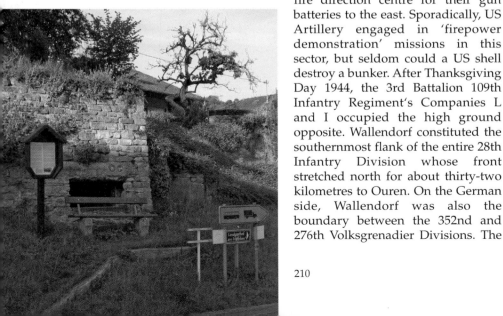

After the American withdrawal from the German side of Wallendorf, the Germans used this bunker as a fire direction centre for their gun batteries to the east. Sporadically, US Artillery engaged in 'firepower demonstration' missions in this sector, but seldom could a US shell destroy a bunker. After Thanksgiving Day 1944, the 3rd Battalion 109th Infantry Regiment's Companies L and I occupied the high ground opposite. Wallendorf constituted the southernmost flank of the entire 28th Infantry Division whose front stretched north for about thirty-two kilometres to Ouren. On the German side, Wallendorf was also the boundary between the 352nd and 276th Volksgrenadier Divisions. The

276th commander, *Generalmajor* Kurt Moehring was killed on 18 December near Beaufort when his staff car was ambushed by American troops.

Return to Wallendorf and take second road on the right uphill (following star markers) for about 400 metres. Here on the left side of the small road to Ammeldingen there is yet another signpost for a bunker.

This bunker suffered very little in the way of shell damage, its function being an observation post over the high ground on the far bank and heights of the Our River. Further downhill on the same road are two additional *C-Werk* type bunkers, located in such a way as to protect the flanks of the present *B-Werk*. As usual, all three were connected by underground telephone and wire equipment.

As can be seen, the service entrance was always in the rear side of the bunker, with a machine gun mounted in a side armour plate gun port, to protect the heavy entrance door. Of special interest are also the concrete bullet deflector housing the machine-gun mount, as well as the air vents of the bunker's ventilation system. Through steel tubes imbedded in the wall, grenades could be thrown outside from the interior, where the steep incline trench around the backside of the bunker would increase the concussion and fragmentation effects of the explosion.

Inside, the bunker has several compartments that could be sealed off with additional gas-tight doors. At the time of writing, several wartime inscriptions can still be seen. A nearby spring and cistern provided drinking water by means of a pump.

In mid-September, incoming units of the US 5th Armored Division knew of its existence thanks to sketches made by a Luxembourg engineer earlier in the war and from which the

This B-Werk bunker is preserved as a timeless and silent testimony to the second World War by the community and tourist office in Wallendorf. (At the time of writing had become overgrown and can be inaccessible after heavy rain)

Americans drew vital intelligence. Shelling ripped off its natural camouflage exposing the concrete structure and the Americans no longer considered it a threat. In spite of this, German soldiers continued to occupy it prior to the Bulge, entering at sunset and leaving at dawn. On one occasion, an American reconnaissance patrol became engaged in close-quarter fighting after clashing with a German patrol near this bunker. American artillery regularly fired

Throughout the Battle of the Bulge this bunker, just south of Gentingen, served as a Company Command Post of the 352nd Volksgrenadier Division.

propaganda rounds across the Our River in attempts to weaken the combat morale of the Westwall defenders in efforts to get them to run over and surrender.

> *Pass through Ammeldingen in the direction of Gentingen and about 500 metres before reaching the village stop by another bunker on the right side of the road.*

As can clearly be seen here, this bunker on the outskirts of Gentingen, had a larger gun port facing the narrow road as well as the banks of the Our River. Originally conceived to house a 37mm anti-tank gun, like others in the area it was stripped of its gun after the campaign in 1940. According to eyewitness narrative, German Volksgrenadiers manned the bunker prior to the start of the attack in preparation for their crossing of the Our River. In his book *The Battle of the Bulge In Luxembourg* (Volume 1) Roland Gaul included the story of 17 year old Private Schmäschke who served as a runner with Grenadier Regiment 916 of the 352nd Volksgrenadier Division.

He told of his memories of bunker life shortly before they received their attack order:

'The company commander took our sealed message envelopes at the bunker; they included detailed maps of our sector. A tense silence

prevailed as we handed him a small stack of pamphlets they had given us at battalion headquarters. Printed on red paper was a daily order to the soldiers of the Western Front, signed by OB West, Field Marshal von Runstedt. It said roughly: "Soldiers of the western front. From the North Sea to the Swiss border, an advance such as the world has never seen has begun. I expect obedience and fulfilment of duty from you to the last; you sense it all, we are gambling everything! It is time to turn the war around." The peaceful silence of the bunker was now replaced by restless muttering. There were even comrades who broke out in wild euphoria. The company commander ordered me to pass the attack order to all lieutenants and lower-rank leaders of the individual platoons by telephone. After half an hour, everyone had assembled. A discussion inside the bunker with the artillery fire-control officer followed. The objective of the attack was made known, as was the time for the crossing of the Our River. Then we had a hot meal which some of the men ghoulishly called our hangman's meal. Our iron rations were distributed and checked. Some of the men turned to their liquor ration to raise their spirits. Then, the soldiers began to check their assault-packs; everything non-essential was left at the bunker. Hand grenades, Panzerfausts and extra small arms ammunition were passed out again and we had to lie down and rest while fully dressed. Now we knew that was it – the unavoidable! The last hours before something we couldn't change, were a strange time for us. It had a numbing effect upon us. Our minds were cleared, resulting in a terrible emptiness. No thoughts of home or family. I could have screamed, and at the same time I knew that it would have been senseless. Other soldiers crawled inside themselves as if they could escape everything, but there was no escape. The morning of 16 December came inexorably. We were to be awakened at 04.00am but that didn't prove necessary since nobody slept. Shortly after 04.00am, we left the bunker and silently climbed down the mined trail in direction of the river.'
NB: Friederich Schmäschke participated in the heavy fighting on the Hoesdorf Plateau opposite the bunker and was wounded on 18 December in the afternoon in Longsdorf, Luxembourg, only four kilometres from here.

Drive into Gentingen stopping by the small footbridge that spans the Our River (adjacent to the small chapel).

At this very spot where today's small bridge spans the Our River to link Germany and Luxembourg, German army engineers constructed an improvised heavy infantry bridge, capable of bearing the weight of smaller armoured vehicles and artillery prime movers. Prior to the attack of 16 December, terrain reconnaissance had indicated that, because of the gently sloping bank on the other side, this was definitely the best location for a heavy infantry bridge in this sector. The bridge was also intended to carry the 352nd Volksgrenadier Division artillery, (partially horse-drawn) and the 18-ton 'Hetzer' tank destroyers and other tracked vehicles.

Normally, the Our River is less than three feet deep, but in December 1944 it was heavily swollen as a result of heavy rain earlier in the month. According to available statistics it was then five to seven feet deep, the depth and fast-moving current thus prohibiting the movement of vehicles across the river.

In the wake of the initial thirty minute long artillery barrage, the 352nd Volksgrenadier division's organic engineer battalion, supported by additional Corps engineer troops, began moving bridging equipment down to the east bank of the Our River. Transportation problems meant that an insufficient amount of such equipment had reached the Westwall supply points in time so it took until the evening of 17 December to get the rest forward.

Again in his book, Roland Gaul tells the story of Lieutenant Günter Stottmeister, a company commander with the 352nd Engineer Battalion:

'Unfortunately due to supply problems, the promised bridging equipment didn't arrive on time so we had to make do with a makeshift wooden bridge that would bear the weight of the Hetzers. When the artillery opened up, with effort unimaginable today, we felled trees up to fifty centimetres in diameter, with axes, two-man saws and NSU chainsaws. We moved the timber down to the river by winch and line. Actual construction of the bridge began at daybreak. Meanwhile, assault troops of the division, crossed the Our in rubber assault boats or on infantry footbridges between here and Ammeldingen then started moving forward. We could clearly hear the sound of combat on the opposite side. A first attempt to equip the bridge with a central pier made of timber, failed when the strong current tore the bridge apart even before it could be fastened in place. Since timing was critical, we dispensed with the central pier and made do with two reinforced end piers. The construction of the various components using improvised equipment and timber as the raw material went on until twilight on 16 December. At that point, we came under direct mortar fire aimed at the bridge site. This American defensive fire forced us to take shelter for about two hours. Throughout the night, the bridge building continued all night with artificial moonlight provided by heavy anti-aircraft searchlight batteries and sporadic US mortar and artillery fire. Medics transported the wounded to the battalion command post bunker. The battalion surgeon Dr. Krause, amputated torn limbs before my eyes, it was horrible.

'Around noon on 17 December, we joined together and reinforced parts of the wooden frame after pushing them over the river. To increase the bridge's carrying capacity, we put another layer of tree trunks over it since we didn't know whether or not it could hold a weight of 25 tons. That evening, we reached the stage where they declared the bridge to be in a

Generalmajor *Kut Moehring, Commander of the 276th Volksgrenadier Division, died on 17 December 1944 on the outskirts of Beaufort on a trip back from visiting his troops. The Division Chaplain retrieved his cap, ear-muffs, belt and leather map case from the shot up VW 82 in which Moehring and three of his staff had died. He returned these to the General's family in 1994. The General's son, a retired Bundeswehr officer, donated his entire uniform to the National Museum of Military History in Diekirch.* (Courtesy Roland Gaul).

state of readiness so the first Hetzer rolled slowly across the makeshift structure and it held. Others followed, then several RSO tractor units with anti-tank and artillery pieces in tow. Much of our engineer transport was badly damaged by incoming American fire so we had few vehicles left with which to move our equipment as we advanced. All through 18 December other units of the division followed with their heavy equipment, mainly artillery pieces, mostly of the horse-drawn type, a few full-tracked vehicles, supply trucks and the infantry field kitchens. Given

the importance of holding this bridge open as a supply route for the division, what remained operational of the 352nd Engineer Battalion stayed in Gentingen to secure it using only mortars and machine-guns.'
A little further upstream at the small town of Roth an der Our, the 5th Pioneer Battalion of the 5th Fallschirmjäger Division completed a similar but more elaborate bridge on 18 December bringing the divisional assault guns and division artillery across the Our. In early and mid-January 1945, American artillery and fighter aircraft constantly harassed both bridge sites. Although both bridges were damaged, under constant repair they remained operational until the latter part of January 1945 as German troops withdrew east across the Our to take up new defensive positions behind the Westwall.

Return to the centre of Wallendorf-Pont crossing back over the river and drive into Kleinreisdorf and about 500 metres further on turning right in the direction of Hoesdorf. At the first intersection turn left looking out for another white star sign on the right a little further on.
This is number 1 Panel of the 'Promenade du Souvenir'.

After the loss of the Wallendorf bridgehead in late September 1944, remaining smaller troop elements of 5th US Armored Division established observation/listening posts on the Hoesdorf Plateau. At an average altitude of 380 meters, these observation posts offered a good view over the north bank of the Our River and into the Westwall. American troops while remaining alert, found time for much needed rest and recuperation during which time, some of them using knives or bayonets, carved their names, addresses, girl-friends' names or states on nearby beach trees. Although many of the wartime trees have long since disappeared, two remain as silent tokens of the American presence on the plateau. Others nearby still sport signs of damage by shell fragments or small arms fire.

Return in the direction of Hoesdorf finally stopping just before you enter the village.
From here, those wishing to do so can follow the Promenade du Souvenir circuit using the map, which is available from the Tourist Office in nearby Reisdorf. With its extension on the Wallendorf side, the entire circuit covers a distance of +/-seventeen kilometres.

After the January 1945 operations in northern Luxembourg, the 80th US Infantry Division took up positions parallel to the Sauer River as of 1 February. German units in this area, especially remnants of the battle-weary 352nd Volksgrenadier Division, having withdrawn from the Sauer River valley and bridgehead, managed to occupy most of the bunkers and pillboxes on the east bank and high ground across the Our River.

American GIs question a group of very young German POWs from a Lutwaffe flak unit.

For about a week, organic elements of the US 80th Division spent their time patrolling the West Bank of the Our and preparing to cross the river to assault the Westwall. More specifically, the division's 319th Infantry Regiment was to attack in the Hoesdorf-Wallendorf sector, whereas the 318th Infantry was to pass through the 3rd Battalion of the 319th to tie in from a jump-off line near Bettendorf. The division's 317th Infantry was to remain as division reserve in Diekirch.

In the early morning hours of 7 February 1945, the 1st Battalion of the 319th Infantry moved forward under cover of darkness, from its assembly area at Kleinreisdorf to the vicinity of the Our River north of Wallendorf. Around 10:00 a.m., the 2nd Battalion 319th, prior to forcing a crossing of the Our, closed into Hoesdorf. The battalion experienced considerable difficulty due to the high flood level of the Our, the swiftness of the current and heavy enemy artillery and rocket concentrations. Engineers in support were unable to complete construction of bridges; thus all crossings had to be made in assault boats. Units that managed to cross the river, got pinned down by heavy mortar and accurate artillery fire on the north shore of the Our.

Division alerted the 319th Infantry to make a crossing early on the morning of 8 February, so troops began moving from their assembly area at Bettendorf into Moestroff and Kleinreisdorf preparatory to crossing. The regiment's 3rd

Battalion started to move to its crossing site but at about 06:00a.m.the attack failed when German artillery fire wrecked the assault boats. The Americans brought forward additional assault boats but two subsequent crossings at 09.00 a.m. and 4.00 p.m. also failed. It was only on 9 February that elements of the 319th Infantry managed to cross the Our near Wallendorf and secure a hold after repulsing attacks by enemy infantry. Units of the 1st and 2nd Battalions assisted in mopping up the high ground Northeast of Wallendorf and protected the north flank of the bridgehead.

On 11 February the 319th Infantry was able to assemble all its troops in an area approximately one kilometre northwest of the confluence of the Our and Sauer after heavy fighting over two days to clear pillboxes, other pockets of resistance and expand its bridgehead to the north and east. Close artillery and mortar support proved invaluable during these operations and on 13-14 February the regiment continued clearing pillboxes north of Wallendorf as well as near Ammeldingen.

Private First Class Robert Harmon was a member of the anti-tank platoon of the Regimental Headquarters Company of the 319th Infantry and as such assigned to patrolling and combat missions in a bazooka team. He told Roland Gaul of his memories:

'None of us had a clear idea of what we were about to attempt. We were told we would make an assault crossing of the Our into the Westwall forts and could expect heavy machine-gun, mortar and artillery fire. We had no experience of working with the plywood assault boats, each of which was quite heavy, but large enough to carry up to ten men together with their weapons and gear. We made an 'approach march' of a few kilometres from some nearby village through the forest under cover of darkness. Unfortunately, just as we organised the final approach toward Hoesdorf, German artillery came in causing a number of casualties. This was not good for morale.

'When we reached the area just above the village of Hoesdorf, where our engineers had placed the assault boats we found that up to half a dozen of these heavy boats were frozen together. We pried them apart and organized soldiers into boat teams. Getting the boats away from where they had been dumped proved a nerve-wrecking chore as more than one GI got his fingers or hand caught between boats as we tried to separate them.

'For my boat crew, the assault that night failed. Shells came in when we got to the river; boats capsized in the icy water and one could hear the cries of wounded drowning men as their equipment dragged them under the water. We were in Hoesdorf for two or three days, I'm not sure. Finally, the division commander arranged for some medium and heavy mortars (81mm and 4.2" chemical mortars) to 'zero in' on the Westwall forts with special attention to the pillbox escape and exit stairways on the German

Security first!

Soldiers of th 28th Division!

For the third time you made your bad experience at the „Siegfried-Line" and it was a big failure. Do you remember what happened to your Inf. Regiment 112 at Wallendorf?

And after that you had to stand the fights in the Wood of Hürtgen where you had to do some „victory-business" for your Präsident's latest Election. You attacked twice and it was of no use. Near to Vossnack your Regiment 112 has been nearly annihilated and also the Regiments 109 and 110 have lost a whole lot of good sports.

Than you have been replaced by the 8th Division and they promised you some time of rest and recreation. They told you that Germany was going to quit. What a nice idea! Come and see yourself!

And now? All what see now is only the beginning, of the migthy German Offensive. Once more you are near to Wallendorf and Wallendorf will be your fate.

German propaganda leaflet aimed at demoralizing GIs of Major General Norman D. Cota's 28th Infantry Division. Both sides engaged in such attempts to undermine the morale of the opposing forces.

side of the hill opposite Hoesdorf. This took at least one full day, then some self-propelled 155mm guns rolled into Hoesdorf at dawn firing 100-pound shells and finished off the pillboxes in a few hours. They fired co-axial .50 calibre tracer rounds until the Germans closed the gun ports on their bunkers. Then, the 155mm would fire, usually one round – end of story! I do not think they fired more than one round at any one fort. The range was short and the shells were accurate. When a high explosive shell burst inside a bunker, everyone inside died.

'As we waited in the houses in Hoesdorf, to make the crossings, there was a good deal of shelling on both sides. There were a number of Quad 50s (4x.50 calibre machine-guns) which were part of our antiaircraft units. We used these highly effective guns, along with 40mm Bofors antiaircraft guns to sweep a barrage of rounds over the German lines as suppressing fire. The night of 7-8 February 1945, the whole valley was lit by tracers, the crash of artillery and the usual mysterious flashes of light, which sweep over battlefields.

'We finally crossed the river downstream at Wallendorf, late in the day and in the dark then proceeded up the hill and into some small village beyond the river and Wallendorf. Somewhere up there, in Germany, I spent part of an afternoon lying on top of the rearmost Westwall bunker, talking to the German troops inside. We were trying to get them to surrender. There was a German mortar in the area, probably firing from a small patch of woods a few hundred yards from where we were. When we heard the shells in the mortar tube, we would scurry off the bunker and into shallow foxholes scraped in the dirt around the construction. Our usual argument to the German soldiers inside was simple: "Der krieg ist verloren"(The war is lost). They finally emerged and surrendered. Another GI and I marched them down the hill into some sort of regimental POW area.

'I was anxious to be one of the guards taking them to a POW concentration point, because we all knew that there would be a chance of a hot meal at regimental headquarters and that's what happened!'

Return to Diekirch to spend the rest of the day in the magnificent National Museum of Military History located on the left side of the main road-leading north out of town in a former brewery.

This museum is without a doubt, the very finest example of a balanced, impartial and objective representation of the historical facts of the Battle of the Bulge to be found on the entire battlefield.

Address:
10 Bamertal
L-9209 Diekirch
Luxembourg.

Tel (352) 808908 or (352) 804719
Website: **www.mnhm.lu/**
Email: **info@mnhm.lu**

Suggested Reading:
MacDonald: Chapters 7 and 17.
Cole: Chapter 9.
Gaul: Volumes 1 + 2 *'The Battle of the Bulge In Luxembourg'.*

MILITARY CEMETERIES

After the battle, Graves Registration units began the complex task of recovering and burying casualties. In the years following World War Two, families in the United States were given the option of leaving their loved ones in Europe or having their remains returned to the United States for burial. This resulted in about two thirds being repatriated and those remaining in Europe were then buried in designated US Military Cemeteries. American casualties from the Bulge buried in Belgium lie in one of two cemeteries at either Henri-Chapelle or Neuville En Condroz while those killed in Luxembourg and the extreme south-east of Belgium are buried in Hamm, Luxembourg. British casualties of the battle lie buried in a British and Commonwealth war graves cemetery at Hotton, Belgium and unlike their American allies, the British did not repatriate the remains of men killed in action.

German casualties are buried in a number of locations. Some of those killed in the opening stages of the battle were buried in small military plots in German civilian cemeteries near the German border with Belgium and Luxembourg, such as that in Stadtkyll, Germany. The majority of Germans killed in the Bulge are buried in a large German military cemetery located near Lommel, near the Dutch border north of Liège. Two smaller German cemeteries can be found at Recogne, near Bastogne, Belgium, and at Sandweiler near Hamm, Luxembourg.

Information about the location of graves in any American military cemetery can be obtained by writing to:

The American Battle Monuments Commission
Courthouse Plaza II Suite 500
2300 Clarendon Boulevard
Arlington, VA 22201   U.S.A.
Telephone: (703) 696 6897

Queries about the British and Commonwealth cemeteries should be addressed to:
CWGC
2 Marlow Road, Maidenhead
Berkshire SL6 7DX   UK.
Tel: International + 1628 634221   Fax : International + 1628 771208

Information about German cemeteries can be obtained from:
Volksbund Deutsche Kriegsgräber – Fürsorge
Bundesgeschäftsstekke
Werner Hilpert Str. 2
D-3500 Kassel

LUXEMBOURG AMERICAN MILITARY CEMETERY

Troops of the U.S. 5th Armored Division liberated Luxembourg City on 10 September 1944. On 29 December 1944, just 13 days after the German offensive in the Ardennes began; this site in nearby Hamm (close to the airport) was chosen as a temporary battlefield cemetery. After the war, this temporary cemetery was re-designated as a permanent shrine, the only American Military Cemetery in the Grand Duchy of Luxembourg, along with 13 others on foreign soil. Control of the cemetery passed from the U.S. Army's Graves Registration Command to the American Battle Monuments Commission in December 1949. After upgrading the infrastructure and enhancement of the grounds, the cemetery was dedicated on 4 July 1960. Architects for the cemetery were Keally and Patterson of New York City; the landscape architect was Alfred Geiffert Jr., also of New York City. Approximately one quarter million people visit it annually, 100,000 of whom are Americans. The cemetery is entered between tall iron gates, each weighs well over a ton and bears gilded laurel wreathes, the ancient award for valor. Each gate pylon bears, in relief, 13 stars representing the 13 original states. Gilded bronze eagles, the national emblem, surmount the pillars. Low curving stone walls, backed by evergreen, outline the entrance.

To the left of the entrance is the visitors' building. It is faced with Virginia creeper, which suffuses the stone with brilliant red in autumn. Inside is a guest register for those who wish to record their visit. Restrooms and easy chairs are available for visitors' convenience. A register for those buried at the cemetery is maintained in the office as well as those buried at other American Military Cemeteries Overseas. Records are not available here for those who were repatriated to the United States after the war, at the request of the next-of-kin.

From the Visitors' Building may be seen the Memorial Chapel, a 50 foot tall rectangular structure built of Valore stone quarried in central France. The dedication on the east wall reads:

In proud remembrance of the achievement of her sons and in humble tribute to their sacrifices this memorial has been erected by the United States of America.

Above the dedication is the Great Seal of the United States. This same dedicatory inscription, in French and the Luxembourg coat of arms is on the west wall. The Memorial Chapel has two large bronze doors bearing eight gilded panels, each symbolizing a different military virtue. Above the doors a 23 foot sculpture of the Angel of Peace is carved out of Swedish Orchid red granite. The angel's right hand is raised in blessing while the left holds a laurel wreath.The Memorial Chapel is non-denominational. Visitors may stop here to meditate or pray. The alter is of Bleu Belge marble from Belgium and bears the text from St. John, 10:28

I give unto them eternal life and they shall never perish.

The stained glass windows behind the altar contain the insignia of the five major military commands, which operated in the region: 12th Army Group, 1st and 3rd Armies, and the 8th and 9th Air Forces. The four massive bronze lamps located in the Chapel interior illuminate the mosaic ceiling. Inset in the floor is a large bronze circular laurel wreath plaque. The interior walls are of Hauteville Perle stone from France.

In Front of the Memorial Chapel lies a cobblestone terrace. Set in granite and taken from a dedication made by General Dwight D. Eisenhower in the Golden Book at St. Paul's Cathedral, London, England, is a bronze inscription reading:

'All who shall hereafter live in freedom will be here reminded that to these men and their comrades we owe a debt to be paid with grateful remembrance of their sacrifice and with the high resolve that the cause for which they died shall live eternally'.

At the east and west sides of the terrace stand large pylons of Valore stone. The west pylon bears a map of the military operations in northwest Europe, from the Normandy landings until the war's end. The east pylon carries a map illustrating operations, which took place in this region. Inscribed on the outer face of the pylons are the names of 371 missing in action.

Looking from the terrace one sees the grave plots; 17 acres of manicured lawns divided into 9 plots framed by 30 acres of deciduous and evergreen trees. Here rest the remains of 5076 Americans who gave their lives for freedom. Among them are 23 pairs of brothers and 101 Unknowns. One hundred and eighteen stars of David mark the graves of those of Jewish faith; all others have Latin crosses. The inscription for the Unknowns reads:

'Here lies in honored glory a comrade in arms known but to God'.

All headstones are of Lasa marble quarried in Italy. The arrangement of the headstones is unusual. The rows are concentric arcs swung from a theoretical center point 500 feet behind the Chapel.

Two radial malls break the plots, each containing two fountains, which flow into three small terraced pools embellished by bronze dolphins and turtles.

General George S. Patton Jr. the Third Army Commander lies buried between the flagpoles, at the head of the grave plots. He rests here overlooking the brave soldiers of his army, thereby remaining alongside his men, as he expressly wished. His gravesite was originally among the other graves but was moved to its present location on 19 March 1947 to accommodate the many visitors. The cemetery's details are:

Luxembourg American Military Cemetery
Val du Scheid 50
L – 2517 Luxembourg
Grand Duchy of Luxembourg

Telephone: (International) +352 43 17 27
Fax: (International) +352 43 03 05

ARDENNES AMERICAN MILITARY CEMETERY

The Ardennes Military Cemetery at Neuville En Condroz just southwest of Liège was established at its present site on 8 February 1945. It served mainly as a U.S. First Army cemetery in Belgium and contains the remains of those who fell in the fighting around Aachen and during the drive to the Siegfried Line. In addition, this cemetery contains Battle of the Bulge casualties as well as U.S. Army Air Force casualties who had fallen in Germany. The cemetery site covers 90.5 acres of rolling woodland, which was once part of the domain of Baron de Torrance. The people of Belgium, through their government, gave to the United States of America the use of this land in perpetuity, in acknowledgement of gratitude for their liberation in World War II. The Congress of the United States to the American Battle Monuments Commission appropriates funds for the construction, maintenance and administration.

The liberation of Neuville-en-Condroz occurred on 6 September 1944 as a result of the U.S. 3rd Armored Division's eastward advance along the Meuse River and its occupation of Huy. The 9th Infantry Division expanded and strengthened its Meuse bridgeheads, encompassing Neuville-en-Condroz. On 8 September 1944 the 3rd Armored Division, reinforced by the 47th Infantry Regiment, 9th Division secured Liège, thereby liberating the whole area.

Following the Battle of the Bulge American troops pushed down the Roer valley. On 23 February, the First and Ninth Armies launched their assault across the river, supported by fighters and medium bombers of the Ninth Air Force, and seized the bridgeheads at Jülich and Düren. As the offensive gathered momentum, units to the south joined the advance. The First Army reached Cologne by 5 March and wheeled to the southeast. The next day, Third Army attacked north of the Moselle. Preceded by aircraft strikes that disorganized the retreating enemy, U.S. ground forces advanced rapidly. On 7 March the First Army seized the undemolished bridge over the Rhine at Remagen, then promptly established and expanded this bridgehead across the mighty Rhine River. American units then swept across Germany to meet their Soviet Allies at Torgau on the Elbe River, 377 days after the initial landings in Normandy.

Some 5,327 American casualties are buried in the Ardennes American Military Cemetery. This figure is subject to change due to the fact that this cemetery is the only one remaining open for additional burial of remains, which still might be recovered in Europe. Some 5,300 others, originally buried in the area, were repatriated to the United States at the request of the next-of-kin. Those who gave their lives in the service of their country came from almost every state in the Union as well as from the District of Columbia. Some 791 headstones mark the graves of Unknowns. Among the headstones are 11 pairs of brothers buried side by side. There are also 3 cases of 2 identified airmen buried in single graves.

Local contractors following plans drawn by the architects Reinhard, Hoffmeister and Walquist of New York built the Memorial. Construction of the cemetery and memorial was completed in 1960. Dedication took place on 11 July 1960 in the presence of His Royal Highness (now King) Albert of Belgium and numerous civic and military personalities form the United States and Belgium, including the personal representative of the President of the United States.

On the south façade of the Memorial is a sculpture depicting the American eagle, which is 17 feet high. The three figures on the lower right symbolize Justice, Liberty and Truth. At the lower left are 13 stars representing the 13 original colonies. Paul C. Jennewein of New York City is responsible for the sculptural arrangement while Jean Juge of Paris executed the work. The entrance doors, bearing the date 1941-1945, are of stainless steel, as are all the doors in the memorial. The interior walls are decorated with 3 huge marble maps made of colored glass mosaics. Bronze and chrome lettering form the topographical and military details. On the west wall are the Overall Military Operations Map Europe, Services and Supply, and on the east wall the Ardennes and Rhineland campaigns over the entrance door on the south wall. Dean Cornwell of New York City also designed the 24 white marble panels depicting functions of combat and Service of Supply, framing the maps.

To the rear of the Memorial, is a non-denominational chapel at the disposition of all visitors who wish to meditate. The altar is a large block of white Carrara marble. On the 12 slabs of polished Danube grey granite flanking the east and west sides of the Memorial, are inscribed the names of 462 members of the U.S. Armed Forces listed as missing in this region and who 'sleep in unknown graves'. (The remains of one of those listed, Private First Class Alphonse M. Sito, a machine-gunner with Company B, 394th Infantry of the 99th Infantry Division, were recovered in September 1988 and subsequently buried in Maryland). The missing soldiers are from 45 states of the Union as well as the District of Columbia.

The north steps behind the Memorial afford a magnificent view of the burial area whose four plots are laid out in the form of a huge Greek cross. The headstones are of Lasa marble, a Star of David for those of the Jewish faith and a Latin cross for all others. At the East End of the central traverse path is a bronze figure symbolizing American Youth, designed by Paul C. Jannewein and cast by Bruno Bearzi of Florence, Italy. At the bottom of the large intersecting footpath stands a 75 feet high flagpole complex built of Danube grey granite. Richard K. Weber of Roslyn, Long Island, designed the setting and horticultural details.

Ardennes American Military Cemetery
Route Condroz 164
4121 Neuville-en-Condroz
Belgium
Telephone: (International) +32 41 71 42 87.
Fax: (International) +32 41 72 03 29.

HENRI-CHAPELLE AMERICAN MILITARY CEMETERY

The Henri-Chapelle American Military Cemetery and Memorial, covering 57 acres, was established in September, 1944 by the 1st Infantry Division of the First U.S. Army, as a combat burial site then named the 'Jayhawk' cemetery. The cemetery and Memorial were completed in 1960 and dedicated during ceremonies on 9 July the same year.

This cemetery commemorates 7,989 American soldiers who died during two periods of fighting; the First Army's drive in September of 1944 through northern France into Belgium, Holland, Luxembourg and Germany, as well as the Battle of the Bulge. Some were formerly buried at Fosse (near Namur) and Recogne (near Bastogne and today a German cemetery), which contained the remains of 2,700 Americans who gave their lives in the Bulge.

The roll call of valiant U.S. divisions, in addition to the 1st, include: the 2nd, 4th, 5th, 9th, 28th, 30th, 35th, 70th, 75th, 78th, 83rd, 84th, 87th, 89th, 95th, 99th, 100th, 102nd, 104th and the 106th. The 99th bore the full brunt of the 6th Panzer Army attack, and along with the 1st, 2nd and 9th Divisions held the vital North Shoulder and the Elsenborn Ridge. The 2nd and 3rd Armored Divisions, which trapped some 40,000 enemy soldiers in the vicinity of Mons then along with the 4th, 6th, 7th, 9th, 10th and 11th Armored Divisions fought in the Bulge The 5th Armored, the first American unit across the German border, the 8th and 12th Armored Divisions and aircrew shot down on missions over Belgium and Germany.

Buried there are the remains of soldiers from the then 48 states, the District of Columbia, Panama and England. In 33 cases, two brothers rest side-by-side and in one instance, three brothers. Some 94 stones mark the graves of Unknowns, 138 Stars of David identify those of the Jewish faith, while Latin crosses mark all others. The cemetery enshrines the remains of three Congressional Medal of Honor recipients. Brigadier General Frederick W. Castle, U.S. Army Air Corps, the highest ranking officer buried in this cemetery, was shot down on 24 December, 1944, in this vicinity, while leading the greatest bomber formation in military history.

West of the highway, which passes through the cemetery, is the overlook and one of the flagpoles. The roadway to the Overlook is lined with Linden trees and provides a beautiful view of the rolling countryside with distant church steeples and the Plateau de Herve.

Landscaping features include hawthorn, yew and boxwood hedges as well as rhododendron beds. In front of the Colonnade are masses of pink and white polyantha roses. The grass terrace, surrounded by clipped box hedging enhances the beauty of the Memorial. The weeping willows and conifers at each end of the Memorial provide massive foliage. The ramps leading to the burial area (beware the steps!) are flanked with clipped box hedges whose adjacent beds are planted with spreading juniper. In the grave plots are groups of beech, birch, hornbeam and yew. Climbing roses and boxwood are grown in front of the perimeter wall. Rose beds and hornbeam trees decorate the Wall of Honor. The cemetery proper is framed with mixed tree plantings and masses of rhododendrons.

The Memorial consists of the Chapel (north end) and the combined Visitors' Museum building (south end) connected by a Colonnade of 12 pairs of rectangular pylons. On the pylons are inscribed the names of 450 missing in action whose remains were never recovered or identified. Also carved on these pylons are the seals of the states and territories. In the Colonnade are 13 stars of golden glass representing the 13 original colonies. East of the Colonnade is a wide terrace with ramps leading to the graves area. The exterior of the Memorial is of Massangis limestone from the Cote D'Or, France. The Colonnade, Chapel and Museum are paved with St. Gothard granite from Switzerland.

The Chapel doors are in bronze, while the altar is of Belgian Blue and Italian green D'Issorie marble. The pews are of walnut and along with the cross were intentionally designed to be off-center. In front of the graves area is a bronze statue of an archangel bestowing a laurel branch upon the heroic dead for whom he expresses special approbation to the almighty. The graves area is divided into 8 plots lettered 'A' to 'H', separated by the broad axial mall and longitudinal grass paths. The headstones are arranged in gentle arcs, sweeping across a broad green lawn sloping gently downhill, overlooking the rolling wooded ground to the east. The central mall terminates in a wall-enclosed flagpole plaza, backed by a coppice of oak and spruce trees.

The architects for the cemetery and Memorial were Holabird, Root and Burgee while the landscaping architect was Franz Lipp, all of Chicago, Illinois.

Photographs of the cemetery may be taken but if they are to be used for commercial purposes, prior approval must be obtained from the European Office of the American Battle Monuments Commission. Information concerning grave decorations may be obtained from the cemetery office.

Henri-Chapelle American Military Cemetery
4850 Aubel
Belgium
Telephone: (International) +87 68 71 73
Fax: (International) +87 68 67 17

The American Battlefield Monuments Commission have a Website that can be viewed on:
http://**www.abmc.gov**

APPENDIX I
BATTLE CHRONOLOGY

In writing this guide to the Ardennes battlefield, the author decided to include a battle chronology of how the action unfurled with emphasis upon the role of the United States Army. Such a chronology already exists as part of the *Special Studies* series on the *US Army in World War Two*, published by the Center of Military History and compiled by Mary H. Williams. Changes made to the original text are indicated as being this author's and not those of Williams. (As marked by a*).

16 DECEMBER
12th Army Group:

Generalfeldmarschall von Runstedt opens all-out counteroffensive in the Ardennes early in the morning. Taking Americans by surprise and penetrating lines of First US Army. 6th Panzer Army on North and 5th Panzer Army on South press vigorously toward the Meuse on a broad front, former directed ultimately toward Albert Canal in Maastricht – Antwerp area and latter toward Brussels – Antwerp area. Enemy paratroopers dropped behind US lines to seize key points succeeded in disrupting communications and causing widespread confusion.

In US First Army's VII Corps area, Corps releases 1st Division to V Corps. In V Corps area, German counteroffensive hits South flank of V Corps and VII Corps line to South. 99th Division holds back enemy in Höfen area, South of Monschau, on North but outnumbered, gives ground to South and Germans penetrate almost to Büllingen. Continuing offensive to North, 2nd Division (and 395th Regimental Combat Team of 99th Division*) seize objectives in Monschau Forest. VII Corps' 106th Division (reinforced by 14th Cavalry Group), 28th Division, 9th Armored Division and North flank elements of 4th Division all fall back under enemy onslaughts. Germans drive several miles west, cutting main north/south highway between Our and Clerf Rivers, encircling Echternach and threatening St. Vith.

17 DECEMBER
12th Army Group:

Reinforcements are being sent to Ardennes sector to defend vital road centers. Two airborne divisions, 82nd and 101st, of XVIII Corps (Airborne), First Allied Airborne Army, are released from SHAEF reserve for action on Ardennes front.

US Ninth Army releases 7th Armored Division to VIII Corps and 30th Division whose zone on XIX Corps front is taken over by 29th Division to V Corps.

In First Army area, VII Corps while rounding up paratroopers and guarding against possible airborne attack, continues to press its right flank toward the Roer, 9th Division gains ground slowly just West of Düren; releases Regimental Combat Team 47 to V Corps. Corps is fully occupied holding current positions north of breakthrough and delaying German offensive, which continues to gain ground slowly toward Malmédy. 1st and 30th Divisions are getting into positions to counterattack. 26th Infantry of 1st Division is attached to 99th Division. Regimental Combat Team 47, 9th Division, assembles in Eupen area. In VIII Corps area, disorganised 14th Cavalry Group continues to fall back on North flank of Corps (*heavily outnumbered). German columns isolate two regiments (422nd and 423rd) of 106th Division in Schnee Eifel salient and push on through Heuem toward St. Vith. Elements of 7th and 9th Armored Divisions are committed to defense of St. Vith. In 28th Division zone, Germans drive almost to Wiltz. Corps releases Combat Command Reserve 9th Armored Division from reserve to block Bastogne-Trois Vierges road. 4th Division halts enemy south of Osweiler and Dickweiler, but units are isolated at a number of points. 10th Armored Division arrives in vicinity of Luxembourg City.

18 DECEMBER

In US First Army's VII Corps area, 83rd and 9th Divisions finish clearing their respective zones. Corps extends southward because of Ardennes breakthrough to take over part of V Corps zone, new boundary running from

Eupen area to the Roer River near Dedenborn. With boundary change, 8th and 78th Divisions and attachments pass to Corps control in current positions. Corps releases Combat Command A of 3rd Armored Division and 9th Division, less Regimental Combat Teams 47 and 60, to V Corps, 104th Division takes responsibility for 9th Division zone as well as its own and is reinforced by Regimental Combat Team 60. 78th Division, reinforced by 2nd Ranger Battalion and 102nd Cavalry Group, is to hold road center North Konzen and Paustenbach knoll. V Corp's mission, on its smaller front, is to stabilise line Monschau – Bütgenbach – Malmédy – Stavelot. Corps holds firmly at Bütgenbach and Elsenborn Ridge but enemy continues to move West through gap South of Bütgenbach.

Regimental Combat Team 26 reverts to 1st Division, which joins in action to keep enemy from Malmédy, combing woods near Eupen and organising perimeter defense of Waimes. 99th Division is attached to 2nd Division. Germans now hold Honsfeld and Büllingen; push into Stavelot (*Kampfgruppe Peiper). 30th Division recovers most of Stavelot northwest of the Amblève River; organises defense positions in Malmédy – Stavelot area; blunts enemy spearheads at Stoumont and Habiemont (*291st Engineer Combat Battalion). In VIII Corps area, 106th Division's encircled 422nd and 423rd Regiments try in vain to break out toward Schönberg. 7th Armored Division is too heavily engaged at St. Vith to assist with eastward push. Germans occupy Recht and cut St. Vith – Vielsalm road at Poteau but Combat Command recovers Poteau. 14th Cavalry group, which falls back to Petit Their, is transferred from 106th Division to 7th Armored Division control. 28th Division is unable to stop enemy in its zone and becomes completely disorganised. Germans get almost to Houffalize and Bastogne; smash through roadblocks of Combat Command Reserve, 9th Armored Division, on Bastogne – St. Vith road. Troops of 4th Division and 10th Armored Division remaining South of the breakthrough are placed under Third Army command. Combat Command B, 10th Armored Division, remains with VIII Corps to help defend Bastogne; Combat Command A attacks North and East through 4th Division to Berdorf and Echternach areas. 4th Division mops up infiltrators beyond Osweiler and Dickweiler and repels thrust from Dickweiler.

19 DECEMBER
21 Army Group:
Because of the Ardennes counteroffensive, Field Marshal Montgomery abandons plan to employ 30 Corps, British Second Army, in Nijmegen area and orders it to assemble in Louvain – St. Trond – Hasselt region to hold Meuse River line.
12th Army Group:
US Ninth Army is ordered to go on the defensive.

In US First Army's area, VII Corps remains generally in place. In V Corps area, 2nd and 99th Divisions repel further attacks and start toward new defensive positions from which they will defend Elsenborn Ridge. 9th Division (Regimental Combat Team 47, which is already in Corps zone, and Regimental Combat Team 60) takes up defensive positions in 2nd Division zone, relieving elements of 2nd and 99th Divisions. 1st Division holds line East of Malmédy. Combat Command A, 3rd Armored Division, relieves 18th Infantry, 1st Division, of defense of Eupen. 30th Division holds at Stavelot and engineers blow bridge across the Amblève River there; keeps enemy (*Kampfgruppe Peiper) from Stoumont in costly battle. CCB 3rd Armored Division is attached to Corps to assist 30th Division. SVIII Airborne Corps takes responsibility for region generally South of the Amblève River, including Houffalize, key road center between St. Vith and Bastogne, with mission of holding north flank of the enemy. 82nd Airborne Division, which reverts to Corps, upon closing Werbomont relieves 30th Division troops in that region. 3rd Armored Division, less Combat Command A and Combat Command B, passes to Corps control and starts toward Hotton – Le Grand Pré area. In VII Corps area, hope of relieving beleaguered 422nd and 423rd Regiments of the 106th Division in the Schnee Eifel fades. 7th and 9th Armored Divisions aggressively defending region just east of St. Vith. 112th Infantry, 28th Division, is attached to 106th Division. 28th Division is ordered to abandon Wiltz and return to friendly lines by infiltration; withdraw from Diekirch area. 101st Airborne Division arrives at Bastogne, which enemy has almost encircled. Also employed in defense of Bastogne are Combat Command B of 10th Armored Division and remnants of Combat Command Reserve, 9th Armored Division, the latter coming under control of the 101st Airborne Division.

US Third Army forms provisional Corps from former First Army units South of the Ardennes salient, 4th Division and 10th Armored Division (Combat Command B). The Corps is to hold enemy on South flank of the penetration and plug gap existing between it and elements of 9th Armored Division near Ettelbruck. III Corps is ordered North for attack against South flank of the "Bulge". 4th Armored Division and 80th Division are being transferred to III Corps.

20 DECEMBER

21 Army Group:

Takes operational control of American forces North of Ardennes breakthrough, US Ninth and First Armies.

In US Ninth Army's XIII Corps area, 84th Division is attached to First Army and starts to Marche (Belgium). 102nd Division takes responsibility for Corps front. In XIX Corps area, 29th Division takes over defense of Corps front. 2nd Armored Division is released as army reserve.

In US First Army's VII Corps area, 5th Armored Division resumes attack toward the Roer River. Although 84th Division is attached to Corps, it is verbally attached to XVIII Corps until 22nd, pending arrival of VII Corps in new zone. In V Corps area, 2nd and 99th Divisions complete withdrawal to new defensive positions before Elsenborn Ridge and organise secondary defense line. Germans makes slight penetration in line of 99th Division west of Wirtzfeld but are sealed off and destroyed. 1st Division clears assigned region South of Eupen and contains attacks in Bütgenbach – Faymonville area. 9th Division takes over new zone on north flank of Corps. 30th Division in Malmédy – Stavelot sector, is attached to XVIII Corps. In XVIII Airborne Corps area, Combat Command B of 3rd Armored Division is attached to 30th Division and assists in attack on La Gleize and Stoumont, which enemy defends effectively. Elements of 30th Division continue to defend Stavelot and Malmédy. 3rd Armored Division (Combat Commands A + B), upon closing in Hotton area, attacks eastward to secure Manhay – Houffalize road. 82nd Airborne Division is attempting to establish contact with friendly forces in Vielsalm – St. Vith area, pushing toward Vielsalm and Hebronval.

VIII Corps units defending St. Vith (7th Armored Division, 106th Infantry Division, Combat Command B of 9th Armored Division, and 112th Infantry of 28th Division) pass to control of XVIII Corps. Enemy pressure on St. Vith is undiminished. Elements of 10th Armored Division, 101st Airborne Division, and 705th Tank Destroyer Battalion fight their way out of local encirclement on perimeter of larger encirclement of Bastogne area. 101st Airborne Division extends defensive line to west and Southwest of Bastogne, assisted by remnants of Combat Command Reserve, 9th Armored Division, and Combat Command B, 10th Armored Division, both of which are later attached to it, along with 705th Tank Destroyer Battalion and stragglers from other units. Marvie, southeast of Bastogne, is cleared in course of tank battle. Some 25 miles Southeast of Bastogne, 109th Infantry of 28th Division establishes defensive line Ettelbruck – Oberfeulen – Merzig and also has forces near Ermsdorf backing up Combat Command A of 9th Armored Division, to which it is attached. Enemy now holds Waldbillig, six miles west of Echternach. Southwest of Bastogne, 28th Division Headquarters and remnants of 110th Infantry block Neufchâteau – Bastogne highway. In effort to halt enemy, engineers block and demolish bridges as far west of Bastogne as St. Hubert. During day, operational control of Corps passes to Third Army.

12th Army Group:

In US Third Army area, III Corps moves its headquarters from Metz to Arlon (Belgium), and 4th Armored, 26th and 80th Infantry Divisions are assembling in Arlon – Luxembourg area. Elements of 4th Armored Division, push to Bastogne area and makes (*radio) contact with 101st Airborne and 10th Armored Division; are temporarily attached to VIII Corps. 80th Division takes up reserve battle positions on heights north and Northeast of Mersch. In provisional Corps area, General Patton strengthens Corps by attaching 5th Division, Combat Command A of 9th Armored Division, and Regimental Combat Team 109 of 28th Division. Combat Command A, 9th Armored Division, is further attached to 10th Armored Division. Combat Command A, 10th Armored Division, withdraws to assembly area as 4th Division moves up to take over its positions near Echternach. Tanks assist 12th Infantry of 4th Division in futile effort to relieve isolated infantry in Echternach.

21 DECEMBER

21 Army Group:

British 51st Division reinforces US NINTH Army as its zone expands. XIX Corps releases 2nd Armored Division to First Army; takes over VII Corps sector at 24:00. Under its command, in current positions, are 104th, 83rd, 5th Armored (Combat Command Reserve), 8th and 78th Divisions, from north to south, XII Corps takes over former XIX Corps front and 29th Division. XVI Corps releases 75th Division to First Army.

In US First Army area, Regimental Combat Team 60, 9th Division, is detached from 104th Division and moves to Ouffet (Belgium). Corps is to operate next against north flank of German salient. In V Corps area, 9th Division, reinforced by 102nd Cavalry Group, round up enemy in Monschau area. 99th Division breaks up enemy formations with artillery fire. Combat Command A, 3rd Armored Division, reverts to parent unit and moves from Eupen to Werbomont area. 1st Division contains further attacks toward Elsenborn Ridge. In XVIII Airborne Corps area, Combat Command B, of 7th Armored Division withdraws from St. Vith at night; Combat Command A contains attack near Poteau; Combat Command Reserve clears Vielsalm – Poteau road. Combat Command B, 9th Armored Division, is attached to 7th Armored Division. 82nd Airborne Division's 504th Parachute Infantry clears Cheneux and Monceau, forcing the enemy back across the Amblève River. 505th Parachute Infantry improves positions from the Salm at Trois Ponts to vicinity of Grand Halleux; 508th and 325th Glider Infantry occupy line Vielsalm – Hebronval – Regné, making no contact with the enemy; Division makes contact with friendly troops in the St. Vith area. 30th Division is unable to take La Gleize and Stoumont; continues to defend Stavelot and Malmédy. 3rd Armored Division, to which Combat Command A reverts, contains enemy at Hotton; continues efforts to secure Manhay – Houffalize road. 84th Division is organising perimeter defense of Marche.

12th Army Group:

In US Third Army's VIII Corps area, enemy lays siege to Bastogne and extends westward; crosses Neufchâteau – Bastogne highway in force. Ammunition and food supplies at Bastogne garrison are running low. Provisional Corps troops are transferred to XII Corps. Combat Command A, 10th Armored Division, tries unsuccessfully to recover Waldbillig. Combat Command A of 9th Armored Division and Combat Command Reserve of 10th Armored Division are formed into Combat Command X, 10th Armored Division. 4th Division repels attacks toward Consdorf and Osweiler; is out of communication with troops in Echternach. Regimental Combat Team 10, 5th Division, is attached to 4th Division. XII Corps opens forward Command Post in Luxembourg. 35th Division's relief is completed.

22 DECEMBER

In US First Army's V Corps area, Germans breach lines of 1st Division at Bütgenbach and of 9th Division in Monschau Forest but are unable to exploit their success. In XVIII Airborne Corps area, withdrawal of delaying forces in St. Vith area through 82nd Airborne line begins. 82nd Airborne Division is under strong pressure along the Salm River in Trois Ponts area. 30th Division column captures Stoumont. 3rd Armored Division maintains roadblocks at strategic points and attempts to clear Hotton area. VII Corps, reconstituted to consist of 75th and 84th Infantry Divisions and 2nd Armored Division, is rapidly concentrating in Durbuy – Marche area of Belgium and organising defensive line. 84th Division completes perimeter defense of Marche and establishes counter reconnaissance screen to south and Southwest.

12th Army Group:

In US Third Army's area, Brigadier General McAuliffe, acting Commanding General, 101st Airborne Division, refuses German demand for surrender of Bastogne. Garrison is holding under heavy fire and sharp attacks. 28th Division troops blocking road Southwest of Bastogne at Vaux-les-Rosières are forced back to Neufchâteau. US ammunition shortage is becoming acute and weather conditions prevent aerial re-supply. III Corps begins northward drive to relieve Bastogne. On west, 4th Armored Division columns reach Burnon and Martelange. 26th Division, to right, marches about sixteen miles before making contact with enemy in Rambrouch–Grosbous area. After 5-mile advance, 80th Division runs into stiff resistance at Merzig and Ettelbruck but clears most of Merzig. XII Corps, in new zone along east border of Luxembourg, attacks with 4th

Division Southwest of Echternach but is held to small gains. 10th Armored Division maintains positions Northeast of Luxembourg and straightens lines. 5th Division closes north of Luxembourg. 35th Division moves from Puttelange to Metz. 2nd Cavalry Group assembles near Vatimont. In XX Corps area, 90th Division completes withdrawal of Dillingen bridgehead.

23 DECEMBER

In US First Army's V Corps area, 1st Division restores line at Bütgenbach, as does 9th Division in Monschau Forest. Regimental Combat Team 60 reverts to 9th Division. 5th Armored Division is attached to Corps. In XVIII airborne Corps area, 7th Armored Division, remnants of the 106th Infantry Division, Regimental Combat Team 112 of 28th Division, and Combat Command B of the 9th Armored Division withdraw from St. Vith area (through the 'Grand Bois' near Commanster) as planned, moving through lines of 82nd Airborne Division. Assault on La Gleize by 30th Division is unsuccessful. 3rd Armored Division passes to control of VII Corps in place. In VII Corps area, 3rd Armored Division attempts to clear Hotton – Soy road but makes little headway; loses key road junction Southeast of Manhay. Germans penetrate 84th Division positions between Hargimont and Rochefort. 4th Cavalry Group, with mission of screaming along Lesse River, organises defensive positions between Ciney and Marche. Combat Command A, 2nd Armored Division, organises Ciney for defense and starts toward Buissonville. 75th Division, in Corps reserve, establishes outposts along the Ourthe River.

12 Army Group:

In US Third Army area, improving weather conditions permit extensive air support, particularly in Bastogne area, where supplies are dropped to the garrison. In VIII Corps area, enemy continues to press in slowly on Bastogne. In III Corps area, Combat Command A of 4th Armored Division clears Martelange and continues two miles up Arlon – Bastogne highway while Combat Command B, on secondary road, drives to Chaumont, from which it is ousted in counterattack; Combat Command Reserve begins drive toward Bigonville (Luxembourg). 26th Division's 104th Infantry clears Grosbous and pushes on to Dellen and Buschrodt and 328th occupies Wahl. 80th Division seizes Heiderscheid and holds it against counterattacks; finishes clearing Merzig; takes Kehmen; continues to battle enemy at Ettelbruck. Roadblocks on Division's south flank are turned over to XII Corps. In XII Corps area, attack Southwest of Echternach still gains little ground. 10th Armored Division continues action to shorten and improve its line. 35th Division passes to Third Army control.

24 DECEMBER

21 Army Group:

In British Second Army's 30 Corps area, 29th Armored Brigade clashes with enemy spearheads between Dinant and Ciney.

In US First Army's V Corps area, 1st Division repels another enemy bid for Bütgenbach. 5th Armored Division closes in Eupen area and is held in reserve. In XVIII Airborne area, 30th Division overruns La Gleize and releases Combat Command B, 3rd Armored Division. 82nd Airborne Division is under strong pressure in Manhay area; loses Manhay, although elements of 7th Armored Division are pressed into action in that region. 17th Airborne Division is being flown to France from England and subsequently operates under VIII Corps. In VII Corps area, Germans reduce 3rd Armored Division's roadblock at Belle Haie, on road to Manhay; Combat Command Reserve columns attacking east from Hotton and west from Soy clear Soy – Hotton road. Elements of 75th Division enter combat for the first time: Regimental Combat Teams 290 and 289 are attached respectively to Combat Command Reserve and Combat Command A, 3rd Armored Division. In 84th Division zone, Germans drive through Verdenne. Combat Command A, 2nd Armored Division reaches Buissonville; 4th Cavalry Group, attached to 2nd Armored Division to cover its assembly and maintain contact with adjacent units, makes contact with British at Sorinnes.

12th Army Group:

In US Third Army's Corps area, heavy fighting continues around Bastogne perimeter. The city is badly damaged by air attacks. 11th Armored Division, released from SHAEF reserve to Corps on the 23rd, is held in mobile reserve west of Meuse. Combat Engineers are guarding Meuse River line and blocking approaches to bridges. In III Corps area, Combat Command B, 4th Armored Division is meeting lively opposition south of Chaumont, as is Combat Command A at Warnack; Combat Command Reserve seizes Bigonville, 318th Infantry (-), 80th Infantry Division, is attached to 4th Armored Division. 6th Cavalry Group (Task Force Fickett) arrives from XX Corps front to guard west flank of Corps in Neufchâteau area; 6th Cavalry Reconnaissance Squadron is assigned sector between 4th Armored and 26 Infantry Divisions. 26th Division secures Rambrouch and Koetschette but is held up at Arsdorf and Hierheck. 80th Division contains determined counterattacks. In XII Corps area, 5th Division, to which Regimental Combat Team 10 has reverted, relieves left flank elements of 4th Division and attacks toward Haller and Waldbillig, making slow progress. 2nd Cavalry Group, designated Task Force Reed, relieves right flank units of 4th Division along the Moselle. Combat Command A, 10th Armored Division, captures Gilsdorf and Mostroff on Sauer River.

25 DECEMBER
21 Army Group:
In British Second Army area, 30 Corps is disposed along the west bank of the Meuse from Givet to Liège.

In US First Army area, V Corps maintains defensive positions and has only light patrol contact with enemy. In XVIII Airborne area, 82nd Airborne Division, to shorten line, withdraws from Vielsalm salient upon order, pulling back to general line Trois Ponts – Basse Bodeux – Bra – Manhay. 7th Armored Division is reinforced by Regimental Combat Team 424, 106h Division tries vainly to recover Manhay. 30th Division clears region north of the Amblève River between Stavelot and Trois Ponts. VII Corps directed to go on the defensive, conducts limited attack to stabilise right flank of First Army. 3rd Armored Division attacks toward Grandmenil and crossroads just east, which enemy has recently seized, and reaches edge of town; is establishing defensive line in Werpin – Amonines area. Task Force cut off in Marcouray radios that it is starting toward Soy through enemy territory. 84th Division recovers Verdenne, but an enemy pocket remains between there and Bourdon. Combat Command B, 2nd Armored Division, seizes Celles, blocking enemy's westward advance on Dinant; reconnoitres to Sorrines and Foy Notre Dame; Combat Command A occupies Havrenne.
12th Army Group:
In US Third Army area, VIII Corps maintains Bastogne perimeter against pressure from all sides. In III Corps area, Combat Command Reserve, moving to west flank of 4th Armored Division from Bigonville, launches surprise attack and gains road from Vaux-les-Rosières to Chaumont, Hollange and Tintange. 26th Division Task Force begins struggle for Eschdorf, gaining weak hold there; other elements of the Division clear Arsdorf. 319th Infantry, 80th Division, clears its sector to the Sauer and makes contact with the 26th Division; assisted by 317th, contains counterattacks and drives almost to Kehmen. Ettelbruck is found clear. In XII Corps area, 5th Division takes Waldbillig and Haller.

26 DECEMBER
In US First Army's area, army halts westward drive short of the Meuse. German supply lines are now overextended, and stalled armor becomes a lucrative target for aerial attacks. XVIII Airborne Corps maintains defensive positions and defeats enemy efforts to break through to the Meuse. In VII Corps area, 3rd Armored Division stabilises its front except on the left, where contact has not yet been established with 7th Armored Division; seizes Grandmenil and heights south of Soy – Hotton road. 84th Division reduces enemy pocket between Verdenne and Bourdon; hurls back enemy thrust toward Menil. 2nd Armored Division repels counterattacks in Celles area and against Havrenne and Frandeux, inflicting heavy losses on the enemy.
12th Army Group:
In US Third Army area, armored units break through to Bastogne. In III Corps area, forward tanks of Combat Command Reserve, 4th Armored Division, push through Assenois to Bastogne, but vehicles are unable to follow. 101st Airborne Division is temporarily attached to Corps. Combat Command A, 9th Armored Division, is detached from 10th Armored Division, XII Corps, and attached to 4th Armored Division for employment on west flank. 26th Division closes along the Sauer, winning Eschdorf in lively battle, and thus begins crossing. 80th Division, after clearing Scheidel, is halted in the Kehmen area and transferred in place to XII Corps.

InterCorps boundary is adjusted accordingly. 35th Division is attached to III Corps to assist in action against south flank of Ardennes salient. In XII Corps area, 5th Division improves positions in Echternach area and takes Berdorf. 6th Armored Division, transferred to Corps from XX Corps, moves into Luxembourg and relieved 10th Armored Division. Latter passes to XX Corps control. 109th Infantry reverts to 28th Division (VIII Corps) from attachment to 10th Armored Division.

27 DECEMBER
21 Army Group:
In US First Army's XVII Airborne Corps area, 30th Division maintains defensive positions while regrouping. 508th Parachute Infantry, 82nd Airborne Division, continues drive Northeast of Bra. 7th Armored Division recaptures Manhay early in day. 9th Armored Division is reinforced by 112th Infantry of 28th Division. In VII Corps area, Germans are infiltrating toward Sadzot in zone of Combat Command A, 3rd Armored Division, where front line is held by Regimental Combat Team 289. 84th Division clears pocket in Verdenne area. 2nd Armored Division columns envelop Humain and clear stubborn resistance there. 83rd Division, upon closing in Havelange area, begins relief of 2nd Armored Division.
12th Army Group:
In US Army's VIII Corps area, 17th Airborne Division takes over Meuse River sector. In III Corps area, trucks and ambulances roll into Bastogne on road opened by Combat Command Reserve, 4th Armored Division, ending siege of the city. 4th Armored Division and reinforcements from 9th Armored and 80th Infantry Divisions are broadening corridor to Bastogne and attempting to open the Arlon – Bastogne highway. From south bank of the Sauer, 35th Division attacks northward between 4th Armored Division and 26th Division, 137th Infantry taking Surre and 320th, Boulaide and Boschleiden. 26th Division pushes northward through 101st Airborne Division, clearing Mecher – Dunkrodt and Kaundorf. In XII Corps area, 80th Division checks attack in Ringel area and blocks roads north and Northeast of Ettelbruck. 6th Armored Division takes responsibility for sector south of the Sauer between Ettelbruck and Mostroff. Beaufort, north of Waldbillig, falls to 11th Infantry, 5th Division. 4th Division patrols find Echternach undefended.

28 DECEMBER

General Eisenhower and Field Marshal Montgomery meet in Hasselt (Belgium) to plan offensive.
21 Army Group:
In US First Army's V Corps area, finally enemy effort to force 1st Division from Elsenborn defenses fails. In XVIII Airborne Corps area, zone is relatively quiet. Combat Command B, 9th Armored Division and Regimental Combat Team 112 move into position to back up 3rd Armored Division and 75th Infantry Division. In VII Corps area, 75th Division, less Regimental Combat Teams 289 and 290, is attached to XVIII Corps. Germans infiltrating in sector of Combat Command A, 3rd Armored Division take Sadzot but are driven out. 83rd Division is relieving 2nd Armored Division and takes responsibility for line east of Buissonville – Rochefort; elements push into Rochefort. 2nd Armored Division regroups.
12th Army Group:
In US Third Army's VIII Corps area, 11th Armored Division is transferred to Corps from SHAEF reserve. III Corps makes limited progress against delaying opposition between Sauer and Wiltz Rivers. 35th Division continues drive on south flank of enemy salient despite very heavy fire southwest of Villers-la-Bonne-Eau. 26th Division makes slight progress toward Wiltz. Elements of 80th Division attached to 4th Armored Division revert to parent unit. 6th Armored Division is transferred to Corps from XII Corps. XII Corps is ordered on the defensive in afternoon. 80th Division repels attack for Ringel.

29 DECEMBER
21 Army Group:
In British Second Army area, 30 Corps begins relief of US 2nd Armored Division on west flank of US VII Corps.

In US First Army area, V Corps front is quiet, with both sides on the defensive. XVIII Airborne Corps zone is also virtually static. 75th Division is attached to Corps and takes over zone of 7th Armored Division. VII Corps mops up infiltrators and patrols. 83rd Division releases 331st Infantry to 3rd Armored Division; attacks toward Rochefort with 329th, making slow progress.

12th Army Group:

In US Third Army area, VIII Corps prepares for drive on Houffalize. 11th Armored Division moves to vicinity of Neufchâteau.

30 DECEMBER

21 Army Group:

In US First Army's XVIII Airborne Corps area, 7th Armored Division releases Regimental Combat Team 424 to 106th Division. 75th Division hold positions previously occupied by Regimental Combat Team 424. VII Corps turns over region southwest of line Marche – Namur to British. Germans abandon Rochefort.

12th Army Group:

In US Third Army area, VIII Corps opens drive on Houffalize. 11th Armored Division progresses slowly and at heavy cost. 87th Division takes Moircy but loses it in a counterattack later in day. 9th Armored Division is ordered to Sedan area as SHAEF reserve. In III Corps area, Germans again attempt to cut Arlon – Bastogne highway and isolate Bastogne, reaching Lutrebois and surrounding two companies of the 137th Infantry, 35th Division in Villers-la-Bonne-Eau. On left flank of Corps, 6th Cavalry Group is relieved by elements of VIII Corps.

31 DECEMBER

21 Army Group:

In US First Army's VII Corps area, 83rd Division, to which 331st Infantry reverts, takes over zone of 3rd Armored Division and is reinforced by Regimental Combat Team 290, 75th Division.

12th Army Group:

In US Third Army area, VII Corps takes command of 4th Armored Division. Elements of 87th Division capture Remagne and close in on Moircy. Combat Command Reserve, 11th Armored Division, drives to Pinsamont and Acul while Combat Command B Attacks Chenogne. In III Corps area, one 6th Armored Division column secures Wardin; another advances to outskirts of Rechrival. 35th Division is unable to relieve isolated forces in Villers-la-Bonne-Eau, and they are presumed lost. Germans still hold Lutrebois. 26th Division repels counterattack and reorganises. Corps Artillery places Time on Target fire on Wiltz.

1 JANUARY

German Air force is unusually active, employing some 800 aircraft and damaging airfields in Holland, Belgium and France.

12th Army Group:

US Third Army continues Ardennes counteroffensive with VIII and III Corps. In VIII Corps area, 87th Division takes Moircy and Jenneville. 11th Armored Division attacks with Combat Command A, toward Hubermont, stopping east of Rechrival, and with Combat Command B, clears Chenogne and woods to north. Combat Command A, 9th Armored Division, drives toward Senonchamps. 101st Airborne Division, in Bastogne area, gives fire support to 11th Armored Division on its left and 6th Armored Division (III Corps) on its right. 17th Airborne Division relieves 28th Division in Neufchâteau area. III Corps contains enemy salient Southeast of Bastogne. 4th Armored Division holds corridor into Bastogne and supports 35th Division with fire. 35th Division partially clears Lutrebois and reaches crossroads Southeast of Marvie, but makes no headway in vicinity of Villers-la-Bonne-Eau (Belgium) and Harlange (Luxembourg). In region east of Bastogne, 6th Armored Division takes Neffe, Bizory and Magaret, but then loses Magaret.

2 JANUARY

21 Army Group:

In British Second Army's 30 Corps area, 53rd Division assumes responsibility for Marche – Hotton sector (Belgium), relieving US 84th Infantry Division; boundary between 30 Corps and US VII Corps is adjusted.

12th Army Group:

In US Third Army's VIII Corps area, Gerimont falls to 87th Division; Mande St. Etienne to 11th Armored Division; and Senonchamps to Combat Command B, 10th Armored Division (attached to 101st Airborne Division), and Combat Command A, 9th Armored Division. 4th Armored Division protects and enlarges corridor leading into Bastogne from the south and helps III Corps clear woods near Lutrebois. In III Corps area, 6th Armored Division's Combat Command B enters Oubourcy and Michamps but is driven out of latter; unsuccessfully attacks Arloncourt; Combat Command A takes Wardin; division withdraws to high ground west of Michamps – Arloncourt – Wardin for night. 35th Division continues fight for Lutrebois. 28th Cavalry Squadron of Task Force Fickett (6th Cavalry Group) is committed between 134th and 137th Regiments, 35 Division. 26th Division's 101st Infantry advances north in area southwest of Wiltz.

3 JANUARY

21 Army Group:

US First Army starts counteroffensive to reduce enemy's Ardennes salient from north. VII Corps attacks Southeast toward Houffalize with 2nd Armored Division followed by 84th Division on the right and 3rd Armored Division followed by 83rd Division on left. 2nd Armored Division gains Trinal, Magoster, positions in Bois de Tave, Freineux, Le Batty, and positions near Belle Haie. 3rd Armored Division takes Malempré and Floret and from latter continues Southeast on Lierneux road to Grumont creek. 75th Division, after attack passes through its line, continues mopping up south of Sadzot. In XVIII Airborne Corps area, 82nd Airborne Division, in conjunction with VII Corps attack, thrusts Southeast improving positions. As a diversion, 30th Division pushes small forces south of Malmédy and then withdraws them as planned.

12th Army Group:

In US Third Army's VIII Corps area, elements of 87th Division are temporarily surrounded in woods east of St. Hubert. 17th Airborne Division attacks north late in day in region some 5 miles Northwest of Bastogne. Northeast of Bastogne, 101st Airborne Division and 501st Parachute Infantry are clearing Bois Jacques. Task Force Higgins (elements of 101st Airborne and Combat Command A, 10th Armored Division) is organised to block enemy attacks toward Bastogne. Combat Command B, 4th Armored Division, continues to defend corridor into Bastogne. 28th Division defends the Meuse from Givet to Verdun. In III Corps area, 6th Armored Division thrusts west of Michamps and places heavy artillery concentrations on Arloncourt, Michamps, and Bourcy; to south, attempts to clear high ground near Wardin and takes road junction just south of the town. 35th Division gains about two thirds of Lutrebois and crossroads west of Villers-la-Bonne-Eau (Belgium) but is unable to take Harlange (Luxembourg). East of Harlange, 26th Division continues attack in region north of Mecher-Dunkrodt and Kaundorf.

4 JANUARY

21 Army Group:

In British Second Army area, 30 Corps opens offensive west of the Ourthe River, protecting US First Army right. From Marche – Hotton road, 53rd Division drives south abreast US VII Corps. 6th Airborne Division meets determined opposition south of Rochefort.

In US First Army's area, 2nd Armored Division captures Beffe, contains counterattacks near Devantave, seizes Lamorménil, and reaches Odeigne. 3rd Armored Division takes Baneux, Jevigne, and Lansival and gains bridgehead at Groumont creek. In XVIII Airborne Corps area, 82nd Airborne Division advances its line to include Heirlot, Odrimont, wooded heights north and Northeast of Arbrefontaine, St. Jacques, Bergeval, and Mont de Fosse; on extreme left patrols push to the Salm.

12th Army Group:

In US Third Army's VIII Corps area, 87th Division attack is halted by resistance near Pironpré. Attack of 17th Airborne Division evokes strong reaction in Pinsamont – Rechrival – Hubertmont area. Enemy attacks in 101st Airborne Division sector are ineffective. In III Corps area, 6th Armored Division is repeatedly attacked in Magaret – Wardin area east of Bastogne, and withdraws to shorten line. 35th Division clears Lutrebois but is still unable to take Harlange. 26th Division gains a few hundred yards.

5 JANUARY
21 Army Group:

In US First Army's VII Corps area, 2nd Armored Division's main effort against Consy makes little headway; elements move toward Dochamps and clear part of Odeigne. 3rd Armored Division is slowed by rearguard action in Bois de Groumont but seizes Lavaux and enters Lierneux. 75th Division moves to Aisne River. In XVIII Airborne Corps area, 82nd Airborne Division makes progress all along line and repels counterattacks near Bergeval.

12th Army Group:

In US Third Army's VIII Corps area, 97th Division meets resistance near Bonnerue and Pironpré, west of Bastogne. Rest of Corps maintains defensive positions. In III Corps area, 35th Division continues to fight for negligible gains.

6 JANUARY
21 Army Group:

In US First Army's VII Corps area, 2nd Armored and 84th Infantry Divisions make converging attacks toward Consy, taking positions east and west of the town, respectively. 2nd Armored Division continues toward Dochamps, completes occupation of Odeigne, and makes contact with 3rd Armored Division on Manhay – Houffalize road. 3rd Armored Division cuts Laroche – Salmchâteau road at its intersection with the Manhay – Houffalize road and captures Fraiture, Lierneux and La Falise; 83rd Armored Recon Battalion clears Bois Houby. In XVIII Airborne Corps area, 82nd Airborne Division consolidates. To protect its left flank, 30th Division attacks south toward Spineux and Wanne with Regimental Combat Team 112, 28th Division.

12th Army Group:

In US Third Army's VIII Corps area, enemy gets tanks into Bonnerue, lightly held by 87th Division. 87th Division makes limited attack toward Tillet. In III Corps area, 6th Armored Division holds against repeated counterattacks. 35th Division attacks into woods Northeast of Lutrebois and maintains positions in Villers-la-Bonne-Eau area; 6th Cavalry Squadron of Task Force Fickett is committed near Villers-la-Bonne-Eau. In XII Corps area, 80th Division's 319th Infantry crosses Sure River near Heidersheidergrund and captures Goesdorf and Dahl.

7 JANUARY
21 Army Group:

In British Second Army's 30 Corps area, 53rd Division takes Grimbiermont. In US First Army's area, co-ordinated attacks of 2nd Armored and 84th Infantry Divisions toward Laroche-Salmchâteau road, intermediate objective before Houffalize, makes notable progress. Dochamps and Marcouray fall. Only rear guards remain in Consy area. 3rd Armored Division seizes Regné, Verleumont, Sart and Grand Sart. In XVIII Airborne Corps area, 82nd Airborne Division, in rapid advance of 2-3 miles, clears most of angle formed by Laroche – Salmchâteau road and Salm River. Some elements secure positions on ridge just north of Comté; others, during advance to Salm river line, clear Goronne, Farniers, Mont, and Rochlinval. Regimental Combat Team 112 seizes Spineux, Wanne and Wanneranval.

12th Army Group:

In US Third Army's VIII Corps area, 87th Division continues attack on Tillet and is engaged sporadically in Bonnerue area. 17th Airborne takes Rechrival, Millomont, and Flamierge and reaches outskirts of Flamizoule. In III Corps area, 6th Armored Division remains under strong pressure in Neffe-Wardin region east of Bastogne. 35th Division makes limited attack toward Lutrebois-Lutremange road, halting just short of it.

8 JANUARY

21 Army Group:

In US First Army's VII Corps area, 4th Cavalry Group and 84th Division pursue enemy on right of Corps to Marcourt and Cielle; other elements of 84th Division start clearing woods south of main road junction Southeast of Manhay, 2nd Armored Division drives on Samrée road. 3rd Armored Division gains intermediate objective line, taking Hebronval, Ottre, Joubieval, and Provedroux. In XVIII Airborne Corps area, 82nd Airborne Division consolidates along line Grand Sart – Salmchâteau – Trois Ponts and clears Comté. (*Grand Sart and Comté are tiny hamlets just north of Joubieval)

12th Army Group:

In US Third Army's VIII Corps area, enemy drives 87th Division units from Bonnerue and maintains pressure in Tillet region. Some 17th Airborne Division elements gain then lost high ground north of Laval and others are forced out of Flamierge. In III Corps area, 6th Armored Division recovers lost ground in Neffe – Wardin sector. Task Force Fickett occupies zone between 35th and 26th Divisions, along high ground before Villers-la-Bonne-Eau, Betlange, and Harlange.

9 JANUARY

21 Army Group:

In US First Army's VII Corps area, 84th Division mops up near Consy, takes commanding ground at Harze, and clears woods south of main crossroads Southeast of Manhay. (*"Parker's Crossroads") 2nd Armored Division continues toward Samrée, which is subjected to heavy artillery fire. 83rd Division attacks through 3rd Armored Division, gaining line from Bihain – which is entered but not captured – west to point Northeast of Petit Langlir. (*Northeast of Houffalize) In XVIII Airborne Corps area, 82nd Airborne Division finishes mopping up within its zone. In 30th Division sector, Regimental Combat team 424 (106th Division) takes over Wanne – Wannereval region, formerly held by Regimental Combat Team 112 (28th Division).

12th Army Group:

In US Third Army's VIII Corps area, 87th Division continues to fight near Tillet; elements are clearing Haies-de-Tillet woods.

506th Parachute Infantry, 101st Airborne Division, attacks with Combat Command B, 4th Armored Division, and Combat Command B, 10th Armored Division, toward Noville, gaining 1,000 yards. 501st Parachute Infantry takes Recogne. III Corps launches attack to trap and destroy enemy pocket Southeast of Bastogne. 90th Division breaks through 26th toward high ground Northeast of Bras, taking Berle – Winseler road. 26th Division's gains are slight but include heights Northwest of Bavigne. Combat Command A, 6th Armored Division, co-ordinating closely with 134th Infantry of 35th Division, advances to high ground Southeast of Marvie and feints toward Wardin. 137th Infantry of 35th Division attacks Villers-la-Bonne-Eau.

10 JANUARY

21 Army Group:

In British Second Army's 30 Corps area, 51st Division which has taken over from 53rd, reaches Laroche.

US First Army prepares to broaden attack on 13th, VII Corps thrusting toward line Houffalize – Bovigny and XVIII Corps toward St. Vith. In VII Corps area, most of the Laroche – Salmchâteau road, intermediate objective of Corps, is cleared. 84th Division patrols toward Laroche. 2nd Armored Division captures Samrée and clears Laroche – Salmchâteau road within its zone. 83rd Division takes Bihain, advances slightly in region north of Petit Langlir, and crosses Ronce River east of Petit Langlir. In XVIII Airborne Corps area, elements of 82nd Airborne Division secure bridgehead across the Salm River near Grand Halleux.

12th Army Group:

In US Third Army's VIII Corps area, 87th Division captures Tillet. Renewing attack toward Noville, 101st Airborne Division clears portion of Bois Jacques. 4th Armored Division units, having passed through 6th Armored Division, attack Northeast with elements of the 101st Airborne Division toward Bourcy but cease attack upon order. III Corps continues attack, with greatest progress on right (east) flank. On left flank, 6th Armored

Division furnishes fire support for neighboring VIII Corps units and outposts north sector of line reached by 4th Armored Division. Elements of 35th Division take Villers-la-Bonne-Eau and high ground Northwest Betlange falls to 6th Cavalry Squadron and Harlange to 28th Cavalry Squadron. One 90th Division regiment advances from Berle to heights overlooking Doncols (*Southeast of Bastogne) another fights indecisively for Trentelhof strongpoint. Elements of 26th Division reach high ground southwest of Winseler. (*West of Wiltz)

11 JANUARY
21 Army Group:

In British Second Army's 30 Corps area, patrols of 6th Airborne reach St. Hubert and make contact with US VIII Corps.

In US First Army's VII Corps area, Laroche, in 84th Division sector, is cleared of enemy; 4th Cavalry Group patrol covers portion east of the Ourthe River. 83rd Division secures road junction on Bihain – Lomre road and attacks Petit Langlir and Langlir. In XVIII Airborne Corps area, 75th Division takes up positions along Salm River that were held by the 82nd Airborne Division. 106th Division assumes control of right of 30th Division zone.

12th Army Group:

In US Third Army's VIII Corps area, 87th Division's 347th Infantry finishes clearing Haies-de-Tillet woods and occupies Bonnerue, Pironpré, Vesqueville and St. Hubert from which the enemy has withdrawn.

Germans are also withdrawing from 17th Airborne Division zone in vicinity of Herpont, Flamierge, Mande Ste. Etienne and Flamizoulle. In III Corps area, Germans are retiring from pocket Southeast of Bastogne. Elements of all divisions from Corps are converging on Bras. 6th Armored Division takes over sector east of Bastogne formerly held by 4th Armored Division (VIII Corps); elements attack toward Bras, clearing woods near Wardin. 35th Division gains additional high ground in Lutrebois – Lutremange area. Task Force Fickett clears Wantrange and attacks Tarchamps, then moves into zone of Task Force Scott (mainly 26th Division units) as it advances on Sonlez. Task Force Fickett reaches Sonlez by midnight and makes contact with 90th Division. Elements of Task Force Scott clear forest east of Harlange then, in conjunction with Task Force Fickett, secure heights southwest of Sonlez. 90th Division overcomes resistance around Trentelhof, cuts Bastogne – Wiltz road at Doncols, and advances on Sonlez. 26th Division improves positions on right flank of Corps. In Corps area, 80th Division takes Bockholtz-sur-Sure and high ground south of Burden.

12 JANUARY
21 Army Group:

In US First Army's VII Corps area, 2nd Armored Division attacks in vicinity of junction of Manhay – Houffalize and Laroche – Salmchâteau roads. Combat Command A takes Chaumont, continues about a mile south in Bois de Belhez and reduces strongpoint east of Bois de St. Jean. Combat Command B captures Les Tailles and Petit Tailles. On 3rd Armored Division right, 83rd Armored Reconnaissance Battalion drives south through Task Force Hogan (Combat Command Reserve) at Regne, crosses Langlir River, and clears Bois de Cedrogne east of Manhay – Houffalize road and blocks road there running west from Mont le Ban. Task Force Hogan moves to Bihain and clears high ground southwest of the town. 83rd Division completes capture of Petit Langlir and Langlir and gains bridgehead south of Langlir – Ronce River. In XVIII (Airborne) Corps 106th Division sector, bridgehead is established across Amblève River south of Stavelot.

12th Army Group:

In US Third Army's VII Corps area, enemy continues withdrawing. 87th Division takes Tonny, Amberloup, Lavacherie, Orreux, Fosset, Sprimont and road junction Northeast of Sprimont. 17th Airborne Division recaptures Flamierge. Flamizoulle is found to be heavily mined. Renuamont, Hubertmont, and villages to the southwest are held by light delaying forces. In III Corps area, Combat Command A of 6th Armored Division captures Wardin and advances to within a few hundred yards of Bras; 357th mops up Sonlez and continues to high ground south-east of Bras; 359th repels attacks on crossroads Northeast of Doncols.

JANUARY

21 Army Group:

In British Second Army area, 30 Corps' Ardennes mission is completed as 51st Division reaches Ourthe River Line southward from Laroche.

In US First Army area, VII Corps pushes steadily toward Houffalize. On right flank, 4th Cavalry Group and 84th Division clear several towns and villages. Combat Command A, 2nd Armored Division, reaches positions north of Wibrin; Combat Command B advances in Bois de Cedrogne to point 5-6 miles due north of Houffalize. 3rd Armored Division's Combat Command Reserve cuts Sommerain – Cherain road at its junction with the road from Mont le Ban, and contains Mont le Ban while Combat Command B takes Lomre. After clearing passage through woods south of Langlir for 3rd Armored Division, 83rd Division mops up and regroups. XVIII Airborne Corps opens offensive, employing its 106th Division on right and 30th on left. 106th Division, with its 424th Infantry on right and 517th Parachute Infantry on left, attacks Southeast from junction of Amblève and Salm Rivers toward La Neuville – Coulee – Logbiermé – Houvegnez line, reaching positions near Heneumont. 30th Division drives south from Malmedy area toward Amblève River, gaining positions near Hédomont, in Houire woods, and in Thirimont area.

12th Army Group:

In US Third Army's VIII Corps area, advance elements of 87th Division reach Ourthe River and make contact with British. 17th Airborne takes Salle, north of Flamierge, without opposition. 11th Armored Division, which has relieved elements of 101st and 17th Airborne Divisions, attacks north with Combat Command Reserve and Combat Command A, along Longchamps – Bertogne axis, cutting Houffalize – St. Hubert highway near Bertogne. Bertogne is enveloped. 506th Parachute Infantry, 101st Airborne Division, seizes Foy, on Bastogne – Houffalize highway; 327th Glider Infantry advances through 501st Parachute Infantry in Bois Jacques toward Bourcy. In III Corps area, 6th Armored Division drives northward, Combat Command partially clearing Magaret. 90th Division drives enemy from Bras and gains Hill 530. 35th Division and Task Force Fickett are pinched out near Bras. 26th Division moves units into positions Northeast and east of Doncols as boundary between it and 90th Division is moved west.

14 JANUARY

21 Army Group:

In US First Army's VII Corps area, 84th Division gains its final objectives, taking Nadrin, Filly, Petit Mormont and Grand Mormont; 4th Cavalry Group patrol makes visual contact with US Third Army patrol. 2nd Armored Division seizes Wibrin, Cheveoumont, Wilogne and Dinez. 3rd Armored Division takes Mont le Ban and Baclain. 83rd Division clears Honvelez and high ground near Bovigny. In XVIII Airborne Corps' 106th Division sector, 517th Parachute Infantry clears Henumont and continues south. 424th Infantry secures Coulée and Logbiermé. Some elements of 30th Division attack toward Hédomont and Thirimont, night 13-14, and take Hédomont before dawn; other elements clear Villers and Ligneuville and gain bridgeheads across the Amblève River at these points.

12th Army Group:

In US Third Army's VIII Corps area, 17th Airborne Division's 507th Parachute Infantry secures Bertogne, from which the enemy has fled, and 194th Glider Infantry takes Givroule; both regiments continue to Ourthe River. A Task Force of Combat Command A, 11th Armored Division clears Falize woods and drives along Longchamps – Compogne highway until stopped by heavy fire. 101st Airborne Division continues attack toward Noville – Rachamps – Bourcy area. Elements are forced out of Recogne and Foy, but both are regained in counterattacks. Enemy is cleared from Cobru. Tank task force of Combat Command B, 11th Armored Division, followed by infantry task force, enters Noville but withdraws under intense fire. In III Corps area, Combat Command A of 6th Armored Division clears woods east of Wardin and captures Benonchamps; Combat Command B finishes clearing Magaret. Elements of 90th Division drive toward Niederwampach. Having cleared small pockets during night, 26th Division moves combat patrols against enemy south of Wiltz River.

On US First Army's VII Corps right, 84th Division consolidates. 2nd Armored Division clears Achouffe, Mont, and Taverneux and sends patrols to Ourthe River and into Houffalize, which has been vacated by enemy. 3rd Armored Division attacks with Combat Command Reserve toward Vaux and Brisy, taking Vaux, and with, Combat Command B toward Cherain and Sterpigny. Elements of Combat Command A are committed as reinforcements. A battalion of the 83rd Division attacks Bovigny but is unable to take it. In SVIII Airborne Corps area, 75th Division attacks across the Salm before dawn and seizes Salmchâteau and Bech. 106th Division consolidates and clears Ennal. 30th Division takes Beaumont, Francheville, Houvegnez and Pont; improves positions south of Ligneuville; clears north part of Thirimont. V Corps opens offensive to clear heights between Büllingen and Amel and to protect left flank of XVIII Corps. 1st Division, reinforced by Regimental Combat Team 23 of 2nd Division, attacks Southeast with 23rd Infantry on right, 16th Infantry in center, and 18th on left gains Steinbach, neighboring village of Remonval, and north half of Faymonville, but is held up south of Bütgenbach by heavy fire.

12 Army Group:

In US Third Army's VIII Corps area, Combat Command A of 11th Armored Division takes Compogne and Rastadt and reaches Vellereux; falls back west of Vellereux under counterattack in Rau De Vaux defile. Combat Command B bypasses Noville and clears woods to east. 506th Parachute Infantry, 101st Airborne Division, occupies Noville. In III Corps area, 6th Armored Division, employing 320th Infantry of 35th Division, overcomes house-to-house resistance in Oubourcy; Combat Command B takes Arloncourt; Combat Command A clears heights southwest of Longvilly. 358th Infantry of 90th Division meets unexpectedly strong resistance as it assumes Northeast attack; 1st Battalion makes forced march into 6th Armored Division sector to attack Niederwampach from Benouchamps area and gains town after artillery barrage by 14 field artillery battalions. 357th Infantry battles strongpoints in and around railroad tunnels along Wiltz River valley while 359th starts to Wardin.

In US First Army's VII Corps area, VII Corps of First Army and VIII Corps of Third Army establish contact (*between Houffalize and Laroche at Rensiwez). 2nd Armored Division occupies that part of Houffalize north of the Ourthe River. Enemy resistance continues on left flank of Corps. 3rd Armored Division captures Sommerain, Cherain and Sterpigny but is unable to take Brisy. Attempt to get tank force from Cherain to Retigny fails. 83rd Division consolidates along east edge of Bois de Ronce. In XVIII Airborne Corps area, 75th Division makes slow progress east of the Salm. After gaining objective line, 106th Division mops up, 424th Infantry along 75th Division boundary and 517th Parachute Infantry on high ground northwest of Petit Thier. 30th Division clears rest of Thirimont and pushes south toward junction of Recht – Born road with Malmedy – St. Vith road, which enemy is blocking. In V Corps area, 1st Division captures Ondenval and rest of Faymonville, but progress in woods south of Bütgenbach is negligible.

12th Army Group:

In US Third Army's VIII Corps area, Combat Command A of 11th Armored Division takes Velleroux and pursues enemy through Mabompré Combat Command B, after advancing Northeast through Wicourt, secures high ground south of Houffalize. Attack of 502nd Parachute Infantry, 101st Airborne Division, is halted near Bourcy, but 506th Parachute Infantry captures Vaux and Rachamps. In II Corps area, 6th Armored Division continues Northeast toward Moinet: 320th Infantry, attached, takes Michamps; Task Force Lagrew, Combat Command A, advances through Longvilly. 90th Division clears heights east of Longvilly and seizes Oberwampach and Schimpach.

Despite further bitter fighting during the second half of January and early February, the junction of First and Third Armies (*at Rensiwez) near Houffalize on 16 January, 1945, is generally viewed as heralding the end of the battle of the "Bulge".

Appendix II
Bulge Medals of Honor

During the period 16 December 1944, through 16 January 1945, some 18 American soldiers in the Bulge earned the nation's highest award for gallantry, the Medal of Honor. In World War II, regulations concerning the Medal of Honor stated:

> 'In their provisions for judging whether a man is entitled to the medal, Army Regulations permit no margin of doubt or error. The deed of the winner must be proved by incontestable evidence of at least two eyewitnesses. It must be so outstanding that it clearly distinguishes his gallantry beyond the call of duty from lesser forms of bravery. It must involve the risk of his life; and it must be the type of deed, which, if he had not done it, would not subject him to any justified criticism'.

The citations for those 18 Medals of Honor speak for themselves:

Corporal Arthur O. Beyer, of Company C, 603rd Tank Destroyer Battalion. On 15 January 1945, near Arloncourt, Belgium.

'He displayed conspicuous gallantry in action. His platoon, in which he was a tank destroyer gunner, was held up by anti-tank, machine gun, and rifle fire from enemy troops dug in along a ridge about 200 yards to the front. Noting a machine-gun position in this defense line, he fired upon it with his 75-mm gun, killing one man and silencing the weapon. He dismounted from his vehicle and, under direct enemy observation, crossed open ground to capture the two remaining members of the crew. Another machine-gun, about 250 yards to the left, continued to fire on him. Through withering fire, he advanced on the position. Throwing a grenade into the emplacement, he killed one crewmember and again captured the two survivors. He was subjected to concentrated small-arms fire but, with great bravery, he worked his way a quarter of a mile along the ridge, attacking hostile soldiers in their foxholes with his carbine and grenades. When he had completed his self-imposed mission against powerful German forces, he had destroyed two machine-gun positions, killed 8 of the enemy and captured 18 prisoners, including two bazooka teams. Corporal Beyer's intrepid action and unflinching determination to close with and destroy the enemy eliminated the German defense line and enabled his task force to gain its objective'.

Private First Class, Melvin E. Biddle of Company B, 517th Parachute Infantry Regiment, on 23-24 December, 1944 near Soy, Belgium.

'He displayed conspicuous gallantry and intrepidity in action against the enemy near Soy, Belgium on 23rd and 24th December, 1944. Serving as lead scout during an attack to relieve the enemy encircled town of Hotton, he aggressively penetrated a densely wooded area, advanced 400 yards until he came within range of intense enemy rifle fire, and within 20 yards of enemy positions killed three snipers with unerring marksmanship. Courageously continuing his advance an additional 200 yards, he discovered a hostile machine-gun position and dispatched its 2 occupants. He then located the approximate position of a well-concealed enemy machine-gun nest, and crawling forward threw hand grenades, which killed two Germans and fatally wounded a third. After signaling his company to advance, he entered a determined line of enemy defense, coolly and deliberately shifted his position and shot three more enemy soldiers. Undaunted by enemy fire, he crawled within 20 yards of a machine-gun nest, tossed his last hand grenade into the position, and after the explosion charged the emplacement firing his rifle. When night fell, he scouted enemy positions alone for several hours, and returned with valuable information, which enabled our attacking infantry and armor to knock out two enemy tanks. At daybreak, he again led the advance and, when flanking elements were pinned down by enemy fire, without hesitation made his way toward a hostile machine-gun position and from a distance of 50 yards killed the crew and two supporting riflemen. The remainder of the enemy, finding themselves without automatic weapon support, fled panic-stricken. Private Biddle's intrepid courage and superb daring during this 20-hour action enabled his battalion to break the enemy grasp on Hotton with a minimum of casualties'.

Staff Sergeant Paul L. Bolden of Company I, 120th Infantry, 30th Infantry Division, on 23 December 1944 in Petit-Coo, Belgium.

'He voluntarily attacked a formidable enemy strongpoint in Petit-Coo, Belgium on 23rd December 1944, when his company was pinned down by extremely heavy automatic and small-arms fire coming from a house 200 yards to the front. Mortar and tank artillery shells pounded the unit, when Sergeant Bolden and a comrade, on their own initiative, moved forward into a hail of bullets to eliminate the ever increasing fire from the German position. Crawling ahead to close with what they knew was a powerfully armed, vastly superior force, the pair reached the house and took up assault positions, Sergeant Bolden under a window, his comrade across the street where he could deliver covering fire. In rapid succession, Sergeant Bolden hurled a fragmentation grenade and a white phosphorous grenade into the building; and then, fully realizing that he faced tremendous odds, rushed to the door. He threw it open and fired into 35 SS troopers who were trying to reorganize themselves after the havoc wrought by the grenades. Twenty Germans died under the fire of his sub-machine-gun before he was struck in the shoulder, chest, and stomach by part of a burst, which killed his comrade across the street. He withdrew from the house, waiting for the surviving Germans to come out and surrender. When none appeared in the doorway, he summoned his ebbing strength, overcame the extreme pain he suffered and boldly walked back into the house, firing as he went. He had killed the remaining 15 enemy soldiers when his ammunition ran out. Sergeant Bolden's heroic advance against great odds, his fearless assault, and his magnificent display of courage in re-entering the building where he had been severely wounded cleared the path for his company and insured the success of its mission'.

Private First Class Richard E. Cowan of Company M, 23rd Infantry, 2nd Infantry Division on 17 December 1944, northeast of Krinkelt, Belgium.

'He was a heavy machine-gunner in a section attached to Company I in the Krinkelterwald, Belgium, 17 December 1944, when that company was attacked by a numerically superior force of German infantry and tanks. The first six waves of hostile infantrymen were repulsed with heavy casualties, but a seventh drive with tanks killed or wounded all but three of his section, leaving Private Cowan to man his gun, supported by only 15 to 20 riflemen of Company I. He maintained his position, holding off the Germans until the rest of the shattered force had set up a new line along a firebreak. Then, unaided, he moved his machine-gun and ammunition to the second position. At the approach of a Royal Tiger (author's note: not a Tiger but a Panther) tank, he held his fire until about 80 enemy infantrymen supporting the tank appeared at a distance of about 150 yards. His first burst killed or wounded about half of these infantrymen. An 88-mm shell (actually 75-mm) rocked his position when the tank opened fire, but he continued to man his gun, pouring deadly fire into the Germans when they again advanced. He was barely missed by another shell. Fire from three machine-guns and innumerable small arms struck all about him; an enemy rocket shook him badly but did not drive him from his gun. Infiltration by the enemy had by this time made the position untenable, and the order was given to withdraw. Private Cowan, was the last man to leave, voluntarily covering the withdrawal of all his remaining comrades. His heroic actions were entirely responsible for allowing the remaining men to retire successfully from the scene of their last-ditch stand'.

Sergeant Francis S. Currey of Company K, 120th Infantry, 30 Infantry Division, on 21 December 1944 at the Pont de Warche paper-mill on the southeast outskirts of Malmédy, Belgium.

Sergeant Francis S. Currey of Company K, 120th Infantry Regiment, who earned the Medal of Honor for bravery at the Pont de Warche paper mill in Malmedy on 21 December 1944. (US Army Signal Corps).

'He was an automatic rifleman with the Third Platoon defending a strong point near Malmédy, Belgium, on 21 December 1944, when the enemy launched a powerful attack. Over running tank destroyers and anti-tank guns located near the strongpoint, German tanks advanced to the Third Platoon's position, and, after prolonged fighting, forced the withdrawal of this group to a nearby factory. Sergeant Currey found a bazooka in the building and crossed the street to secure rockets, meanwhile enduring intense fire from enemy tanks and hostile infantrymen who had taken up position at a house a short distance away. In the face of small arms, machine-gun, and artillery fire, he, with a companion, knocked out a tank with one shot. Moving to another position, he observed three Germans in the doorway of an enemy-held house. He killed or wounded all three with his automatic rifle. He emerged from cover and advanced alone to within 50 yards of the house, intent on wrecking it with rockets. Covered by friendly fire, he stood erect and fired a shot, which knocked down half of one wall. While in this forward position, he observed five American who had been pinned down for hours by fire from the house and three tanks. Realizing that they could not escape until the enemy tank and infantry guns had been silenced, Sergeant Currey crossed the street to a vehicle, where he procured an armful of anti-tank grenades. These he launched while under heavy enemy fire, driving the tankers from the vehicles into the house. He then climbed onto a halftrack in full view of the Germans and fired a machine-gun at the house. Once again changing his position, he manned another machine-gun whose crew had been killed; under his cover five soldiers were able to retire to safety. Deprived of tanks and with heavy infantry casualties, the enemy was forced to withdraw. Through his extensive knowledge of weapons and by his heroic and repeated braving of murderous enemy fire, Sergeant Currey was greatly responsible for inflicting heavy losses in men and material on the enemy. He also rescued five comrades, two of whom were wounded, and for stemming an attack which threatened to flank his battalion's position'.

Technical Sergeant Peter J. D'Alessandro of Company E, 39th Infantry, 9th Infantry Division, on 22 December 1944, near Kalterherberg, Germany.

'He was holding an important road junction on high ground, near Kalterherberg, Germany, on 22 December 1944. In the early morning hours, the enemy after laying down an intense artillery and mortar barrage, followed through with an all-out attack that threatened to overwhelm the position. Sergeant D'Alessandro, seeing that his men were becoming disorganized, braved the intense fire to move among them with words of encouragement. Advancing to a fully exposed observation post, he adjusted mortar fire upon the attackers, meanwhile firing upon them with his rifle and encouraging his men in halting and repulsing the attack. Later in the day the enemy launched a second determined attack. Once again, Sergeant D'Alessandro, in the face of imminent death, rushed to his forward position and immediately called for mortar fire. After exhausting his rifle ammunition, he crawled 30 yards over exposed ground to secure a light machine-gun, returned to his position, and fired upon the enemy at almost point-blank range until the gun jammed. He managed to get the gun to fire one more burst, which used up his last round, but with these bullets he killed four German soldiers who were on the verge of murdering an aid man and two wounded soldiers in a nearby foxhole. When the enemy had almost surrounded him, he remained alone, steadfastly facing almost certain death or capture, hurling grenades and calling for mortar fire closer and closer to his outpost as he covered the withdrawal of his platoon to a second line of defense. As the German hordes swarmed about him, he was last heard calling for a barrage, saying, 'Okay mortars, let me have it – right on this position!' The gallantry and intrepidity shown by Sergeant D'Alessandro against an overwhelming enemy attack saved his company from complete rout.'

Staff Sergeant Archer T. Gammon of Company A, 9th Armored Infantry Battalion, 6th Armored Division, on 11 January 1945, near Bastogne, Belgium.

'He charged 30 yards through hip-deep snow to knock out a machine-gun and its three-man crew with grenades, saving his platoon from being decimated and allowing it to continue its advance from an open field into some nearby woods. The platoon's advance through the woods had only begun when a machine-gun supported by riflemen opened fire and a Tiger Royal tank sent 88-mm shells screaming at the unit from the left flank. Sergeant Gammon, disregarding all thoughts of personal safety, rushed forward, then cut to the left, crossing the width of the company's skirmish line in an attempt to get within grenade range of the tank and its protecting foot troops. Intense fire was concentrated on him by riflemen and the machine-gun positioned near the tank. He charged the automatic weapon, wiped out its crew of four with grenades, and, with supreme daring, advanced to within 25 yards of the armored vehicle, killing two hostile infantrymen with rifle fire as he moved forward. The tank had started to withdraw, backing a short distance, then firing, backing some more, and then stopping to blast out another round. Gammon, whose single-handed relentless attack had put the ponderous machine on the defensive was struck and instantly killed by a direct hit from the Royal Tiger's heavy gun. By his intrepidity and extreme devotion to the task of driving the enemy back no matter what the odds, Sergeant Gammon cleared the woods of German forces, for the tank continued to withdraw, leaving open the path for the gallant squad leader's platoon'.

Staff Sergeant James R. Hendrix of Company C, 53rd Armored Infantry Battalion, 4th Armored Division, on 26 December 1944, near Assenois, Belgium.

'On the night of 26 December 1944, near Assenois, Belgium, he was with the leading element engaged in the final thrust to break through to the besieged garrison at Bastogne when halted by a fierce combination of artillery and small-arms fire. He dismounted from his halftrack and advanced against two 88-mm guns; and, by the ferocity of his rifle fire, compelled the gun crews to take cover and then to surrender. Later in the attack, he again left his vehicle, voluntarily, to aid two wounded soldiers, helpless and exposed to intense machine-gun fire. Effectively silencing two hostile machine-guns, he held off the enemy by his own fire until the wounded men were evacuated. Sergeant Hendrix again distinguished himself when he hastened to the aid of still another soldier who was trapped in a burning halftrack. Braving enemy sniper fire and exploding mines and ammunition in the vehicle, he extricated the wounded man and extinguished his flaming clothing, thereby saving the life of his fellow soldier. Sergeant Hendrix, by his superb courage and heroism, exemplified the highest traditions of the military service'.

Staff Sergeant Isadore S. Jachman of Company B, 513th Parachute Infantry Regiment, 17th Airborne Division, on 4 January 1945 in Flamierge, Belgium.

'For conspicuous gallantry and intrepidity above and beyond the call of duty at Flamierge, Belgium, on 4th January 1945, when his company was pinned down by enemy artillery, mortar, and small-arms fire, two hostile tanks attacked the unit, inflicting heavy casualties. Staff Sergeant Jachman, seeing the desperate plight of his comrades, left his place of cover and with total disregard for his own safety dashed across open ground through a hail of fire and seizing a bazooka from a fallen comrade advanced on the tanks, which concentrated their fire on him. Firing the weapon alone, he damaged one and forced both to retire. Staff Sergeant Jachman's heroic action, in which he suffered fatal wounds, disrupted the entire enemy attack, reflecting the highest credit upon himself and the parachute infantry'.

Technician Fourth Grade Truman Kimbro of Company C, 2nd Engineer Combat Battalion, 2nd Infantry Division, on 19 December 1944, near Rocherath, Belgium.

'On 19 December 1944, as scout, he led a squad assigned to the mission of mining a vital crossroads near Rocherath, Belgium. At the first attempt to reach the objective, he discovered it was occupied by an enemy tank and at least 20 infantrymen. Driven back by withering fire, Technician Fourth Grade

Kimbro made two more attempts to lead his squad to the crossroads but all approaches were covered by intense enemy fire. Although warned by our own infantrymen of the great danger involved, he left his squad in a protected place and, laden with mines, crawled alone toward the crossroads. When nearing his objective he was severely wounded, but he continued to drag himself forward and laid his mines across the road. As he tried to crawl from the objective his body was riddled with rifle and machine-gun fire. The mines, laid by his indomitable act of courage delayed the advance of enemy armor and prevented the rear of our withdrawing columns from being attacked by the enemy'.

Sergeant Jose M. Lopez of Company M, 23rd Infantry, 2nd Infantry Division at the western edge of the Krinkelterwald, Belgium.

'On his own initiative, he carried his heavy machine-gun from Company K's right flank to its left, in order to protect that flank which was in danger of being overrun, by advancing enemy infantry supported by tanks. Occupying a shallow hole offering no protection above his waist, he cut down a group of 10 Germans. Ignoring enemy fire from an advancing tank, he held his position and cut down 25 more enemy infantry attempting to turn his flank. Glancing to his right he saw a large number of infantry swarming in from the front. Although dazed and shaken from enemy artillery fire, which had crashed into the ground only a few yards away, he realized that his position would soon be outflanked. Again, alone, he carried his machine-gun to a position to the right rear of the sector; enemy tanks and infantry were forcing a withdrawal. Blown over backward by the concussion of enemy fire, he immediately reset his gun and continued his fire. Single-handed, he held off the German horde until he was satisfied his company had effected its retirement. Again he loaded his gun on his back and in a hail of small-arms fire he ran to a point where a few of his comrades were attempting to set up another defense against the onrushing enemy. He fired from this position until his ammunition was exhausted. Still carrying his gun, he fell back with his small group to Krinkelt. Sergeant Lopez" gallantry and intrepidity, on seemingly suicidal missions in which he killed at least 100 of the enemy, were almost solely responsible for allowing Company K to avoid being enveloped and to withdraw successfully. It gave other forces coming up in support time to build a line which repelled the enemy drive.'

Sergeant Jose M. Lopez of Company M, 23rd Infantry is presented with the Medal of Honor by Major General James van Fleet for heroism in the Krinkelterwald on 17 December 1944 in support of Company I of the same Battalion.

Technical Sergeant Vernon McGarity of 1st Platoon, Company L, 393rd Infantry, 99th Infantry Division, on 16/17 December 1944 in the Krinkelterwald, Belgium.

'He was painfully wounded in an artillery barrage that preceded the powerful counter-offensive launched by the Germans near Krinkelt, Belgium, on the morning of 16 December 1944. He made his way to an aid station, choosing to return to his hard-pressed men instead. The fury of the enemy's great Western Front offensive swirled about the position held by Sergeant McGarity's small force, but so tenaciously did these men fight on orders to stand firm at all costs that they could not be dislodged despite murderous enemy fire and the breakdown of their communications. During the day the heroic squad leader rescued one of his friends who had been wounded in a forward position, and throughout the night he exhorted his comrades to repulse the enemy's attempts at infiltration. When morning came and the Germans attacked with tanks and infantry, he braved heavy fire to run to an advantageous position where he immobilized the enemy's lead tank with a round from a rocket launcher. Fire from his squad drove the attacking infantrymen back, and three supporting tanks withdrew. He rescued, under fire, another wounded American, and then directed devastating fire on a light cannon, which had been brought up by the hostile troops to clear resistance from the area. When ammunition began to run low, Sergeant McGarity, remembering an old ammunition hole about a hundred yards distant in the general direction of the enemy, braved a concentration of hostile fire to replenish his unit's supply. By a circuitous route the enemy managed to position a machine-gun to the rear and flank of the squad's position, cutting off the only escape route. Unhesitatingly, the gallant soldier took it upon himself to destroy this menace single-handedly. He left cover, and while under steady fire from the enemy, killed or wounded all the hostile gunners with deadly accurate rifle fire and prevented all attempts to re-man the gun. Only when the squad's last round had been fired was the enemy able to advance and capture the intrepid leader and his men. The extraordinary bravery and extreme devotion to duty of Sergeant McGarity supported a remarkable delaying action which provided the time necessary for assembling reserves and forming a line against which the German striking power was shattered'.

Staff Sergeant Curtis F. Shoup of Company L, 346th Infantry, 87th Infantry Division on 7 January 1945, near Tillet, Belgium.

'On 7 January 1945, near Tillet, Belgium, his company attacked German troops on rising ground. Intense hostile machine-gun fire pinned down and threatened to annihilate the American unit in an exposed position where frozen ground made it impossible to dig in for protection. Heavy mortar and artillery fire from enemy batteries was added to the storm of destruction falling on the Americans. Realizing that the machine-gun must be silenced at all costs, Sergeant Shoup, armed with an automatic rifle, crawled to within 75 yards of the enemy emplacement. He found that his fire was ineffective from this position, and, completely disregarding his own safety, stood up and grimly strode ahead into the murderous stream of bullets, firing his low-held weapon as he went. He was hit several times and finally knocked to the ground. But he struggled to his feet and staggered forward until close enough to hurl a grenade, wiping out the enemy machine-gun nest with his dying action. By his heroism, fearless determination, and supreme sacrifice, Sergeant Shoup eliminated a hostile weapon which threatened to destroy his company and turned a desperate situation into victory'.

Private First Class William A. Soderman of Company K, 9th Infantry, 2nd Infantry Division, on 17 December 1944, at the Lausdell crossroads east of Rocherath, Belgium.

'Armed with a bazooka, he defended a key junction near Rocherath, Belgium on 17 December 1944, during the German Ardennes counteroffensive. After a heavy artillery barrage had wounded and forced the withdrawal of his assistant, he heard enemy tanks approaching the position where he calmly waited in the gathering darkness of early evening until the five Mark V tanks which made up the hostile force were within point-blank range. He then stood up, completely disregarding the fire that could be brought to bear upon him, and launched a rocket into the lead tank, setting it afire and forcing its crew to abandon it as the other tanks pressed on before Private Soderman could re-load. The daring bazooka-man remained at his post all night under severe artillery, mortar and machine-gun fire, awaiting the next onslaught. It was made shortly after dawn by five more tanks. Running along a ditch to meet them, he reached an advantageous point and there leaped to the road in full view of the tank gunners, deliberately aimed his weapon and disabled the lead tank. The other vehicles, thwarted by a deep ditch in their attempt to go around the crippled machine, withdrew. While returning to his post, Private Soderman, braving heavy fire to attack an enemy infantry platoon from close range, killed at least three Germans and wounded several others with a round from his bazooka. By this time, enemy pressure had made Company K's position untenable. Orders were issued for withdrawal to an assembly area where Private Soderman was located, when he once more heard enemy tanks approaching. Knowing that elements of the company had not completed their disengaging maneuver and were consequently extremely vulnerable to an armored attack, he hurried from his comparatively safe position to meet the tanks. Once more he disabled the lead tank with a single rocket, his last; but before he could reach cover, machine-gun bullets from the tank ripped into his right shoulder. Unarmed and seriously wounded, he dragged himself along a ditch to the American lines and was evacuated. Through his unfaltering courage against overwhelming odds, Private Soderman contributed in great measure to the defense of Rocherath, exhibiting to a superlative degree the intrepidity and heroism with which American soldiers met and smashed the savage power of the last great German offensive'.

Corporal Horace M. Thorne of Troop D, 89th Cavalry Reconnaissance Squadron, 9th Armored Division, on 21 December 1944, near Grufflingen, Belgium.

'He was the leader of a combat patrol, on 21 December 1944, near Grufflingen, Belgium, with the mission of driving German forces from dug-in positions in a heavily wooded area. As he advanced his light machine-gun, a German Mark III tank emerged from the enemy position and was quickly immobilized by fire from American light tanks supporting the patrol. Two of the enemy tankers attempted to abandon their vehicle but were killed by Corporal Thorne's shots before they could jump to the ground. To complete the destruction of the tank and its crew, Corporal Thorne left his covered position and crept forward through intense machine-gun fire until close enough to toss two grenades into the tank's open turret, killing two more Germans. He returned across the same fire-beaten zone as heavy mortar fire began falling in the area, seized his machine-gun, and without help, dragged it to the knocked-out tank and set it up on the vehicle's rear deck. He fired short rapid bursts into the enemy positions from his advantageous but exposed location, killing or wounding eight. Two enemy machine-guns abandoned their positions and retreated in confusion. His gun jammed; but rather than leave his self-chosen post he attempted to clear the stoppage; enemy small-arms fire, directed on the tank, killed him instantly. Corporal Thorne, displaying heroic initiative and intrepid fighting qualities, inflicted costly casualties in the enemy and insured the success of his patrol's mission by the sacrifice of his life'.

Sergeant Day G. Turner of Company B, 319th Infantry, 80th Infantry Division, on 8 January 1945, at Dahl, Luxembourg.

'He commanded a nine-man squad with the mission of holding a critical flank position. When overwhelming numbers of the enemy attacked under cover of withering artillery, mortar and rocket fire, he withdrew his squad into a nearby house, determined to defend it to the last man. The enemy attacked again and again and was repulsed with heavy losses. Supported by direct tank fire, they finally gained entrance, but the intrepid Sergeant refused to surrender although five of his men were wounded and one was killed. He boldly flung a can of burning oil at the first wave of attackers, dispersing them, and fought doggedly from room to room, closing with the enemy in hand-to-hand encounters. He hurled hand grenade for hand grenade, bayoneted two fanatical Germans who rushed a doorway he was defending and fought on with the enemy's weapons when his own ammunition was expended. The savage fight raged for 4 hours, and finally, when only three men in the defending squad were left unwounded, the enemy surrendered. Twenty prisoners were taken, 11 enemy dead and a great number of wounded were counted. Sergeant Turner's valiant stand will live on as a constant inspiration to his comrades. His heroic, inspiring leadership, his determination and courageous devotion to duty exemplify the highest tradition of the military service'.

Corporal Henry F. Warner of Anti-tank Company, 26th Infantry, 1st Infantry Division, on 20-21 December 1944, near Dom Bütgenbach, Belgium.

'Serving as a 57-mm, anti-tank gunner with the Second Battalion, he was a major factor in stopping enemy tanks during heavy attacks against the battalion position near Dom Bütgenbach, Belgium, on 20-21 December, 1944. In the first attack, on the early morning of the 20th, Corporal Warner disregarded the concentrated cannon and machine-gun fire from two tanks bearing down on him. He ignored the imminent danger of being overrun by the infantry moving under tank cover, destroyed the first tank and scored a direct and deadly hit upon the second. A third tank approached to within five yards of his position while he was attempting to clear a jammed breach lock. Jumping from his gun pit, he engaged in a pistol duel with the tank commander standing in the turret, killing him and forcing the tank to withdraw. Following a day and night during which our forces were subjected to constant shelling, mortar barrages, and numerous unsuccessful infantry attacks, the enemy struck in great force on the early morning of the 21st. Seeing a Mark IV tank looming out of the mist and heading toward his position, Corporal Warner scored a direct hit. Disregarding his injuries, he endeavored to finish the loading and again fired at the tank, whose motor was now aflame, when a second machine-gun burst killed him. Corporal Warner's gallantry and intrepidity at the risk of life above and beyond the call of duty contributed materially, to the successful defense against the enemy attacks'.

Staff Sergeant Paul J. Wiedorfer of Company G, 318th Infantry, and 80th Infantry Division, on 25 December 1944, near Chaumont, Belgium.

'He alone made it possible for his company to advance until its objective was seized. Company G had cleared a wooded area of snipers and one platoon was advancing across an open clearing toward another wood when it was met by heavy machine-gun fire from two German machine-gun positions dug in at the edge of the second wood. These positions were flanked by enemy riflemen. The platoon took refuge behind a small ridge approximately 40 yards from the enemy positions. There was no other available protection and German fire pinned down the entire platoon. It was about noon and the day was clear, but the terrain extremely difficult due to a 3-inch snowfall the night before over ice-covered ground. Private Wiedorfer, realizing that the platoon advance could not continue until the two enemy machine-gun nests were destroyed, voluntarily charged alone across the slippery open ground with no protecting cover of any kind. Remaining in a crouched position, under a hail of enemy fire, he slipped and fell in the snow, but quickly rose and continued forward with the enemy concentrating automatic and small arms fire on him as he advanced. Miraculously escaping injury, Private Wiedorfer reached a point some 10 yards from the first machine-gun emplacement and hurled a grenade into it. With his rifle, he killed the remaining Germans, and, without hesitation, wheeled to the right and attacked the second emplacement. His fire wounded one of the enemy and the other six immediately surrendered. This heroic action by one man enabled the platoon to advance from behind its protecting ridge and continue successfully to reach its objective. A few minutes later, when both the platoon leader and the platoon sergeant were wounded, Private Wiedorfer assumed command of the platoon, leading it forward with inspired energy until the mission was accomplished'.

Appendix III
LOST GRAVES OF '88 HILL'

On a snowy morning in April 2001, fifty-six years after they were killed, the skeletal remains of three American soldiers were found on a remote hillside in Germany. The discovery of their long-lost graves ended a Second World War mystery and closed a dark chapter in the lives of three families.

PFCs Jack C. Beckwith of LaMoure, North Dakota, Saul Kokotovich of Gary, Indiana, and David A. Read of Hudson, Ohio, died in December 1944. They were battle casualties of the 395th Infantry Regiment, part of the 99th Infantry Division. The trio were killed during an American attack launched in mid-December 1944.

Beckwith and Kokotovich, both twenty years old, were BAR (Browning Automatic Rifle) gunners with Company C, 395th. Read, nineteen, was a radio operator with Cannon Company, 395th. Less than five months after the three died, the war in Europe ended, but their bodies remained missing.

Vernon Swanson, a close comrade of Beckwith, returned home to Chicago in January 1946. Shortly thereafter, he penned a note to the army asking for the location of Beckwith's grave. The reply was disconcerting. The remains had not been recovered or positively identified. Search efforts were underway. The same was true of Kokotovich and Read. Their relatives wrote letters asking for answers. But the army offered only 'deep regret' and folded American flags. In 1951, the army deemed the remains of Beckwith, Kokotovich and Read to be 'non-recoverable.' Their case files were closed.

As decades passed the Second World War became, to many, as remote as ancient Greece. But the war was of great interest to a pair of young Belgians, Jean-Louis Seel of Ensival and Jean-Philippe Speder of Thirimont. They met in 1978 and began searching together for battlefield relics as a hobby.

In September 1988, Seel and Speder were digging in the Ardennes forest, near the Belgian-German border, when they made an extraordinary discovery. In an old foxhole, they chanced upon the complete skeleton of PFC Alphonse M. Sito of Baltimore. Sito, a machine gunner with the 99th Division, had been missing since 16 December, 1944, the day German armies launched a surprise attack in the Ardennes forest that became know as the 'Battle of the Bulge.' Sito's remains were turned over to the U.S. Army and then interred by the family at St. Stanislaus cemetery in Baltimore.

I was a student at The Ohio State University at the time and an associate member of the 99th Infantry Division Association. News of Sito's recovery piqued my imagination. If the two Belgians could find a missing GI by sheer luck, the remains of other 'Missing in Action' GIs might well be located if a more scientific approach were taken.

Using records of the American Battle Monuments Commission, I compiled a list of thirty-three missing soldiers from the 99th, most of whom were lost during the Battle of the Bulge. I showed the list to Richard H. Byers of Mentor-on-the-Lake, Ohio. Byers, who died in March 2001, was a 99th Division veteran and a seminal member of the 99th Division Association. I proposed publishing the list in the *Checkerboard*, the association newspaper. In March 1990, the thirty-three names were published along with this request: 'If you have knowledge of what happened to any of these men, please contact Dick Byers. With a few facts, a search could be started.' Byers received a flood of mail. We then evaluated the data. Some of the best information concerned the death of 2nd Lt. L.O. Holloway Jr. of Corpus Christie, Texas.

Based on the evidence, I prepared a map pinpointing the location where I believed Holloway's body was last seen. Byers's hand carried the map to Europe and to the two Belgians. Armed with this information Seel and Speder entered the Ardennes in November

1990. After a two-day search, Holloway's remains were found along with his dogtags and other personal effects.

The following week, an army team received the remains from the Belgians. The bones and artifacts were shipped to the army's Central Identification Laboratory in Hawaii. After forensic analysis, Holloway's identification was confirmed and his family notified. In September 1991, he was interred in Texas at Fort Sam Houston National Cemetery.

In suburban Chicago, the Holloway case inspired Vernon Swanson. Perhaps the remains of his buddy, Jack Beckwith, could be found. Swanson enlisted the cooperation of his wartime comrade, Ron Whitmarsh of Richardson, Texas. Both men had seen Beckwith's shallow grave and other graves only a few feet away. A rifle stuck in the ground marked at least one burial spot. Other graves had only a twig with a dogtag attached. This makeshift cemetery stood on a wooded hillside southeast of Monschau, Germany. The Americans dubbed the place '88 Hill'. The name came from the fearsome 88-mm artillery projectiles used by the Germans.

Beckwith, Kokotovich and Read died on the hill from enemy shellfire. The entire area was abandoned to the Germans when their attack started before dawn on December 16. During the retreat, dead GIs were hastily buried where they fell.

In 1991, hoping to find Beckwith's grave, Swanson and Whitmarsh joined forces with Byers, Seel, Speder and myself. The hunt was on. The search – expanded to include Saul Kokotovich and David Read – gradually dwarfed the effort to locate Holloway.

Reams of correspondence and army documents were collected. There were trips to the National Archives, the National Personnel Records Center and the U.S. Army Military History Institute. The families of all three missing men helped. Above all, Swanson and Whitmarsh pursued the project as if it was the sole reason for their existence. Ironically, it was a single sheet of paper that offered the best hope for success. It was a crude map drawn in 1948 by Donald O. Woolf Jr. who had also known Beckwith and had seen his grave. The map, drawn to aid the army's search effort after the war, was found in Beckwith's army file.

Woolf noted the graves near a cluster of trees at the edge of a clearing. Unfortunately, he had got the compass direction wrong as well as the grid coordinates. The army considered the map useless. I found it valuable. Woolf's errors were easy to see. But finding the clearing and the cluster of trees was problematic. They had long since disappeared. The hill had been solid fir trees for years. The key was an aerial photograph from the National Archives. It showed 88 Hill in December 1944. I found the clearing and the grouping of trees, then transferred their locations to a modern topographic map.

Armed with my findings, Seel and Speder hiked to 88 Hill in February 1992. The two diggers found an M1 rifle, three U.S. Army combat shoes and an American handgrenade at the precise spot where I had pinpointed the graves. Surely, they had found the right place. The rifle must have been one of the grave makers. Seel and Speder dug countless holes and trenches, but found nothing. The area yielded only frustration. One possibility was that the graves had been discovered in 1945 and the bodies disinterred. If so, they would have been buried as 'unknowns' at one of the U.S. military cemeteries in northwest Europe. Sadly, the quest for Beckwith, Kokotovich and Read was at an end again. It was tough news to deliver to their families, especially to Beckwith's eighty-eight year-old mother.

A bit more was done for one of Read's four brothers. In October 1995, Verne Read, a World War II veteran, traveled to Europe. He and a friend rendezvoused with Swanson, his wife, Seel and Speder. The foursome escorted Read and his friend to 88 Hill. The graves area was among the spots on the tour. After Read's visit, Seel and Speder had little cause to return. Years passed. The aborted search effort faded into a memory.

Beckwith's mother passed away in 1997. Read's oldest brother, 'Tommy,' died in 2000. But the ghosts of 88 Hill lingered.

In March 2001, Seel and Speder heard an astounding rumor. Another digger had supposedly found dogtags and a wallet belonging to Beckwith. But there was cause for disbelief. 'Knowing the guy, we had doubts about the discovery,' Seel said. Within days, it became clear the discovery was no hoax. Anxiety gripped Seel. Had Beckwith's grave been looted by this relic hunter? On March 26, Seel returned to 88 Hill with Erich Hönen, a forest ranger. There was no sign of fresh digging. The place had remained untouched since 1992. The dogtags and wallet apparently came from someplace other than the hill. But where? On April 11, 2001, Seel decided to double-check the hill. He scanned the suspected graves area with his metal detector, crossed a forest trail and continued exploring. He quickly unearthed an American handgrenade. This dangerous device was missed in 1992.

Three steps from the grenade, he heard a familiar sound through his earphones. It was the tell-tale ping of a stainless steel dogtag. Seel flipped it from the soil with his shoe. After grabbing the shiny object, he starred in bug-eyed amazement at the name – READ, DAVID A. Had the dogtag marked a grave?

Seel ran out of time and departed without further investigation. He made plans to return with Speder and two friends who were new to their search team since 1992. The newcomers were Marc Marique of Visé, Belgium and Jean-Luc Menestrey of Stembert, Belgium. Early on Tuesday, April 17, Seel and Marique ascended 88 Hill. Two hours later, Speder joined them as did forest ranger Hönen.

In late afternoon, Speder fired a short e-mail to Vernon Swanson, Byron Whitmarsh and myself:

'Jack Beckwith, Saul Kokotovich and David Read no longer on the MIA list. Bodies found today. Complete report tonite.'

After more than five decades, 88 Hill had finally relinquished the last of its dead. The three were found a scant 30 yards from the 1992 search area. Read's dogtag had indeed marked his resting place. The graves of Beckwith and Kokotovich were easily found several feet away. For two days, Seel, Speder, Marique and Menestrey labored to exhume the remains. Each of the dead had a single dogtag around his neck. Rotted clothing was also found, along with boots and overshoes. Apparently, most personal effects were removed in 1944 before the men were buried. What about Beckwith's dogtags and wallet found in March 2001? They must have been among his personal effects and were lost elsewhere in the forest. It was not uncommon for a GI to have more than one pair of dogtags.

Once excavation work in the forest ended, Seel e-mailed David Roath, director of the U.S. Army Memorial Affairs Activity, Europe. A meeting was arranged for April 26. As planned, Roath met the diggers and viewed the skeletons and artifacts. Before returning to his office at Landstuhl, Germany, another visit was scheduled. Roath would bring a recovery team and take custody of the remains. The team arrived on 14 May, 2001. With Roath were four specialists from Memorial Affairs Europe as well as two other members of the organization. There was also a DNA expert from Austria who came along as an observer. They took possession of the remains, set up camp on 88 Hill and began the formal identification process. 'It was impressive to watch,' said Seel, who found their depth of knowledge, precision and professionalism phenomenal.

After three days, Roath's team placed each soldier in a metal casket. International politics dictated the remains be given to the German government, then officially handed over to the United States. On May 18, a solemn ceremony took place at the German military cemetery near the village of Hürtgen. A U.S. Army honor guard from the 1st Infantry Division accepted three flag-draped caskets from the German War Graves Commission.

Across the Atlantic, on June 7, the army telephoned the next-of-kin with official word of recent events. The call came from the Casualty and Memorial Affairs Operations Center in

Alexandria, Virginia. Two weeks after receiving official word, the three families met for the first time. They gathered at Fort Mitchell, Kentucky, site of the 52nd annual reunion of the 99th Division. Besides getting to know each other, they met the four diggers along with Vern Swanson, Byron Whitmarsh and myself. At Fort Mitchell, the families learned about an incredible story that unfolded in the wake of the 88 Hill discovery.

Energized by their recent success, the diggers decided to revisit the location of a 99th Division aid station used during the Battle of the Bulge. In the 1990s, Seel and Speder combed this area many times. They had hoped to find three infantrymen whose bodies were last seen there, but no trace of them ever surfaced.

One thought now weighed on Seel and Speder. Maybe they had missed the soldiers by only a few yards, just like the graves on 88 Hill. Marc Marique took up the quest on May 25. He trekked to the aid station site and began searching with his metal detector. With uncanny ease, he uncovered a corroded brass dogtag. It belonged to one of three soldiers. This stunning development sparked plans to scour every inch of the aid station. One week after finding the dogtag, Marique returned to the spot and began excavating a hole about three yards away. Seel and Speder accompanied him and began cleaning out another hole. Suddenly, Marique called out. 'Hey guys, come see ... I have a snow boot.' Together, the Belgians probed deeper. Bones emerged. They had found the man named on the dogtag. Besides his skeleton, they hit upon the remains of the other two men last seen at the aid station. For fifty-six years, the three warriors laid buried in this common grave.

Seel telephoned David Roath with the news. He could hardly believe it. Once more, he assembled a recovery team and traveled to meet the diggers. On June 29, 2001, a ceremony took place at the church in Krinkelt, Belgium. The sanctuary was packed with spectators and officials, including the U.S. Ambassador to Belgium. Three caskets were formally turned over to the U.S. Army. In less than two months, the diggers had located six 99th Division soldiers missing since December 1944. This achievement brought feelings of pride and accomplishment. Yet, the end was nowhere in sight for the Belgians and their American colleagues. Today, the search continues for other missing Second World War soldiers.

William
Warnock
July 4, 2001

The Color Guard of the 82nd Engineer Battalion based in Germany escort the remains of 399th Division soldiers from the Church in Krinkelt. Photo Scott Long

Allen, Robert: *Lucky Forward.* (New York: Manor Books 1977).

Ambrose, Stephen E.: *The Supreme Commander: The war years of General Dwight D. Eisenhower.* (Garden City, N.Y.: Douyleday 1970).

Arend, Guy F.: *L'Offensive Des Ardennes ET la Bataille de Bastogne* (Brussels, Belgium: Sagato 1977).

Astor, Gerald A.: *A Blood Dimmed Tide: The Battle of the Bulge by the Men who fought it.* (New York: Donald L. Fine Inc. 1992).

Baldwin, Hanson W.: *Battles Lost and Won:* (New York: Harper and Row, 1966).

Bauserman, John M: *The Malmedy Massacre,* (Shippensburg, White Mane 1979).

Bennett, Ralph: *Ultra In The West,* (New York: Charles Scribner's Sons, 1980).

Blumenson, Martin: *The Patton Papers 1940-45,* (Boston: Houghton Mifflin, 1974).

Blumenson, Martin: *Patton, The Man Behind The Legend 1885-1945, and* (N.

Booth, Michael T. & Spencer, Duncan: *Paratrooper The Life Of General James M. Gavin,* (New York: Simon & Schuster 1994).

Bradley, Omar N.: *A Soldier's Story* (New York: Henry Holt and Company, 1951).

Breuer, William B.: *Bloody Clash at Sadzot* (New York: Jove Books, 1981).

Brett-Smith, Richard: *Hitler's Generals* (San Rafael, CA.: Presidio Press, 1977).

Browlow, Donald G.: *Panzer Baron; The Military Exploits of General Hasso von Manteuffel* (North Quincy: Mass. The Christopher Publishing House 1975).

Burgett, Donald R.: *Seven Roads To Hell: A Screaming Eagle At Bastogne,* (Novato. CA: Presidio, 1999).

Cavanagh, William C.C.: *Krinkelt-Rocherath, The Battle For The Twin Villages,* (Norwell, Mass.: Christopher Publishing House, 1986).

Cavanagh, William C.C.: *Dauntless - A History of the 99th Infantry Division,* (Dallas TX: Taylor Publishing Company, 1994).

Cole, Hugh M.: *The Ardennes: Battle of the Bulge, U.S. Army In World War Two,* (Washington D.C.: Government Printing Office, 1965).

Collins, Lawton J.: *Lightning Joe, An Autobiography,* (Baton Rouge LA. Louisiana State University Press 1979).

Curley, Charles D. Jr.: *How A Ninety-Day Wonder Survived the War* (Richmond, VA. Ashcraft, 1991).

Delaval, Maurice: *St. Vith Au Cours De L'Ultime Blitzkrieg De Hitler* (Vielsalm, Belgium: Editions J.A.C., Mid 1980's).

D'Este, Carlo: *A Genius for War - A Life of General George S. Patton* (London, England: Harper Collins, 1995).

Doherty, Joseph C.: *The Shock of War 2 volumes plus a Photo Annex* (Alexandria, VA. Vert Millon Press, 1994/95 and 1996).

Dupuy, Trevor N.: *Hitler's Last Gamble - The Battle of the Bulge, December 1944 - January 1945* (New York: Harper Collins, 1994).

Eisenhower, Dwight D.: *Crusade in Europe* (Garden City, N.Y.: Doubleday, 1948).

Eisenhower, John S.D.: *The Bitter Woods* (New York: Putnam's Sons, 1969).

Ellis, William Donohue, Cunningham, Thomas J. Jr., and Pattison, Hal C.: *Clarke of St. Vith - The Sergeant's General* (Cleveland, Ohio: Dillon Liederbach Inc., 1974).

Elstob, Peter: *Hitler's Last Offensive* (London, U.K.: Martin Secker and Warburg Ltd., 1971).

Fowle, Barry W. and Wright, Floyd D.: *The 51st Again: An Engineer Combat Battalion In World War II* (Shipensburg, PA. The White Mane Publishing Company Inc. 1992).

Gable, Kurt: *The Making of A Paratrooper, Airborne Training and Combat in World War II* (Lawence, Kansas: University of Kansas Press, 1990).

Gaul, Roland: *Schicksale Zwischen Sauer Und Our* (Diekirch, Luxembourg: Two Volumes, St. Paulus Druckerei, 1986/87).

Gaul, Roland: *The Battle of the Bulge in Luxembourg, Volumes 1 & 2*(Atglen, PA. Schiffer, 1995).

Gavin, James M.: *On To Berlin - Battles Of an Airborne Commander 1943/1946* (New York: The Viking Press, 1978).

Giles, Janice Holt P: *The Damned Engineers* (Boston: Houghton Mifflin, 1970).

Giles, Janice Holt P: *The GI Journal of Sergeant Giles* (Reprint by U.S. Army Corps of Engineers, 1988).

Gregoire, Gerard: *Les Panzer De Peiper Face à L'U. S. Army* (Stavelot-Malmedy, Belgium: Printed by Chauvehid s.p.r.l. no date).

Irving, David: *The War Between The Generals: Inside The Allied High Command* (New York: Congdom and Lattes, 1981).

Karen, Fred: *Kriegsereignisse Im Frontsektor Der Untersauer* (Diekirch, Luxembourg: St. Paulus Druckerei, 1989).

Kreisle, James E.: *Forty Years after* (San Antonio TX Published Privately, 1992).

Laby, Hubert: *Ardennes 44 Stavelot* (Waremme, Belgium: published privately, 1996).

Lauer, Walter E.: *Battle Babies* (Nashville, TN.: The Battery Press, 1985).

Leinbaugh, Harold P. and Campbell, John D.: *The Men of Company K,* (New York: William Morrow, 1985).

Lombardo, Samuel: *O'er The Land Of The Free* (Shippensburg PA: Beidel Inc, 2000).

MacDonald, Charles B.: *Company Commander* (New York: Bantam Books, 1978).

MacDonald, Charles B.: *The Mighty Endeavor: American Armed Forces In The E.T.O.* (New York: Oxford University Press, 1969).

MacDonald, Charles B.: *The Siegfried Line Campaign, U.S. Army In World War II* (Washington D.C.: Government Printing Office, 1963).

MacDonald, Charles B.: *The Last Offensive* (Washington D.C.: The Government Printing Office, 1973).

MacDonald, Charles B.: *A Time for Trumpets* (New York: William Morrow and Company Inc., 1985).

Merriam, Robert E.: *The Battle of the Bulge* (New York: Bantam Books, 1978).

Messenger, Charles: *Hitler's Gladiator:* A Biography of Sepp Dietrich (London, U.K.: Brassey's, 1988).

Messenger, Charles: *The Last Prussian:* A Biography Of Field Marshall Gerd Von Runstedt 1875-1953 (London, U.K.: Brassey's, 1991).

Myers, Tom and Scheidweiler, Marcel: *Tom Myers' War Memories* (Diekirch, Luxembourg: St. Paulus Druckerei AG, 1991).

Nyquist, Gerd: *Bataljon 99* (Oslo, Norway: H. Aschehoug & Co., 1981).

Pallud, Jean-Paul: *The Battle Of The Bulge: Then And Now* (London, U.K.: After The Battle Prints, 1984).

Parker, Danny S.: *Battle Of The Bulge: Hitler's Ardennes Offensive 1944-1945* (Conshohocken, PA: Combined Books, 1991).

Parker, Danny S.: *To Win The Winter Sky: Air War Over The Ardennes 1944-1945* (Conshohocken, PA: Combined Books, 1994).

Parker, Danny S.: *(Edited By) Hitler's Ardennes Offensive: The German View Of The Battle Of The Bulge* (London, U.K.: Greenhill Books, Lionel Leventhal Ltd., 1997).

Pergrin, David E. with Eric Hammel: *First Across The Rhine: The Story Of The 291st Engineer Combat Battalion* (New York: Atheneum, 1989).

Phillips, Robert H.: *To Save Bastogne* (New York: Stein and Day, 1983).

Pogue, Forrest C.: *The Supreme Command* (Washington D.C.: O.C.M.H. Dept of the Army, 1954).

Pulver, Murray S.: *The Longest Year* (Freeman S.D.: Pine Hill Press, 1986).

Rapport, Leonard M. And Northwood, Arthur Jr.: *Rendezvous With Destiny: A History Of The 101st Airborne Division* (Washington D.C.: Infantry Journal Press, 1948).

Reichelt, Walter E.: *Phantom Nine: The Ninth Armored (Remagen) Division* (Austin TX: Presidial Press, 1987).

Reynolds, Michael: *The Devil's Adjutant: Jochen Peiper Panzer Leader* (Staplehurst U.K.: Spellmount Ltd., 1995).

Ridgway, Mathew B. and Martin, Harold H.: *Soldier: The Memoirs Of Mathew B. Ridgway* (New York: Harper and

Bros., 1958).

Ronningen, Thor: *Butler's Battlin' Bastards* (Lawrenceville, VA: Brunswick Publishing Corporation, 1993).

Sayer, Ian and Botting, Douglas: *Hitler's Last General: The Case Against Wilhelm Mohnke* (London, U.K.: Bantam Press, Transworld Publishers, 1989).

Skorzeny, Otto: *Special Missions* (London, U.K.: Futura, 1974).

Strowson, John: *The Battle of the Ardennes* (London, U.K.: B.T. Batsford, 1972).

Swanson, Vernon E.: *Upfront With Charlie Company: A Combat History Of Company C, 395th Infantry Regiment, 99th Infantry Division* (Deerfield, ILL. 1977).

Toland, John: *Battle: The Story Of The Bulge* (New York: Random House, 1959).

Van Arsdol, Ted: *Battalion From The Mohave* (2 volumes Vancouver, Washington: published privately, 1976).

Weingartner, James J.: *Crossroads Of Death: The Story Of The Malmedy Massacre And Trial* (Berkley, CA.: University of California Press, 1979).

Weingartner, James J.: *Peculiar Crusade: Willis M. Everett and the Malmedy Massacre Trial* (Possibly University of California Press)

Whiting, Charles: *Decision at St. Vith* (New York: Ballantine Books, 1969).

Whiting, Charles: *Massacre at Malmedy* (London, U.K.: Leo Cooper, 1971).

Whiting, Charles: *Death of A Division* (London, U.K.: Arrow Books, 1979).

Whiting, Charles: *The Last Assault* (London, U.K.: Leo Cooper Ltd., 1994).

Wilmot, Chester: *The Struggle For Europe* (New York: Harper and Row, 1952).

Wilson, George: *If You Survive* (New York: Ivy Books, published by Ballantine, 1987).

Ziak, Karl Heinz: *Ich War Kein Held, Aber Ich Hatte Glück* (Vienna, Austria: OVA, 1977

In addition to commercially available publications, there exists a multitude of U.S. Army unit histories published immediately at or just after the cessation of hostilities. Yard sales and second hand bookstores can be a rich source of such histories and in some cases, reprints are available through:

The Battery Press
P.O. Box 3107
Uptown Station
Nashville, TN 37219.

Official records such as unit journals, after action reports and combat interviews are available through the National Archives, while unit morning reports are kept by the VA Records Center in St. Louis, MO.

The Army War College, in Carlisle PA. is home to an extensive collection of documents including the papers of Charles B. MacDonald and the late Dr. Maurice Delaval, a Belgian historian concerned with the battles in and around St. Vith. A well-stocked library and collection of unit association newspapers are also available to visiting researchers. The premises are open Monday through Friday, from 0830 until 1630, except federal holidays. Prior to visiting the facility, prospective researchers should write to fix an appointment. The address is:

Dept. Of The Army
U.S. Army Military History Institute
Carlisle Barracks
Carlisle, PA 17013-5008.

INDEX